T0323347

Innovation and the Evolution of Industries

The revolutionary impact of technological innovation on the dynamics of industrial structures has been one of the distinguishing features of modern capitalism. In this book, four leading figures in the field of Schumpeterian and evolutionary economic theory draw on decades of research to offer a new, "history-friendly" perspective on the process of creative destruction and industrial change. This "history-friendly" methodology models the complex dynamics of innovation, competition and industrial evolution in a way that combines analytical rigor with an acknowledgment of the crucial role of history. The book presents a comprehensive analysis of the determinants and patterns of industrial evolution and investigates its complex dynamics within three key industries: computers, semiconductors and pharmaceuticals. It will be of great value to scholars and students of innovation and industrial change, from backgrounds as varied as economics, management, history and political science. Its coverage of new methodological tools is also useful for students who are new to evolutionary economic theory.

FRANCO MALERBA is Professor of Applied Economics at Bocconi University in Milan and President of ICRIOS. He is the former president of the International Schumpeter Society and of EARIE (European Association of Research in Industrial Economics). He is an Editor of the journal *Industrial and Corporate Change* and author of a large number of articles and several books on industrial economics, innovation and the dynamics and evolution of sectors.

RICHARD R. NELSON is George Blumenthal Emeritus Professor of International and Public Affairs, Business and Law at Columbia University, and heads the program on Science, Technology, and Global Development at the Columbia Earth Institute. He is a seminal figure in evolutionary economics and is the coauthor of *An Evolutionary Theory of Economic Change* with Sidney Winter.

LUIGI ORSENIGO is Professor of Applied Economics at IUSS (School of Advanced Studies), Pavia. He is coeditor of the *Journal of Evolutionary Economics*, the author of several books, and more than 100 publications in major international journals.

SIDNEY G. WINTER is the Deloitte and Touche Emeritus Professor of Management at the Wharton School, University of Pennsylvania. With Richard Nelson, he coauthored the highly cited book *An Evolutionary Theory of Economic Change*. He was the winner of the Viipuri Prize in Strategic Management in 2008 and the Global Award for Entrepreneurship Research in 2015.

Innovation and the Evolution of Industries

History-Friendly Models

FRANCO MALERBA
Bocconi University

RICHARD R. NELSON
Columbia University

LUIGI ORSENIGO
IUSS, Pavia

SIDNEY G. WINTER
The Wharton School, University of Pennsylvania

CAMBRIDGE
UNIVERSITY PRESS

CAMBRIDGE
UNIVERSITY PRESS

University Printing House, Cambridge CB2 8BS, United Kingdom

Cambridge University Press is part of the University of Cambridge.

It furthers the University's mission by disseminating knowledge in the pursuit of education, learning and research at the highest international levels of excellence.

www.cambridge.org
Information on this title: www.cambridge.org/9781107641006

First published 2016

Printed in the United Kingdom by Clays, St Ives plc

A catalogue record for this publication is available from the British Library

Library of Congress Cataloging-in-Publication Data
Malerba, Franco, 1950– author.
Innovation and the evolution of industries : history-friendly models / Franco Malerba, Richard R. Nelson, Luigi Orsenigo and Sidney G. Winter.
Cambridge, UK : Cambridge University Press, 2016. | Includes bibliographical references and index.
LCCN 2016011386| ISBN 9781107051706 (hardback) | ISBN 9781107641006 (paperback)
LCSH: Industries – Technological innovations. | High technology industries. | Technological innovations – Economic aspects.
LCC HD2328 .M35 2016 | DDC 338/.064–dc23
LC record available at https://lccn.loc.gov/2016011386

ISBN 978-1-107-05170-6 Hardback
ISBN 978-1-107-64100-6 Paperback

Additional resources for this publication at www.cambridge.org/malerba

Contents

Figures

Tables

Preface and acknowledgments

This book is about innovation and the evolution of industries. It is the result of more than a decade of exciting collaboration and intense interaction among the four of us. Although we have been publishing articles on this topic over the years, the book represents an original contribution, in that the chapters are new or revised significantly from previously published articles. This book is also novel in that for the first time it provides the reader with a consistent, integrated and complete view of the nature and value of what we call "history-friendly" models, which aim at a deeper and more articulated theoretical analysis as well as empirical understanding of the dynamics of technologies, market structure and industries.

It all started during the nineties, as the four of us met at conferences in Europe and the United States. While listening to presentations and discussing papers, we were always impressed by the richness of industry and firm case studies, which told complex dynamic stories and highlighted the key role played by technological and organizational capabilities and learning in innovation and the evolution of industries. Often, powerful qualitative theories lay behind these cases. In the late nineties, Malerba and Orsenigo developed detailed studies of the evolution of respectively the computer industry and pharmaceuticals for the book Dick was putting together with David Mowery, *The Sources of Industrial Leadership* (Cambridge University Press, 1999). During this time in our meetings with Sid, we often discussed the industry histories that were being put together for the book.

Thus it was natural for the four of us to start talking about the relationship between the rich qualitative theories that were associated with the industry histories and the then prevalent terse and compact modeling of industry dynamics. We started to discuss how formal models could complement appreciative theory and histories. So, the idea was launched to start a research project that would try to capture and represent in a formal way the gist and richness of the different patterns of industrial evolution as described in the histories that we were familiar with, and the theories that went with these histories, by developing models that would highlight the specific dynamics of those sectors. At that time we became also convinced that this research inquiry would represent a second generation of evolutionary models, following the seminal contributions originated by the book by Nelson and Winter (1982) and by the efforts of a long list of evolutionary scholars such as Stan Metcalfe, Giovanni Dosi, Gerry Silverberg, Peter Allen, Esben Andersen, Paolo Saviotti, Bart Verspagen, John Foster and, more recently, Thomas Brenner, Koen Frenken, Peter Murmann, Andreas Pyka, Claudia Werker, Murat Yildizoglu, Keun Lee and others.

This was the first step into an exciting period where we encountered an unexplored terrain. Meetings and discussions would not only take place during conferences and workshops where any random subset of three out of the four of us were present. A long series of ad hoc meetings of "the Gang of Four" (as Tim Bresnahan used to call us) was initiated in Milan, New York or Washington. These meetings took place frequently at our university sites (Bocconi University, Columbia or Wharton School) or at our homes, on both sides of the Atlantic. In fact often the Gang of Four would invade one house and would camp out there for a couple of days, where discussions on industries and models would be interrupted for enjoyable lunches and dinners with our spouses Pamela, Katherine, Roberta and Alice. Within our group, and with other friends (and our families!), the "New York week-ends" became famous: Franco and Luigi would take the Milan-New York flight (economy, of course) on Saturday morning, arrive in New York at noon, work with Dick and Sid from Saturday afternoon to Sunday early afternoon, and then take the Sunday evening flight New-York Milan, in order to arrive early

Monday morning in Milan and go directly to class. And the frequent Milan meetings, when not hosted in one of our apartments, turned the hotel in which Dick and Sid stayed into the "Nelson and Winter Hotel."

Of course, as one can imagine, the discussion on history-friendly models did not occupy all our time together. Often our discussions about our project took place during long pleasant walks, such as those in Washington starting from Sid's home or the ones from Dick's house on the way to Columbia University. Other times, in New York, our Sunday morning discussions were interrupted when AC Milan was playing: so we would gather in front of the TV, with an audience whose comments reflected history and culture: tension, excitement and big shouting by the Italian side, gentle and profound intellectual comments about the game by the American side. And beyond the usual topics of conversation (politics, the economy or recent books), we often ended up having long discussion on sports, where Sid would lead on football, Dick would talk about tennis and the likely winner of the US Open and Dick and Sid would engage with Stevie and Dani (Malerba) on the difference between Italian basketball and American NBA.

For the completion of this book, we greatly benefitted from the excellent work of our great coauthors for some of the chapters. A very special thanks goes to Gianluca Capone – who provided a fundamental and intelligent contribution in working on the code, fixing the notation and checking the consistency between history, text, models and code. Christian Garavaglia and Michele Pezzoni have substantially contributed to Chapter 5 and coauthored related papers. Davide Sgobba and Luca Bonacina have tremendously helped on the simulation side and have worked hard on the final simulations for the book. Along the way, the cause of clarity was advanced by the editorial efforts of Mendelle Woodley, while Dario Lamacchia, Alessia de Stefani, Giorgio Tripodi and Verdiana Venturi pushed it further in their editing of the final manuscript.

This book benefitted from the comments, suggestions and feedbacks from our invisible college, composed by friends and colleagues with whom we have been interacting over the years. The list is too long to name all of them. At the risk of forgetting some key names, we would like to thank (in strict alphabetical order) Franco Amatori, Esben Andersen, Cristiano Antonelli, Ashish Arora, Tim Bresnahan, Gianluca Capone, Uwe Cantner, Bo Carlsson, Paul David, Richard Day, Kurt Dopfer, Giovanni Dosi, Gunnar Eliasson, Jan Fagerberg, Giorgio Fagiolo, Dominique Foray, John Foster, Lou Galambos, Giovanni Gavetti, Horst Hanusch, David Lane, Richard Langlois, Daniel Levinthal, Richard Lipsey, Brian Loasby, Francisco Louca, Luigi Marengo, Mariana Mazzucato, Maureen McKelvey, Stan Metcalfe, David Mowery, Alessandro Nuvolari, Hiro Odagiri, Vanessa Oltra, Carlota Perez, Gary Pisano, Jason Potts, Daniel Raff, Sandra Tavares Silva, Ed Steinmueller, Aurora Teixeira, Pierangelo Toninelli, Nick Von Tunzelmann, Marco Vivarelli, Paul Windrum and Ulrich Witt. We would like to remember here our dear friends Chris Freeman, Keith Pavitt and Nate Rosenberg, giants in the economics of innovation and history of technology. Paul Geroski and Steve Klepper passed away while the book was being written: we want to recognize here our intellectual debt to their key contributions to the field of industrial dynamics.

Cespri (later ICRIOS) of Bocconi University provided a stimulating and friendly environment, with the presence of Stefano Breschi, Stefano Brusoni, Nicoletta Corrocher, Lucia Cusmano, Roberto Fontana, Alfonso Gambardella, Francesco Lissoni, Maria Luisa Mancusi, Roberto Mavilia, Fabio Montobbio, Andrea Morrison and Fabrizio Onida. In particular, among CESPRI researchers, Marco Guerzoni, Nicola Lacetera, Andrea Pozzi and Lorenzo Zirulia gave a significant contribution in the writing of the code, running simulations and performing history-friendly exercises. We also recognize the precious contributions by Luca Berga, Anna De Paoli, Luca Giorcelli and Alessandro Politano in developing the code.

Along this long journey we presented our work on history-friendly models in a lot of places: the International Schumpeter Society Conference in Rio; the Madrid EARIE Conference; the Pretoria Globelics Conference; the DIME Conference in Maastricht; and then at workshops and seminars at INSEAD, SPRU, Open University, University of Edinburgh, Beta Strasbourg, UNU-Merit, Wharton School, Harvard Business School, University of Manchester, Max Plank Gesellschaft, University of Jena, University of Queensland, TUE Eindhoven, Universidad Complutense de Madrid, Zentrum für Interdisziplinäre Forschung Bielefeld, University of Porto and others too numerous to list.

We gratefully acknowledge the financial support received from Bocconi University, Columbia University, Italian CNR, FIRB – Italian Minister of University and Research, and the Mack Institute for Innovation Management at the Wharton School.

Chris Harrison, Phil Good, Jeevitha Baskaran and Adam Hooper of Cambridge University Press and three anonymous referees have been quite helpful with comments and suggestions in the last stage of the preparation of the final manuscript. We thank them.

After all these remarks and thanks to all these friends, colleagues and collaborators who have shared this exciting enterprise in one way or another, we acknowledge that the responsibility for the remaining errors and mistakes is ours alone.

It is also customary to acknowledge in the end the support from the authors' families. In this case, the recognition goes much beyond any standard formulation. At least as the Italian subset is concerned, our children grew up with Dick, Sid and the book. And our wives Pamela, Katherine, Roberta and Alice were a fundamental component of the Gang of Four. We dedicate the book to them.

Codes

The codes of the models, with related instructions and comments, are available at http://download.unibocconi.it/ICRIOS/HistoryFriendly ModelsCodes.zip and at www.cambridge.org/malerba

Some remarks about notation

The formal representation of the history-friendly models presented some notable issues, first of all because of the huge amount of variables and parameters defining the models: some of these elements were common or at least analogous across the models, while others referred to completely different domains. In order to reduce the number of the main symbols to a manageable size, we adapted from computer programming languages the idea of overloading notation: a main symbol can have slightly different meanings according to the presence or absence of further details, such as superscripts and subscripts. For example, the symbol T indicates the total number of periods of a simulation, T_k indicates the period of introduction of technology k, and T^I the minimum number of periods a firm has to stay integrated after its decision to switch to internal production of components. In general, we use as subscripts the indices for elements (products, firms, markets, technologies) that take different values, without changing the meaning of the main symbol. Instead, we use as superscripts further identifiers of the main symbols that are not instances of a general category: for example, PT is the symbol of patents and E is the symbol of exit. In a very limited number of cases an identifier can be used both as a subscript identifier (TR and MP in most of the cases are used as instances of component technology k) and as a superscript identifier (TR and MP are used as superscripts of the main symbol α, as they refer to different parts of the same equation).

Upper and lowercase letters are considered as different, although whenever it is possible they take related meanings: for example, i indicates the propensity to integrate and I the corresponding probability. The symbols used for specific variables and parameters are not used across models, unless these variables and parameters have the same or a very similar meaning and role in the different models. The values that parameters take and the range of values that heterogeneous parameters and variables can take are indicated in the tables in the Appendices. To this purpose, we use standard notation: (a; b) indicates a point with coordinates a and b; [a, b] indicates a continuous set from a to b; {a, ..., z} indicates a discrete set containing all elements from a to z; $\mathbb{R}_+$ indicates the set of nonnegative real numbers; $\mathbb{N}$ represents the set of natural numbers.

I Innovation and industrial evolution

I.I WHAT THIS BOOK IS ABOUT

This book is about technological progress and its relationships with competition and the evolution of industry structures. It presents a new approach to the analysis of these issues, which we have labeled "history-friendly" modeling. This research stream began more than a decade ago and various papers have been published over the years. Here, we build on those initial efforts to develop a comprehensive and integrated framework for a systematic analysis of innovation and industry evolution.[1]

The relationships among technological change, competition and industry evolution are old and central questions in industrial economics and the economics of innovation, a subject matter that dates back to Marshall and of course to Schumpeter. We authors are indeed Schumpeterians in that we believe the hallmark feature of modern capitalism is that it induces, even compels, firms to be innovative in industries where technological opportunities exist and customers are responsive to new or improved products. The evolution of these industries – like computers or semiconductors – is often characterized by the emergence of a monopolist or of a few dominant firms. The speed at which concentration develops varies drastically,

---

[1] The book is novel in that the original papers have been revised and improved in their structure, code and technical apparatus; moreover, they are presented together to convey to the reader the idea that those models are not simply "stand-alone" efforts but are parts of a broader and more systematic analytical approach. Our aim here is to describe and implement the methodological inspiration and implementation of history-friendly models of industrial evolution. Thus, we do not present here specific extensions of these models that are meant to investigate either specific theoretical points or broader conceptual issues about industrial dynamics. We will briefly mention some of them in the concluding chapter of this book. Nor do we aim at proposing a fully fledged theory of innovation and industry evolution. This is work in progress.

1

however, across sectors and over time, and, often, monopoly power is not durable. In other significant industries – e.g. pharmaceuticals – no firm actually succeeded in achieving such an undisputed leadership. In some cases, the characteristic drift toward concentration is interrupted by significant exogenous change, such as new technologies appearing from outside the sector.

Long ago, Schumpeter proposed that the turning-over of industrial leadership was a common feature in industries where technological innovation was an important vehicle of competition. In recent years economists studying technological change have come to recognize a number of other important connections between the evolution of technologies and the dynamics of industries' structure. Progress in this area has come from different sources. The availability of large longitudinal databases at a very high level of disaggregation has allowed researchers to unveil robust stylized facts in industrial dynamics and to conduct thorough statistical analyses, which show strong inter-industry regularities, but also deep and persistent heterogeneity across and within industries. New sophisticated models have been created that attempt to explain the regularities. A wealth of case studies of firms and industries has provided detailed new knowledge, puzzles and exciting hypotheses to be further developed. But despite this remarkable progress in recent decades, the subject still resists clear-cut and sweeping generalizations. Our position is that there is significant variety in the key relationships across industries, and over time, and this variety needs to be recognized explicitly.

This book follows an evolutionary approach to innovation and industrial change. Evolutionary theory emphasizes the variety of ways of doing things developed by heterogeneous actors, the selection processes that tend to suppress some of these practices while increasing the role of others, and the continuous generation of new ways of doing things. As we will explain more in detail in Section 1.3, since agents are only boundedly rational and since innovations continuously appear in the economic system, at any time different agents do different things, even when they face similar conditions, and some of them do better than others. Evolutionary economic systems tend to generate innovation, variety and progress with a changing population of heterogeneous economic agents, and with continuous entry and exit. Over the past thirty years, evolutionary economists have illuminated these dynamics with a broad range of first-generation evolutionary models. These models generate a number of empirically observed phenomena, such as the patterns of technology diffusion, the relationships between innovation and market structures and typical distributions for firm size and growth rates. However, few of these models have been focused on the dynamics and evolution of specific industries, technologies or countries.

This is what this book aims to do. It presents a new form of evolutionary modeling that aims to investigate the complex dynamics of particular cases with "History-Friendly Models" (HFM). HFM are inspired by reflections on the empirical analyses of industrial dynamics and industry evolution and on the nature of fruitful theorizing in economics regarding them. We note that, since the time Schumpeter was writing, empirically oriented economists have learned a lot about how technological advance proceeds, and how the industrial structures are themselves changed by technological innovation. But they have also learned that there are important differences among economic sectors. In this book we will describe, in some degree of detail, various aspects of what has gone on in the industries our models deal with. The inter-industry differences and the changes that have occurred over time will be revealed by the case studies we treat. HFM are based on the historical reconstruction of the main elements that characterize the evolution of an industry; on the identification of the key factors that might explain the specific observed patterns; on the construction of a model that incorporates the crucial explanatory assumptions suggested by the historical analysis; on the testing of the ability of such a model to broadly simulate the observed phenomena and to produce distinctively different patterns when one or some of the key assumptions are removed or modified. If and when results are deemed satisfactory, the analysis can proceed further by using the model to address new conceptual (and perhaps more general) questions. New models can be developed for different industries' histories.

We certainly subscribe to the view that it is the task of theorizing to develop a simplified characterization of the phenomena to be explained, highlighting the "essential" aspects and stripping away the peripheral, and then to try to develop an explanation that is consistent with the former. However, we believe that today there is too wide a gap between the complex and messy historical phenomena and the simple and abstract theories used to explain and predict them. If we agree about the need to understand the economic circumstances, and about the need to look toward the future on the basis of a solid understanding of the present and the relevant economic history, then theories that do not illuminate the past properly cannot meet our aspirations. The rest of this introductory chapter is organized as follows. First, we present the broad phenomena that HFM are designed to analyze, i.e. innovation and industrial evolution (Section 1.2). Then in Section 1.3 we provide a roadmap of the book.

I.2   THE SUBJECT MATTER: INNOVATION AND INDUSTRY EVOLUTION

I.2.I   *Innovation and market structure*

Over the past twenty-five years or so, the analysis of industrial change has witnessed significant progress. First, it has now become almost unanimously recognized that innovation – in its various forms – is a fundamental determinant of industrial structures and of their transformations over time. Firm size, market structures and forms of competition affect the incentives and capabilities to innovate and are shaped in turn by innovation. Thus, it is now commonplace to start from the premise that market structure and innovation co-evolve or – in the equilibrium language of neoclassical economics – they are endogenously and simultaneously determined. In this respect, the old debate on the "Schumpeterian hypotheses" concerning the relationship among concentration, firm's size and innovation in its simplest form has been largely superseded. Yet, it has still proven very difficult to establish any robust general result concerning the Schumpeterian hypotheses on the relationships between innovation and market structure. As John Sutton remarks, "there appears to be no consensus as to the form of the relationship, if any, between R&D intensity and concentration" (Sutton, 1998, p. 4). Similarly, Cohen and Levin (1989) argue that the results on the relation between size and innovativeness are "inconclusive" and "fragile," although stronger regularities are found at the sectoral level (see also Pavitt, 1984; Marsili, 2001; Cohen, 2011). Thus, for example, Pavitt *et al.* (1987) found that while innovative firms are likely to be rather small in industrial machinery, big companies prevail in chemicals, metal working, aerospace and electrical equipment, and many "science-based" sectors (such as electronics and pharmaceuticals) tend to display a bimodal distribution with high rates of innovativeness associated to small and very large firms.

Analyses have increasingly emphasized the relevance of various factors that impact the co-evolving relationships among innovation, firm size and market structure. To begin with, it is now acknowledged that technology often develops according to its own internal logic, following trajectories that are only partially responsive to market signals (Nelson and Winter, 1977; Dosi, 1982; Dosi and Nelson, 1995). Moreover, there is no such thing as "technology in general" but rather an array of different technologies, with different properties and characteristics, yielding different patterns of technological advance (Pavitt, 1984). Technologies differ in terms of opportunities for innovation, and in terms of the degree of appropriability of its benefits (Mowery and Rosenberg, 1982; Levin *et al.*, 1987; Klevorick *et al.*, 1995). Including measures of these variables in the analysis (either statistical or qualitative) almost always improves results and reduces the significance of market structure *per se* (Levin *et al.*, 1985; Cohen, 2011). Typically technological change proceeds cumulatively, but in some technologies and industries – pharmaceuticals being a clear example – it is harder to use cumulated knowledge to develop new products and processes. This difference has implications for the evolution of industry structure. In some industries, largely public or semi-public organizations produce much of the relevant knowledge base on which innovation depends, which is in principle available to everybody who has the requisite scientific and technological absorptive capabilities. In other cases, technological advances do not rely much on publicly available knowledge, but on private and firm-specific know-how and expertise. Clearly, innovation can arise in very different industry structures.

As is well known, Schumpeter himself distinguished two (extreme) patterns of innovation. In the first one, as theorized in *The Theory of Economic Development* (1911) and often labeled as Schumpeter Mark I (Freeman *et al.*, 1982), innovation is created by the bold efforts of new entrepreneurs, who are able and lucky enough to displace incumbents, only to be challenged themselves by imitative entrants. At the other extreme, as described in *Capitalism, Socialism and Democracy* (1942) and often referred to as Schumpeter Mark II, the main sources of innovation are instead large corporations, which accumulate difficult-to-imitate knowledge in specific domains, and are therefore able to gain long-lasting and self-reproducing technological advantages (and economic leadership)[2]. Following this intuition, the notion has been developed that innovation and market structure evolve according to different technological regimes. Nelson and Winter (1982a) distinguished between science-based and cumulative regimes. Winter (1984) further developed this concept by modeling the different evolution of industries under an "entrepreneurial" as opposed to a "routinized" regime. Malerba and Orsenigo (1995, 1997) and Breschi *et al.* (2000) provided further empirical evidence concerning the relationships among the properties of technologies, the patterns of innovation and market structure.

---

[2]   For more detailed analysis of the evolution of Schumpeter's thought on these matters, and new translations of some of the key materials, see Becker *et al.* (2011).

I.2.2 *Stylized facts about industrial dynamics*

Research on the relationship between market structure and innovation has gone much beyond the almost exclusive focus on concentration and firm size that was common earlier. Empirical analysis has identified a series of "stylized facts" that have substantially changed the conventional way of looking at industries, by highlighting the rich dynamics underlying the changing structures of industries.

First, relatively high rates of entry of new firms are seen in virtually all industries, even those marked by high capital intensity and other apparent barriers to entry. Further, and contrary to what standard economic textbooks would suggest, rates of entry do not appear to be particularly sensitive to the average rate of profit in an industry (Geroski, 1995). And in most industries there is considerable exit as well as entry. Indeed, exit and entry rates tend to be strongly correlated (Dunne *et al.*, 1988). As we will discuss later, both entry and exit tend to be significantly higher in new industries, and decline somewhat as the industry matures. However, even relatively mature industries often are marked by continuing entry and exit.

The vast majority of entrants are small firms, and most of them exit the industry within a few years. Survivors grow faster than incumbents, reaching average levels of productivity gradually over time (around a decade). Only a few outliers in an entry cohort are able to attain superior performances, but, especially in the presence of significant technological and market discontinuities, they sometimes displace the incumbents and become the new industry leaders. Even in relatively mature industries one often observes persistent turbulence and churning in the profile of industrial evolution, due not only to continuous entry and exit flows but also to changes in the incumbents' market shares (Acs and Audretsch, 1989, 1990; Beesley and Hamilton, 1984; Baldwin and Gorecki, 1998; Bartelsman and Doms, 2000; Bartelsman *et al.*, 2005). Even in mature industries there tends to be persistent heterogeneity among firms regarding any available measure of firms' traits and performance: size, age, productivity, profitability, innovativeness, etc. (For overviews see Bloom and Van Reenen, 2010; Syverson, 2011; for a theoretical perspective see Jacobides and Winter, 2012). As Griliches and Mairesse (1997) vividly put it:

> we ... thought that one could reduce heterogeneity by going down from general mixtures as "total manufacturing" to something more coherent, such as "petroleum refining" or "the manufacture of cement." But something like Mandelbrot's fractal phenomenon seems to be at work here also: the observed variability-heterogeneity does not really decline as we cut our data finer and finer. There is a sense in which different bakeries are just as much different from each other as the steel industry is from the machinery industry.
>
> *(Griliches and Mairesse, 1997, p. 23)*

The distributions of these variables tend to be highly asymmetric, and often display fat tails in their rates of change. What is even more interesting though is that heterogeneity is persistent: more efficient firms at time t have a high probability to be highly efficient also at time t+T, and the same applies for size, profitability and (more controversially) innovation. The degree of persistence tends to decline the longer the time span considered, and regression to the mean is usually observed. However, this tendency is weak. Autocorrelation coefficients are quite high and thus heterogeneity decays slowly. Moreover, firms tend in any case to converge to different (notional) steady states: the limiting distributions remain extremely skewed. Although sharply at odds with accounts of firms and industries found in economics textbooks, these dynamic phenomena are hardly mysterious when considered in the light of the underlying processes promoting heterogeneity (Nelson, 1991b and 2008; Jacobides and Winter, 2012; Jacobides *et al.*, 2012). Not surprisingly, positive relationships are typically found among these variables: more efficient firms tend to be also more innovative and profitable and to gain market shares as time goes by. The magnitude of these relationships, however, is extremely variable across samples and across industries. Thus, for example, Bottazzi *et al.* (2010) find no relationship between productivity and profitability, on the one hand, and growth, on the other, in the case of Italy. Innovations tend to have a positive impact on profitability and growth, but not in all industries, and often this effect fades away rather quickly (Brusoni *et al.*, 2006). Firms' expansion appears to be independent from size, possibly with smaller companies exhibiting higher but more variable growth rates. And in general, firms' growth remains very hard to explain. While some studies describe it as driven by small, idiosyncratic and independently distributed shocks – and therefore as essentially erratic – others find highly complex underlying structures (Sutton, 1997; Geroski, 2000; Bottazzi and Secchi, 2006. For an overview, see Dosi, 2007).

These findings suggest that heterogeneous processes drive industry dynamics. Continuous change and turbulence and permanent differences among firms coexist with the emergence of remarkably stable structures at higher levels of aggregation. These results are very well in tune with the basic tenets of a Schumpeterian, evolutionary approach, whereby industries are subject to continuous change and their dynamics are driven by the interaction between processes of learning and selection. However, the strength, speed and directions of these processes vary significantly across sectors and countries. Indeed, various evolutionary models are able to replicate most of these stylized facts at the same time. And also in the more mainstream literature on industrial dynamics, the Schumpeterian and evolutionary metaphors are increasingly and explicitly used (Jovanovic, 1982; Aghion and Howitt, 1992; Ericson and Pakes, 1995; Klette and Kortum, 2004; Luttmer, 2007).

I.2.3 *The evolution of industries and the industry life cycle*

In another, conceptually distinct, stream of analysis, economists have investigated the properties and patterns of the evolution of industries over time. The main focus is on questions like these: How do variables such as concentration, the patterns of entry and exit or the rates and directions of innovation, change over time? Can we observe regularities and/or differences among industries? And what are the micro-economic determinants of these patterns? How can the distinctive aspects of specific industry histories be analyzed and explained? A large literature is now available that investigates the history of different economic sectors in different countries, for different spans of time. Perhaps not surprisingly, these studies are extremely heterogeneous in their inspirations and methodologies, the majority of them being grounded in management, but also in business history, and of course in economics. Most of them, though, share a distinct multidisciplinary orientation. For example, see Klein (1977), Abernathy (1978), Clark (1985) and Klepper (2002b) on autos; Dosi (1984) and Malerba (1985) on semiconductors; Orsenigo (1989) and Gambardella (1995) on biotechnology and pharmaceuticals; Dorfman (1987), Flamm (1988) and Bresnahan *et al.* (2012) on computers; Klepper and Simons (2000a, 2000b) on TV sets and on tires; Greenstein (2010) on the Internet; Phillips (1971) and Mowery and Rosenberg (1982a) on aircraft; Henderson and Clark (1990) on photolithographic alignment equipment; and Rosenberg (1976) on machine tools. See also the cases of seven industries collected in Mowery and Nelson (1999). The study of the evolution of specific industries addresses fundamental questions. What are the sources of firms' competitiveness? How durable can industrial leadership be? Is the emergence of particular leaders the inevitable outcome of the evolution of technology and the general forces driving competition, or is it the result of firm-specific strategies, behaviors and forms of organization? Or is it simply luck? Why is it that, in some instances, episodes of sustained dominance are observed, while in others leadership is transient or even absent?

No unique answer has so far been given to these questions. The main and more popular attempt to draw some generalization about the patterns of industrial evolution is the "industry life cycle (ILC) model" (Abernathy and Utterback, 1978; Gort and Klepper, 1982; Abernathy and Clark, 1985; Klepper and Graddy, 1990; Agarwal and Gort, 1996; Klepper, 1996, 1997). This model is beautifully simple and convincing. At the beginning, an industry is characterized by a radical innovation that sets in motion a stream of product innovations, stimulated by users' needs and/or advancements in science and technology. Many firms – the majority of them newly founded – start designing and producing new products. The design of those products is widely different and production occurs at a small scale. In this early period, competition is intense and driven by functional product performance: turbulence is high. Entry barriers are low and R&D and capital requirements are limited. Entry increases rapidly, driven by the perceived profit opportunities inherent in the new family of products. Exit is also high, since many firms are just unable to deliver products that users appreciate enough. As time goes by, however, product designs are developed that significant numbers of customers find attractive, and demand starts growing at higher rates. Concentration begins to increase, often quite rapidly. Two processes underlie this latter phenomenon. Entry slows down, and a few firms rapidly grow toward dominance. Thus, a shakeout is observed in the industry, with a drastic reduction in the number of producers over a relatively short time span. The life cycle of the industry then reaches its mature stage, with few leaders dominating the sector, a stabilizing or even decreasing demand and lower rates of entry. Tendencies to increased concentration may persist for a long time, albeit at a much reduced rate.

Simple and intuitive as it is, this model presents a number of problems. To begin, there are different explanations for why these patterns arise, in particular, why does concentration emerge and the shakeout take place? According to some classic accounts, these phenomena are linked to the emergence of a "dominant design" of the product (Abernathy and Utterback, 1978; Clark, 1985; Utterback and Suarez, 1993). The emergence of such a design provides a guiding framework for future product development and thereby facilitates a stream of process innovations that make the production process more efficient and at the same time less flexible. Still, it is not necessarily the case that the dominant design is actually better than competing ones. Dominance can arise through the action of network externalities – like those affecting adoption of the Windows operating system or the QWERTY keyboard (David, 1985; Arthur, 1989) – with no presumption that the winning standard is in any meaningful sense better than the competing ones, let alone that the alternatives could never have become better if they were not given some time to be further developed.

Further, the dynamics of shakeout may not be fundamentally linked to the design superiority of the product. Klepper (1996) argues that in the various cases he studied (automobiles, tires, penicillin, television among others), the key mechanism lies in the impact of firm scale on the incentive to search out and develop process innovations. Since larger firms can spread R&D expenditures for process innovation over a larger number of units, they have an incentive to invest more, gaining a growing cost advantage vis-à-vis smaller competitors. Falling costs and prices imply also lower expected profits for potential entrants and the exit of smaller firms. Different mechanisms and processes have been identified in other sectors. Continuous and cumulative innovation figures prominently in the accounts of the chemical industry, computers and semiconductors (Malerba, 1985; Dorfman, 1987; Flamm, 1988; Chandler, 1990, 2005a, 2005b; Arora et al., 1998). Marketing is obviously relevant in sectors like soft drinks, beer, etc., but also in computers and drugs.

Besides identifying the specific processes that might lead to the patterns described in the ILC model, researchers have identified sectors that do not conform fully to the model. The exception cases take several forms. The model's basic message regarding increasing concentration may not hold, or the tide running toward concentration may come in for a period and then reverse. The turn may come from a technological discontinuity arising outside the industry, or from factors emerging from the industry dynamics itself.

Regarding concentration trends, consider, for example, the case of pharmaceuticals. The same firms have dominated the industry for almost a century, but the degree of concentration has been quite low in the industry as a whole, considering that the industry has been highly R&D and marketing intensive, both over time and across countries. Klepper (1997) discusses several other instances where no shakeout occurred and no dominant position was ever achieved by any company: lasers, business jets, petrochemicals, zippers, diapers, etc. Possible reasons have to do first with the existence of a fragmented demand (Klepper 1997; Sutton 2001). The existence of different market niches may allow for the survival and growth of leaders in each market segment. If knowledge accumulated in the development of one set of products cannot be easily transferred and used for other applications, economies of scope are limited and the entry cost in any additional niche is large: pharmaceuticals are a classical example. New companies can create new niches through innovation, and extant leaders may find it unprofitable or difficult to follow suit. The case of personal computers might also be interpreted this way, as we subsequently discuss it at some length.

The development of vertical specialization in a sector can complicate the picture and introduce significant deviations from the canonical life cycle patterns. In some instances, firms enter the market and achieve significant market shares by specializing in new production processes, methods or equipment, or in the manufacturing of key inputs. The emergence of specialized firms enables other firms, which did little process innovation but specialized in manufacturing and/or marketing, to enter (Arora *et al.*, 2001). This appears to have forestalled and, in some instances, even reversed shakeouts in the products. Moreover, the emergence of process specialists can undermine first-mover advantages and contribute to a decline in the market shares of the leaders. In other cases, new firms specialized in product innovation are joined by manufacturing and marketing specialists entering later (e.g. medical instruments and automatic teller machines).

Lastly, the model does not explain when a life cycle ends, what happens afterward and what the relevant level of aggregation is. In several cases, the objects of analysis are relatively specific products such as typewriters or mainframe computers rather than industries defined more broadly (office equipment, including typewriters, computers and microcomputers). So, should the introduction of the microcomputer be considered as the onset of new (product) life cycle or an episode in the evolution of the computer industry? The ILC model describes industry histories marked by an initial major discontinuity associated with a radical product innovation, followed by the emergence and consolidation of a dominant design or dominant firms. But things look different in other sectors: not all industries conform to this pattern. For example, in the semiconductor industry, during the 1950s, the emergence of a dominant design – the planar transistor and the planar process – led to a new discontinuity, the integrated circuit. Similarly, in the integrated circuit period, the introduction of several generations of products was associated with several dominant designs that kept the industry in a highly turbulent state, all the way to the new discontinuity characterized by the introduction of the microprocessor.

After the first pioneering firms have begun to try to produce and sell the new product, the ILC model suggests that they generally are followed by a stream of other firms, pursuing more-or-less imitative innovations. While this may have been true for industries such as typewriters and automobiles, the initial conditions at industry birth differ markedly across industries. In some cases, diversifying entry by established firms plays a major role. For example, while a large telecommunications firm (AT&T) first introduced the transistor, several of the early entrants in the semiconductor industry consisted of the major US and European receiving-tube producers. In the case of computers, entrants were mainly large established firms diversifying from other industries (see Chapter 3).

Research guided by the ILC model has illuminated and appropriately emphasized patterns in innovation, firm entry and exit, and changes in concentration. As we have discussed earlier, however, the patterns identified as typical in the ILC literature do not hold with anything such as universality. Thus, the "stylized facts" describing those patterns cannot be the exclusive target for theoretical explanation; the observable variety of patterns must be accounted for.

1.2.4 Further patterns in the evolution of industries

In this section, we discuss some important patterns in industrial evolution that are outside the scope of the ILC model as it is usually understood. As in the case of those emphasized in the ILC literature, these patterns are not universal. We argue that they are frequently encountered; more research generally would be needed to develop a grounded estimate of just how "frequently" that is. Claims of universality are problematic in any case because of the unsettled state of understanding regarding the population of instances to be addressed (product vs. industry, scale differences, time durations, etc.).

First, as noted previously, technologies, processes and products often improve following relatively well-defined trajectories (Nelson and Winter, 1977; Dosi, 1982). Such trajectories are time paths in some space of design attributes – for example, the scale or speed of a device, the degree of mechanization of a process. Trajectories are understood to be the reflection of the repetitive application of a relatively constant set of problem-solving methods ("heuristics") grounded in a body of understanding of the technology ("technological paradigms"). Perhaps the single, most striking example of the phenomenon is the miniaturization trajectory in semiconductor devices, the technological underpinning of Moore's Law. Moore himself characterized the logic of the paradigm as follows:

> By making things smaller, everything gets better simultaneously. There is little need for trade-offs. The speed of our products goes up, the power consumption goes down, system reliability, as we put more of the system on a chip, improves by leaps and bounds, but especially the cost of doing things electronically drops as a result of the technology.
>
> *(Moore, 1995, p. 51)*

As this example illustrates, a powerful paradigm can create patterns of change that ripple through the economy in both the horizontal and vertical dimensions. The miniaturization trajectory depends upon, and guides, continuing change upstream – in semiconductor equipment, particularly lithography equipment. Better semiconductor devices expand the scope for improved designs, and entirely new product forms, in computers, phones and other products. Better computers dramatically facilitate inventory control and lower transaction costs across the economy, especially when coupled with bar code scanners and complementary innovations in organizational routines. In this sense, the miniaturization trajectory in semiconductors is a powerful shaper of the contemporary economy. It would be quite incorrect, however, to ascribe all of this progress to a single source. In each of the named contexts, innovation presents distinctive challenges that have to be overcome – often with the aid of locally relevant heuristics and paradigms.

While technological paradigms are frequently influential across entire industries and beyond, this influence leaves abundant room for firms to differ. It is one thing to recognize possible directions and methods of improvement, another to recognize and seize the particular improvements that the environment will reward. Typically, firms face high degrees of uncertainty and place their bets in different directions (Nelson, 1991b). Their strategies are path-dependent; for that and other reasons they often become quite rigid (Jacobides and Winter, 2012). Firms find it hard to change their orientations quickly and drastically.

This observation leads us to a second, quite general pattern, the fact that industry leaders often seem to be vulnerable to challenges based on new technologies. Many accounts of why the leaders lost their hegemony claim that (persistent) failure to recognize and adapt to changes in technology and market conditions was a crucial factor (Tushman and Anderson, 1986; Henderson and Clark, 1990; Christensen 1997; Tripsas and Gavetti, 2000). Conversely, cases where firms were able not only to survive but to actually maintain leadership over prolonged periods of time are often linked to the ability to continuously innovate and adapt (e.g. Disney Corporation, Boeing and IBM (at least until the 1990s); see also the accounts in Miller *et al.*, 1995; Tripsas, 1997).

A substantial literature has grown around these issues. The challenge has been to identify the causes of the contrasting examples of inertia and adaptability, and the related phenomena of success and failure for challenged incumbents. It is clear that the basic fact that organizational capabilities are grounded in organizational routines has much to do with the case. This consideration is fundamental in evolutionary theory, and we give it more attention in the following chapters. There are, as usual, other contending explanations that deserve respect – particularly those that focus on questions of entrants' access to complementary assets (Teece, 1986; Tripsas, 1997; Winter, 2006), or on issues of managerial attention (which may or may not be comfortably accommodated under the broad rubric of "organizational routine").

A third noteworthy pattern involves the powerful role of increasing returns phenomena in the establishment of dominant positions in an industry. Increasing returns can arise from conventional (and still extremely important) mechanisms such as economies of scale and scope in production and distribution. Beyond that familiar sphere, there are mechanisms involving scale economies in R&D, learning curves, marketing efforts or so-called network externalities. What is particularly interesting is that market power does not usually arise simply by one firm outspending competitors in one or another of these dimensions but by the fact that these activities – properly managed – can have long-lasting effects. First-mover advantages are often shown to be critical in determining firms' fortunes. For example, Klepper (1996) shows that in all of the four sectors he studied, which conformed to the life cycle model, the market leaders were invariably early entrants in the industry, and that later entrants faced much higher rates of exit (see also Lieberman and Montgomery, 1988; Helfat and Lieberman, 2002; Suarez and Lanzolla, 2007). Also, it is well understood that the competitive value of marketing expenditures does not reside simply in the immediate increase in sales but also in the fact that they make it more difficult for competitors to catch up with the cumulated investments. Similarly, R&D may yield better products and processes, or even drastic innovations, but in addition it endows the firm with new knowledge and new opportunities for further improvements. IBM gained thirty-five years of leadership in the computer industry by developing a strong sales force and service/support organization, which gave it the opportunity to reach, for each innovation, a customer base much larger than the rest of the domestic industry combined. What made IBM unique was not its ability to reap gains from a single innovation but the ability to extract returns from its established position across a wide range of innovations. IBM, in that period, created a strong dynamic capability – an ability to make continuing improvements in a related set of products and processes, by re-deploying related assets and capabilities in R&D, manufacturing, marketing and other functional areas (Teece *et al.*, 1997; Teece, 2009).

Finally, patterns of industry evolution are strongly shaped by various aspects of the institutional background in which the industry appears. In some cases, an innovative founder is significantly protected by intellectual property law. An extreme case in point is that of the Bell patents on the telephone, which permitted AT&T to extract rents from a quasi-monopoly position while forestalling for two decades the typical explosion of imitative entry. In 1894, when the Bell patents expired, there were about 100 firms in the US telephone industry, many involved in patent litigation with Bell. By 1902, there were over 9,000 organizations (most of them very small) in the industry (Barnett and Glenn, 1995). Sometimes, a new industry in the for-profit sector is an almost trivial extension of technical achievements purchased at great expense by the government. Consider, for example, the advent of passenger aircraft propelled by jet engines, which exploited for private gain the massive investments by the US government in the technologies both of the airframes and of the jet engines (Mowery and Rosenberg, 1982b). Consider also the case of electronic computers, where the key advances by nonprofit and private entities were funded by the US government in the 1940s and 1950s, with national security objectives in view (Dorfman, 1987; Flamm, 1988; Mowery and Rosenberg 1998). Reaching farther back, consider how fundamentally the German institutions of advanced education were involved in the origins of the modern, science-based chemical industry – as it has been brilliantly expounded by Murmann (2003).

The picture of the relationships between innovation and the dynamics of industrial structure that comes out of recent empirical research is a complex one, with important aspects of it varying from sector to sector. Economists, social scientists more broadly and policy makers, ask many different kinds of questions about the relationships involved in this picture. It is the task of theoretical analysis to identify those aspects that are particularly salient for the questions being asked, and to build around these an explanation for the phenomena in question that is illuminating and persuasive.

For some questions it is reasonable to ignore the sectoral differences and, with that, much of the complexity, and to build a stylized general model of what is going on. But many important questions directly involve particular sectors: for example, why was it that one firm came to dominate the mainframe computer industry? And a number of questions that are first posed generally – for example, how important is patent protection in motivating innovation – have answers that differ significantly from sector to sector. To illuminate these kinds of questions, the theoretical structure must have built into it the details of the sectoral contexts that empirical analysts have argued to be important.

It is this understanding that has led us to develop the art form of history-friendly modeling.

I.3 A ROADMAP FOR THE VOLUME

The following chapter develops the background of our modeling approach. It recapitulates previous work in the evolutionary tradition that offers a realistic view of firm behavior in domains where ongoing change is a key feature of the competitive environment. We also offer our perspective on the nature of fruitful theorizing in economics, and on related issues of method and methodology. While either or both of these discussions may be largely familiar to many of our readers, we consider it important to provide an adequate entry path for readers who are new to the intellectual territory of evolutionary economics.

In the next three chapters of the book, we explore the following cases: the rise of concentration in the mainframe computer industry, the changing pattern of upstream integration into semiconductors that has marked the history of that industry and the role of market fragmentation in shaping the evolutionary patterns in the pharmaceuticals industry.

In Chapter 3, the central phenomenon we aim to explain is that a large dominant firm emerged quickly, producing mainframes, and it was then able to maintain its leadership for an extended period. It accomplished this sustained dominance despite the appearance of radical technological discontinuities (from transistors to integrated circuits, to microprocessors). These new technologies, however, not only allowed firms to design better computers but also to develop new classes of products (e.g. microcomputers), which appealed to different market niches and offered opportunities for new entrants. Our model explores the conditions that might explain these patterns.

In Chapter 4, we address the changes over time in the extent to which computer firms integrated into semiconductors. Throughout the history of the computer industry, the vertical scope of firms changed substantially, with phases when vertical integration dominated and others when vertical specialization prevailed. In some shorter periods, the two forms coexisted and competed with each other. Our model explores the factors accounting for the identified trends marking the co-evolution of firm capabilities and scope, market size and industrial structures.

The pharmaceutical industry (Chapter 5) provides a very different story. Here, despite high rates of innovation, concentration remained quite low. Our explorations tend to support the view, mentioned previously, that, in addition to the nature of the innovative process, the structure of markets on the demand side plays a distinctive role in restraining concentration. This is also an arena in which patents have long been recognized to play a key role. Our modeling effort aims at sharpening understanding under both of these headings, and also at identifying implications for policy.

Finally, as we close the book with Chapter 6, we point to conclusions, future challenges and suggestions for the way ahead.

2 History-friendly models

Methods and fundamentals

Having sketched the domain of our inquiry, we turn now to the task of bringing new light to that domain. While the empirical phenomena discussed in the first chapter are complex and variegated, the broad subject matter of innovation and industrial evolution is familiar to a great many economists. Most of our readers know what it is about. On the other hand, the promise of "history-friendly modeling" as an approach to that subject matter is less widely appreciated. A principal purpose of this book is to lay out this new methodological approach and to demonstrate its usefulness. In this chapter, we develop the basic argument for this approach, which we then apply in the remainder of the book. We explain our reasons for believing that history-friendly modeling is a valuable addition to the economists' analytic tool kit. In doing so, we discuss considerations ranging from the extremely general – "what forms of economic theory help us to understand the world" – to the very specific – "how does one construct a history-friendly model?" We follow the indicated order, from the general to the specific.

2.1 COMPLEMENTARY APPROACHES TO MODELING: "FORMAL" VS. "APPRECIATIVE" THEORY

Our development of the concept and technique of history-friendly modeling reflects our belief that present notions of what constitutes "good theory" in economics are inadequate to the task of analyzing and illuminating the kind of phenomena this book addresses. Theorizing about complex phenomena involves, first of all, discriminating between the most salient facts that need to be explained, and phenomena that can be ignored as not relevant or interesting, and second, identifying the most important determining variables, and the mechanisms or relationships between these and the salient phenomena to be explained. This requires screening out or "holding constant" variables and mechanisms that seem relatively unimportant, at least given the questions being explored. There is probably little disagreement about these general points. Regarding the principles for assessing theories, there is more controversy.

The illumination provided by a theory can be assessed on at least two grounds. The criterion most recognized by economists today is its power to suggest hypotheses that will survive sophisticated empirical tests, where confirmation is found in the statistical significance levels achieved in the tests and in measures of "goodness of fit." We note, first, that this way of judging a theory forces the analyst to select the dependent and independent variables from among the candidates that are inherently quantitative – or, alternatively, to accept quantitative measures or indicators for inherently qualitative variables (for the latter purpose, familiar statistical techniques involve a generous use of dummy variables on the right-hand side of regression models, and of categorical "count" variables on the left-hand side). It seems to be widely believed that these characteristics of current practice in economics simply reflect the nature of science, and of scientific research, in general. In fact, practice varies enormously across the sciences. Practices akin to those that presently are common in economics are certainly characteristic of some of the physical sciences, but not of all natural sciences. For example, much research in biology does not conform to the model offered by neoclassical economics. More on this will be discussed later.

Deep in the intellectual heritage of today's economics discipline, there resides the view that "only prediction matters." Whatever the lines of descent in particular cases, it seems clear that the strength of this view has much to do with the methodological arguments put forward by Milton Friedman (1953). Since Friedman advanced the argument that the only important attributes of a theory is how well it predicts, economists have not talked much about another criterion for judging a theory – the extent to which the explanation it provides is persuasive, in the sense that someone well-informed about activity in the arena under consideration would agree that the theory captures the most important causal aspects behind the observed phenomena.

Judged in the Friedman-derived methodological paradigm, a good theory does not *need* to be persuasive. The mechanisms built into the theory that generates its results need not be assessed empirically themselves. Indeed, there has been uncritical acceptance of the idea that readily available information – on firm decision processes, for example – can safely be ignored. In contrast to this Friedman-derived account, and in conflict with it, we hold that theory should aspire to being a reasonable abstraction of what is going on – as that is described by close observers of what is "actually" going on. Such an account does, of course, have to be an "abstraction." That is not the issue. The issue is between a conception of theory, which involves a high level of comfort with drastic simplifications and instrumental falsehoods, as against a conception that theories should reflect an aspiration to provide an account of truth – though it is necessarily a limited and imperfect account.

Two aspects of our view of theory assessment are particularly significant given the nature of our subject matter. First, in a range of contexts that in general are complex, and which vary considerably from case to case, development of a theory that encompasses them all may be impossible unless the "salient phenomena to be explained" are defined quite narrowly. This means excluding from the analysis a lot of the actual variation, and similarly holding constant or simply ignoring many factors that likely have some influence. Therefore, in areas of study where economists see a wide range of likely interacting phenomena as the subject matter that needs to be understood, and are wary of over-simplification, the main virtue of a "good" theory may be that it gives a better understanding of the operative causal mechanisms, even though its detailed predictive power is not great. This, of course, is the case with evolutionary theory in biology (see, for example, Philip Kitcher's essay "Darwin's Achievement," 2003).

The alternative is to greatly simplify or abstract starkly what the theory is designed to illuminate.

Second, this alternative view of evaluating a theory does not require that its variables and causal relationships all be specified quantitatively. This is an important consideration in view of the fact that much of what we know empirically about many economic phenomena is qualitative, and in many cases the quantitative indicators that can be used or constructed are not very satisfactory. This is strongly the case regarding the empirical subject matter of this book – innovation and industrial dynamics. Consider, for example, how much knowledge we have about the many manifestations and processes involved in the tremendous increases in computational power since World War II – and how hard it would be to summarize that understanding in any list of numbers.

Of course, one could hope for a theory that has both virtues: it predicts/explains a good portion of the interesting phenomena well, and the explanation fits well with what is known about the causal mechanisms generating what is observed. But in a field like economics, trade-offs are inevitable. We have proposed that these typically involve choices about the scope of the phenomena and the evidence considered relevant, and, on the other hand, the extent to which insight and confirmation are found in aspects that cannot easily be captured in quantitative measures. In both cases, the narrow choices that are generally favored in the discipline tend to detract from the persuasiveness of the explanation, since the causal driving mechanisms are represented very imperfectly, in highly truncated and abstracted form.

Recognizing this problem, two of us (Nelson and Winter) have argued that economic theorizing should proceed at more than one level of abstraction, and in fact it generally does. To flesh out the discussion begun earlier, what we call "appreciative theory" is theorizing relatively close to the observed empirical phenomena and generally is expressed verbally. The advantage of verbal theorizing in economics is that the language used can be rich and nuanced.

Therefore, it can express the understandings and beliefs of the economists knowledgeable about the empirical phenomena under study regarding the key facts and mechanisms – including the varying degrees of conviction with which various beliefs are held. The drawback is that the logical machinery built into theory expressed this way is not strong. It may be difficult to check out the theory for consistency, or to check whether the causal arguments in the theory in fact generate the conclusions they purport to explain. However, a persuasive appreciative theory at least can make sense of those phenomena – and "sense" is not primarily a quantitative matter.

We note that from Adam Smith, through Marshall and Schumpeter and until close to the present time, most of what economists considered as economic theory was of this kind. True, there has also been a rising tide of mathematical theorizing, going back at least to the days of Cournot. But this was long viewed as a different kind of theorizing, and until quite recently, not the standard kind.

Mathematical analysis is one variety of what Nelson and Winter called "formal" theorizing, which we define as theory that presents an explicit logical account of the relationships among the variables it addresses. Formal theory, of whatever kind, is generally developed at a relatively high level of abstraction. The advantage of expressing a theory formally is that it greatly facilitates the ability to check for both consistency and completeness and enables rigorous deduction of implications to a far greater extent than is possible in theory expressed verbally. On the other hand, mathematics and other formal languages lack the richness and nuance that is possible with verbal expression, and therefore formal models inevitably are more distanced from the actual complex reality of economic phenomena and activity than is appreciative theory. There is a real issue, then, regarding whether they really "explain" that reality, even if they generate hypotheses that survive tests, and successfully guide efforts to produce good statistical fits between the limited sets of dependent and independent variables included in the model.

Thus, both appreciative and formal theories have their strengths and their weaknesses. Our point is that economics fruitfully can use both kinds of theorizing. The two kinds complement each other best when their strengths can be combined, and the weaknesses of each are offset by the strengths of the other. We believe that this goal can best be approached if formal theorizing is regarded as the helpful servant of appreciative theorizing. In that frame, it is appreciative theory that is understood as where the basic understandings of the phenomena are articulated. Formal theory is developed as a simplified and abstract model of the appreciative theory, or, more typically, a portion of it. It often happens that formal theory can greatly illuminate particular questions within the larger appreciative structure, but cannot encompass the full scope and richness of that structure.

What we have described here is a very different view of the usefulness of formal theorizing than is common today in economics. The idea of seeing formal theorizing as the servant of appreciative theorizing, in particular, certainly is not currently standard in economics. Our argument is that something like this view is needed if the discipline is to come to grips with the complexity of some of the subject matter it addresses, such as innovation and the evolution of industries.

We would argue that, in fact, formal modeling is often motivated by the modeler's understanding of the explanations of what is going on in an arena of economic activity that are put forth by empirically oriented economists active in that arena – that is, by their appreciative theorizing – and the model is an attempt to build an abstract, formal version of that. In what we are calling history-friendly modeling, this orientation is explicit.

These general issues are not new to the discipline. Over a century ago, an intellectual battle raged among European, principally German, economists regarding explanation in economics. It concerned whether economic phenomena were so complex and dependent upon particular circumstances that the search for broadly applicable economic laws was a fool's quest, or whether on the contrary it was possible to cut through the noise of the particular and discover or deduce general economic laws. From the vantage point of the present, it seems clear that both sides of the argument were too hung up on nineteenth-century physics as a model of what a science should be.[1]

It is interesting that at around the same time Alfred Marshall was proposing that "The Mecca of the economist lies in economic biology ..." We agree with the judgment that biology provides a much better model for economics than physics, in two respects. One involves the role of formal modeling. Unlike in physics, most of theorizing in biology is laid out verbally, often supported by pictorial representations, figures and flow charts, but seldom casting mathematical analysis in a central role. And the expressed "theory" generally stays close to the empirical reality as understood by biologists, often involving a good deal of descriptive material. This tradition in biology dates back to Darwin (1859), a quintessential "appreciative theorist" if there ever was one. In more recent times, good examples are provided by the work of Stephen Jay Gould, or Edward O. Wilson.

It might be objected that formal modeling has a long history in some branches of biology, especially population genetics, as in Fisher (1958). The models are used, however, not so much as a way of expressing the general theory but to explore how parts of the theory work under certain conditions. That is, the mathematical formulations are not the articulation of the theory itself but rather the theory's servants, helpful in gaining a better understanding of what the theory implies, and checking on its logic. And we note that, as with the models in this book, today much of the formal modeling in biology comes in the form of computer simulations.

The second strand we draw from biology is the use of "evolutionary" theory to characterize and analyze the process of change. Our theory of how technologies change over time is evolutionary in the

---

[1]   Something like this assessment is frequently encountered in the literature that is critical of the current state of the economics discipline. For a vigorous statement, see Mirowski (1989).

sense that it stresses the variety of ways of doing things that coexist at any time, the forces of selection that tend to winnow out some of these practices and increase the relative importance of others, and the continuing generation of new variety that keeps the process going. On the other hand, economic evolutionary theory differs radically from evolutionary theory in biology in that the actors are treated as purposeful and intelligent, within their limits.

2.2 BEHAVIORAL ASSUMPTIONS IN EVOLUTIONARY ECONOMICS

In our evolutionary theory economic agents are represented as rational, in the sense that they have objectives and try to achieve them as best they can, given what they think they know. Rationality in this everyday sense is, however, a far different thing than the "rational choice" that is treated as a foundational assumption in the economics discipline, and in significant parts of social science beyond it. Following Herbert Simon (1955, 1976, 1991), Cyert and March (1963), and many others, we hold to the contrasting view that agents display "bounded rationality." They never know all that it would be helpful for them to know, and never can see clearly into the future. They cannot fully anticipate the results of their own problem-solving efforts, let alone what may emerge from other actors. At a more fundamental level, they do not come equipped with innate insight into the causal structure of the situations they confront, nor do they have the logic-processing power of perfect mathematicians (as many mainstream theorists commonly assume). Nevertheless, some actors do manage to find, through exploratory activity, new and better ways of doing things, as judged in the contexts they actually confront. Widely accepted beliefs about the limits of the possible are confounded with some frequency, to the amazement of onlookers. Innovation is always going on somewhere in the system. As a result of the bounded rationality of all agents and the gradual diffusion of effective innovations being made by some, different economic agents are going to be doing different things at any given time, even when their challenges and conditions are similar. Some are going to do better than others. As we mentioned in the previous chapter, the striking degree to which firms are heterogeneous has been recognized for a long time, and its importance has been emphasized by evolutionary economists in particular. A recent surge of excellent empirical work has brought the phenomenon to the fore and it is now considered one of the most robust stylized facts about industrial dynamics and evolution.

Better practices tend to expand in relative use in part because the agents employing them tend to prosper and grow, while those doing poorly tend to contract. The mechanism here is analogous to selection processes in evolutionary biology. In economic evolution, however, agents are not locked into the processes they employ at any time, and indeed can attempt to imitate the behaviors of others who are doing better, as well as to innovate. The relative importance to economic progress of the two mechanisms just mentioned – expansion of progressive firms and decline of less progressive ones, and wide-scale adoption by firms in the industry of productive new practice – varies from case to case. A number of empirical studies suggest that the latter mechanism tends to be even more important than the former. However, outcomes are shaped by time and chance to a significant extent, and some of the agents doing poorly are not able to reform their practices before going bankrupt. Most evolutionary economic models reflect the realities of entry and exit: as we noted in Chapter 1, consistent with empirical observations, continuing churning in the population of firms is part of the picture at the industry or market level (Dunne et al., 1988).

Such an evolutionary system tends to generate continuing progress on the part of most operative economic agents, along with a changing population of agents, with some expanding and some declining, and some exiting and some entering. Over the last thirty years a considerable number of evolutionary models of this broad design have been constructed. The history-friendly evolutionary models developed in this book can be regarded as a new genre of them, different from most of the earlier models in several related ways. We return to this point in the next section.

In the Friedman (1953) methodology essay referred to earlier, a significant role was played by the claim that neoclassical behavioral assumptions ("maximization of returns") could be defended on the ground that they captured firm survival conditions in such an evolutionary system. As Friedman put it,

> The process of "natural selection" thus helps to validate the hypothesis [of maximization of returns] – or rather, given natural selection, acceptance of the hypothesis can be based largely on the judgment that it summarizes appropriately the conditions for survival.
>
> *(Friedman, 1953, p. 22)*

Exploring the *logical* limits and limitations of this claim was the purpose of some of the earliest attempts at formal, analytical modeling in the evolutionary tradition (Winter, 1964, 1971). From today's perspective, one can say that there is essentially no merit in the suggestion that there are *generally valid* theoretical conclusions to be found along the lines that Friedman suggested. In well-specified contexts involving interesting pre-selection variety in firm behavior, the conditions for survival generally turn out to be complex, and the implied constraints on firm behavior much weaker than Friedman implied (see the review of this question in Nelson and Winter, 2002). In particular, simple arguments along Friedmanian lines generally founder on the point that the selection environment is endogenous – that is, the survival tests imposed on any given behavior are jointly determined by all of the behaviors in the system.

Nevertheless, the idea that selection can be an important force in economic evolution is quite correct. Almost any evolutionary model can be viewed as, in part, an exploration of that idea, whatever other purposes it may have. Simulation models like those in this book have significant virtues in that they deal explicitly with the endogenous environment problem and also provide quantitative and temporally situated insights into "survival" conditions: it is not a simple matter of whether behavior A or behavior B remains present in the system but a question of whether the relative importance of the two behavioral patterns changes, and if so how much, and how fast.

Theoretical ideas about organizational routines and capabilities, and the search behaviors that modify them, were an important component of the Nelson and Winter (1982a) contribution. That statement itself had, of course, a number of different antecedents in the prior literatures of economics, management and organization. At this point the literature on these matters has become so extensive and developed so many differentiated branches that it would be quite impossible to review it here. For overviews and numerous references to these literatures, we refer the reader to broad-scope volumes such as Dosi *et al.* (2000), Helfat (2003), Becker (2008).[2]

When general ideas of routines and capabilities are invoked in the context of simulation modeling, some distinctive issues arise that are obviously relevant to our current undertaking. These we discuss briefly in the concluding section of this chapter.

2.3   THE EARLIER GENERATIONS OF EVOLUTIONARY MODELING

Previous evolutionary models often have been oriented toward showing that various stylized economic phenomena, which may score as theoretical successes or as puzzles when viewed from the perspective of neoclassical economics, could have been generated by evolutionary processes along the lines sketched earlier. The presence and nature of diffusion curves is one example; typical responses to price changes are another. Evolutionary models have been shown to

---

[2]   The recent flurry of interest in the "origins and microfoundations of organizational routines and capabilities" is reflected in special issues or special sections of a number of journals; these also provide useful insight into the current state of the general subject. See the *Journal of Institutional Economics* (special issue, June 2011), *Organization Science* (special issue, September–October 2012), *Journal of Management Studies* (special issue, December 2012), *European Management Review* ("Hegelian Dialogue," Winter 2012) and *Academy of Management Perspectives* (symposium, May 2013).

be capable of generating the kind of distribution of firm sizes, and of firm growth rates, that have been observed empirically. Other evolutionary models have explored factors that call out for attention once the evolutionary nature of economic processes is understood. Thus, several models have been concerned with the factors that influence whether or not successful innovators can gain durable monopoly power in an industry.

Many of these evolutionary models have been motivated by prevailing appreciative theories of the areas of economic activity they model. However, few have been as closely linked to particular industrial cases and their appreciative explanations as the history-friendly models we develop here. To a large extent, evolutionary economists have tried to show how their models can reproduce "stylized facts" at a fairly high level of generality. The history-friendly models we develop here thus face the stronger empirical challenge of reproducing salient features of economic change in particular industries.

To highlight what is different about history-friendly modeling, it is useful to describe in more detail some characteristics of earlier modeling efforts in the evolutionary tradition. Like the history-friendly models we develop in this book, most of the earlier evolutionary models were motivated by the author's perception that important empirical phenomena were inconsistent with neoclassical economic theory, or at least were repressed by that theory – while, on the other hand, they seemed readily explainable as aspects of an evolutionary economic process. As suggested earlier, one such important feature of the empirical economic reality is the significant differences among firms in the same industry in their productivity and profitability. Another related phenomenon is the great variation in the time it takes different firms to adopt profitable new innovations, as reflected in diffusion curve analysis.

Several of the models contained in Nelson and Winter (1982a) generate these phenomena. Nelson's "A Diffusion Model of International Productivity Differences in Manufacturing Industry"

(Nelson, 1968), which involves both inter-firm differences and slow diffusion of superior practice, was published in 1968. Preliminary reports on the earliest versions of the evolutionary model of economic growth by Nelson and Winter appeared in 1973 and 1974 and the full report (coauthored with Herbert Schuette) appeared in 1976 (Nelson *et al.*, 1976). Other models based on the methodology pioneered by Nelson and Winter, for example Silverberg *et al.* (1988), and Dosi *et al.* (1995), generate typical "S" shaped diffusion curves, and also patterns of entry and exit and survival among firms that broadly resemble the empirical data on these phenomena. So do a number of models by Metcalfe (1998).

Several of the earlier models were concerned directly with the phenomena that are the focus of this book. Earlier we described Nelson and Winter's modeling of industrial dynamics as driven by, and in turn influencing, the pace of innovation in an industry (Nelson and Winter, 1982a: chapters 13–15). Earlier versions of these models were published as Nelson and Winter (1977, 1982b). Their treatment of Schumpeterian competition, with its emphasis on the co-evolution of R&D intensity, innovation and industrial concentration, was echoed in many subsequent works, including Andersen (1994).

In a series of papers dating back to 1982, the late Steven Klepper greatly extended the empirical understanding of patterns of industrial evolution and contributed significantly to the fund of theoretical models (see, among others: Gort and Klepper, 1982; Klepper and Graddy, 1990; Klepper, 1997; Klepper and Simons, 2000a, 2000b; Klepper, 2002a; Klepper and Sleeper, 2005). Leaving statistical details aside, the empirical contributions include the documentation of typical industry life cycle patterns such as the diffusion of innovations and the "shakeout" phenomenon, the illumination of the important role of the prior experience of entrants, the "spinoff" phenomenon and new perspectives on industrial agglomeration. On the theoretical front, Klepper's approach has similarities and differences relative to our own. Crucially, his models do not represent firm behavior as foresighted, but as responsive to the unfolding situation. Consistent with the models of Nelson and Winter (1982a), he emphasized that innovative effort is an overhead cost, and the net payoff from it is therefore strongly affected by firm scale. On these grounds, we classify Klepper's theoretical models as evolutionary.[3]

However, these various evolutionary models differed from the history-friendly ones we develop here in certain important respects. First, their orientation to empirical economic phenomena was typically at a higher level of aggregation and abstraction (though this is not so in Klepper's examples). Thus, for example, the empirical targets for the Nelson and Winter economic growth model (1976 [with Herbert Schuette], 1982a) were the broad pattern that had been traced out over the first half of the twentieth century by the statistics for real GNP in the United States, the overall capital stock and labor input, and the time paths of real wages and the rate of return on capital over that period. Broad similarity between the time paths generated by the model and the actual time paths was their objective, and their claimed accomplishment. The important message was that the data emphatically did not compel the sort of neoclassical interpretation offered by Solow (1957). The authors did not even try to deal with what happened during the Great Depression, which was such an important part of that economic history; in this, they reproduced a deficiency also present in the neoclassical account. Similar deficiencies in attention to macroeconomic issues also pervaded most of the subsequent evolutionary literature, but there have been significant efforts to rectify that situation (Verspagen, 2002; Dosi *et al.*, 2010; Foster 2011 [1987]).

The difference here between what this earlier model aimed to do, and the objectives of history-friendly modeling, are a matter of

---

[3]   The point to the contrary is that his modeling of the short-term responsiveness of firms is essentially neoclassical, rather than behavioral/evolutionary in spirit. While we disagree with that choice, we would argue that the consequences are often of second-order importance, once the impossibility of foresight is conceded and the central role of feedback affirmed. Indeed, our own evolutionary models also involve many elements of maximizing choice – if by that one only means the postulate that an alternative *perceived* as best will be chosen from some *limited* set of alternatives that is itself the product of the firm's *past behavior* (among other things).

degree, not kind. As we will elaborate shortly, our history-friendly models aim to generate time paths that fit the empirical phenomena qualitatively, rather than to reproduce particular descriptive data.

On the other hand, with the exception of this evolutionary growth model, all of the earlier evolutionary models of which we are aware aimed for at most a rough consistency with stylized characterizations of empirical phenomena. This is very much the case with the models of industry evolution we have cited. And for the most part, while motivated by appreciative theory of what was going on in an arena of economic activity, the authors of these earlier models paid nowhere near the attention to the details of the appreciative accounts that we do in our history-friendly modeling efforts.

2.4   PRIOR WORK ON HISTORY-FRIENDLY MODELING

In the last ten years several history-friendly models have appeared in the literature. Some models, starting from the first one proposed in 1999, tackled the analysis of innovation and industry evolution in specific sectors. In addition to the models proposed for computers (Malerba *et al.*, 1999), pharmaceuticals (Malerba and Orsenigo, 2002) and semiconductors and computers (Malerba *et al.*, 2008a, 2008b) – which are ancestors of those presented in Chapters 3, 4 and 5 – other industries have been examined.

Murmann and Brenner (2003) examine the synthetic dye industry in the late nineteenth century and early twentieth century. They study the emergence of scientific capabilities in organic chemistry, the new key role of advanced human capital in innovation and the rise of new actors in research (such as German universities), in the evolution of the chemical industry and in the change of international leadership from British firms to German firms. Kim and Lee (2003) focus on the semiconductor DRAM industry from the early 1970s to the late 1980s. The industry is modeled as being highly cumulative in its technological advance, with process innovations playing an important role in productivity increases. These technological features lead to a market structure dominated by large diversified firms. Malerba and Yoon (2011) examine the industrial dynamics associated with the change in the knowledge base of the semiconductor industry toward more application-specific knowledge and more modularity. These changes in the knowledge base led to a vertical division of innovative and productive labor, marked by the emergence of specialization between "fabless" (design) firms and foundries.

Other history-friendly models focus either on the evolution of specific technologies or on the dynamics of the international specialization of some countries in specific technologies. Fontana *et al.* (2008) model technological bifurcation between United States and Britain in the nineteenth century, which was shaped by the nature of technological opportunities and the patterns of demand. Oltra and Saint Jean (2005) examine the dynamics of environmental technologies – in particular the pattern of evolution of clean technology and the related industrial structure – as affected by the selection among different strategies regarding the combination of environmental and productive performance attributes in new products. Yoon (2011) models the emergent specialization of Korea and Taiwan in electronics industries, in which firms in one country focused on process innovation and in the other on product innovation, with resulting differences between the Korean and Taiwanese settings in terms of firm size, cost structures, knowledge diffusion and potential entrants.

History-friendly models can also facilitate the examination of more general issues. Starting from the models developed for specific industries, the use of these models has allowed us to explore different aspects and more general issues regarding innovation and industry evolution. Examples are the role of experimental users (Malerba *et al.*, 2007), user-producer interactions (Malerba and Orsenigo, 2010), public policy of support for innovation, entry and diffusion (Malerba *et al.*, 2001, 2008b), and entry and the dynamics of concentration (Garavaglia *et al.*, 2006). We will come back to these issues in the concluding chapter of this book.

2.5   CREATING AND EVALUATING HISTORY-FRIENDLY
MODELS

As we have said, the empirical subject matter analyzed in this book is the historical record of the development of technology and the evolution of industry structure in a number of economic sectors. Researchers who have studied those particular histories have developed an appreciative theory, or set of them, that they believe explains or at least is consistent with what has happened. In the analyses that follow in this book, we first summarize those appreciative theories and develop our own version of them based on our own reading of the historical record and the factors that have molded it. We highlight the causal arguments in those theories. Then we construct a formal model that we believe captures the central causal arguments of the appreciative theory, albeit in stylized and simplified form. The building of that model provides a vehicle for checking out the consistency and completeness of those arguments, at least to the extent that they are represented in the model. And with a formal model in hand it is possible to explore whether the causal arguments, in their stylized form, are capable of generating the phenomena (again in stylized form) that they propose to explain.

Like most of the earlier evolutionary models, our history-friendly models take the form of computer simulations.[4] Various objections against simulation methods have been raised over the years; in particular there is the claim that simulation models are inherently less rigorous and illuminating than ones that can be dealt with mathematically. It is often complained that the presence of a large number of parameters allows the simulator to obtain whatever result might be desired. We challenge this. The requirement that a simulation model actually "runs" provides a logical discipline analogous to the

---

[4]   In principle, however, the history-friendly methodology is not fundamentally linked to simulation. Should a history-friendly model turn out to be analytically tractable, there would be no need for computer simulation. More plausibly and hence more importantly, to the extent that *some portion* of a model is analytically tractable, there is to that extent no need for simulation.

requirement that a mathematical formulation be "solvable." And most parameters are not "free" at all, being fixed throughout all the simulations – of course except those which are changed precisely to probe the theoretical argument. While models that are explored by simulation tend to be more complex than models that can be solved mathematically, the latter also pose, very commonly, the interpretive problem of understanding exactly what is producing the result. Some are open to reasonable doubt regarding whether a claimed "proof" is in fact a proof. The problem of designing the model so that the origin of the results can be seen clearly is especially salient for simulation models, but not unsolvable. In our models we have taken great care to set them up, and explore them, in a way that illuminates the principal forces that are generating the results of interest.

Similar issues have long been identified and extensively discussed across a broad range of applications of simulation techniques. Like many of the earlier evolutionary models, our history-friendly models can be viewed as lying in a small subset of "agent-based modeling," which is itself a small subset of micro-simulation approaches in social science, within the much larger category of simulation applications in general. As compared with many other examples of "agent-based" approaches, however, our models generally contain a larger amount of specific structure that is not explicitly agent-based. For example, firms in our models operate in markets whose functioning is not attributed to specific agents but is part of the specified environment. Similarly, we stylize firm R&D processes in terms of inputs and (stochastic) outputs, and do not treat individual scientists and engineers as "agents." In making the specific modeling choices for these sorts of purposes, we are guided by the ambition to stay close to the appreciative theories of the modeled industries, and not by the ambition to ground all assumptions at the agent level.

Like many users of micro-simulation methods, we are particularly interested in exploring "emergent" properties of our models – by which we mean that they display *"behavior not inherent in or predictable from a knowledge of their constituent parts"* (Holland, 1998,

p. 122, emphasis added). Industry structure, on which we focus much attention, is an emergent property in this sense, as is any feature that is similarly grounded in firm heterogeneity. While it is "emergent" in the sense defined, concentrated structure as a qualitative phenomenon is not an *unexpected* outcome, since the appreciative theories that we draw upon, and many past modeling efforts, provided us with suggestions about its sources in the dynamics of the system. Beyond that, we share the general enthusiasm for the discovery of properties of agent-based models that are both emergent and unexpected, and report some examples in the following chapters.

The core of the model development process consists of translating the relevant appreciative theory into a specification of model agents and their behavior. The characterization of the structure of evolutionary models provided in Nelson and Winter (1982a, pp. 14–21) provides an overall guide to this development process. A crucial step is the specification of the "firm state variables" – the dated quantities that distinguish firms from each other, including their routines (Winter, 1971). Other variables enter at the industry level; these are typically functions of firm state variables (e.g. industry output is the sum of firm outputs). There may also be autonomous industry-level variables, such as some representation of an exogenously changing state of technological opportunity or demand.

Next comes the challenging task of specifying plausible routines or behavioral rules for the model firms. This step is taken under two severe constraints. First, there is the constraint that the only information invoked in a behavioral rule at time t is information that the model calculations have actually made available by time t. True foresight is not allowed – though, of course, a rule involving *attempted* foresight based on explicit modes of inference from past data is perfectly permissible.[5] The second constraint is a vague limit on the overall complexity of the model, which derives ultimately from the

---

5   Acceptance of this "no foresight" principle is in our view a key aspect of what the word "behavioral" means in economic modeling. It crucially distinguishes behavioral models from those that have a "rational expectations" flavor.

requirement that the model offers *understandable* causal explanations for the results it generates. In practice, this means that strong simplifications are required in individual rules. To understand how this happens – and why observers often call a model "complex" in spite of the simplifications – consider this thought experiment. Let us say that a model rule for a particular decision is "simple" if it is expressed as a formula that has no more than three parameters. These might be, for example, the weights placed on three considerations that might plausibly drive that particular decision. But how many decisions does a model firm make? Let's see ... price, output, R&D expenditure, expansion rate, technological focus, suppliers, which rival to imitate, whether to integrate or not, etc. Clearly, it is easy to identify a large number of potential parameters for the model as a whole, and such a model might plausibly be viewed as "complex." It is actually not as complex as it looks, when the near-decomposability of the structure is taken into account, but the complexity can be challenging nevertheless. Endowing model firms with more subtle rules for inference and attempted foresight would increase the complexity very rapidly. Thus, there is an interaction between the two constraints mentioned: limiting model complexity forces reliance on quite simple, feedback-based formulations of how present decisions depend on past events. This in turn means that the modeling process involves repeated engagement with the question, "What are the *main forces* likely to be affecting this sort of decision?" This, of course, is a quintessentially *theoretical* problem.

For guidance in answering those questions, we turn first to the appreciative theory for the industry in question. Beyond that, we gain hints from a wider range of sources that offer insight into the realities of business behavior – including particularly the behavioral theory of the firm and subsequent work in that tradition, and the broader literature on technology, organization and management. Finally, the evolutionary modeling community has developed, over the years, a rich fund of ideas about how such modeling problems can be handled.

The process of specifying the model is temporally interleaved with the process of testing it. This includes repeated checking of the correspondence between the computer code and the intentions of the modelers. Throughout, modeling choices depend on the specific purposes and details of the particular exercise, and are guided by assessments of tentative results.[6] With the model at least tentatively in hand, the next step consists in running, calibrating and conducting the sensitivity analysis of it. With that accomplished, it is time to pursue the principal objectives of the research. We ask whether the main qualitative features of the observed history can be reproduced. We ask whether things could have been different, and if so, why.

---

[6]   For discussion of the use of empirical knowledge in developing simulation models, see Werker and Brenner (2004); Boero and Squazzoni (2005); Murmann and Brenner (2003); Windrum *et al.* (2007).

3   The US computer industry and the dynamics of concentration

3.1   INTRODUCTION

In this chapter we develop a history-friendly model of the development of the US computer industry in the latter half of the twentieth century. The history is marked by a pattern of emergent concentration and subsequent de-concentration, from the industry's birth based on mainframe computers through the advent of personal computers (PC). Our principal analytical purpose in the chapter is to illuminate the explanation for this pattern. We begin in Section 3.2 by laying out the relevant features of that history, the appreciative theorizing about that history and the challenges for history-friendly modeling. In Section 3.3 we develop the model. In Sections 3.4 and 3.5 we display some history-replicating and history-divergent simulations and discuss the major factors affecting the specific evolution of the computer industry and competition among firms. In Section 3.6 we draw our conclusions.

3.2   THE EVOLUTION OF COMPUTER TECHNOLOGY AND THE COMPUTER INDUSTRY

3.2.1   *A stylized history*

A detailed recounting of the industry's history is beyond the scope and purpose of this chapter. We offer only a stylized history of computer technology and the industry, drawing from Flamm (1988), Langlois (1990), Bresnahan and Greenstein (1999) and especially Bresnahan and Malerba (1999).

This chapter is a major revision of previously published work: Malerba *et al.* (1999). The original paper has been improved in the structure, code and technical apparatus.

The computer industry's history shows continuous improvements in machines that serve particular groups of users, punctuated from time to time by the introduction of significant new component technologies that permit the needs of existing users to be better addressed, but also open up the possibility of serving new market segments. In the United States these punctuations were associated with the entry of new firms, which almost always were the first to venture into the new market. However, this happened to a significantly lesser degree in Europe, and hardly at all in Japan.

The evolution of the industry divides naturally into four periods. The first began with the early experimentation, which culminated in designs sufficiently attractive to induce large firms with massive computation tasks, as well as scientific laboratories, to purchase computers. This opened the era of the mainframes. The second period began with the introduction of integrated circuits and the development of minicomputers. The third era is that of the PC, made possible by the invention of the microprocessor. The fourth era, in which we remain today, features networked PCs and the use of the Internet: we do not model this last era. Across these eras, the computational power of computers advanced more or less continuously.

During World War II, and the years right after, public policies in several countries funded projects aiming at the development of computers useful for governmental purposes. In the late 1940s and early 1950s, a number of companies in both the United States and Europe began investing their own funds in computer R&D. They hoped to develop a computer sufficiently attractive to win the market of scientific laboratories, large firms and other organizations with large-scale computation needs. The early 1950s saw the entry of IBM, which at the time was a major punched-card and tabulating machinery company, but with significant capabilities in electronic computing derived in good part from government R&D contracts.[1]

---

[1] See Usselman (1993) for an account of how the capabilities of the "electronic" IBM built on the capabilities of the "electro-mechanical" IBM.

Five other early entrants comprised a group that became known as "the Bunch" (Burroughs, Univac Rand, NCR, Control Data and Honeywell); GE and RCA also entered. These companies differed in the strategies they developed, and in their ability to ideate and produce machines that would sell at a profit. By 1954, with the introduction of the 650, IBM began to pull ahead of the Bunch, and with the introduction of the 1401 in 1960, it came to dominate the world market for electronic computers designed for large-scale accounting applications.

IBM dominated not only in the American market but also in Europe and Japan. A small-scale domestic industry was able to hold on in Europe, and later in Japan, only by virtue of a combination of government subsidy, a guaranteed government market and protection.

Component technology improved greatly during the mainframe era, and transistors gradually replaced vacuum tubes as the basic circuit elements. These developments enabled significant improvements in mainframes' performance, and some reduction in production costs. In the early 1960s IBM introduced its System 360 – a whole family of computers of varying power, with an array of compatible peripheral equipment also offered by IBM. The mix-and-match and upward migration features of System 360 gave IBM the flexibility to address the needs of a wide range of users with varying needs and computing budgets. As a result, IBM seized an even larger share of the mainframe market.

The invention of integrated circuits enabled further improvements in mainframes, stimulating IBM's growth. The use of integrated circuits in computers also reduced barriers to entry. In particular, integrated circuits not only permitted large computers to be made even more powerful, they opened the possibility of designing smaller-scale but still high-powered computers, and of producing them at a much lower cost than mainframes. DEC's PDP8, the first minicomputer, was developed in 1965. Minicomputers opened up a new demand class, not tapped by mainframes, that included medium-sized research laboratories, manufacturing firms and some small businesses.

In the United States, new firms like DEC were the first into the new minicomputer market; these new firms seized and held in it a significant market share. IBM lagged in getting into minicomputers, and never achieved the dominance it held in the mainframe market. While the availability of integrated circuits provided an opportunity for European and Japanese firms to gain a foothold in the minicomputer market, these firms lagged behind, as had been the case with mainframes: American companies took a considerable fraction of the minicomputer market both in Europe and Japan, while domestic firms held onto a limited share of the market and they held that only through a combination of subsidies and protection.

The introduction of microprocessors marked another punctuation in the history of the industry: it enabled significant improvements in mainframes and minicomputers, but the most important impact was to permit the design of reasonably powerful computers that could be produced at quite low costs. PCs based on microprocessors opened up a new demand segment that had not been served by mainframes and minicomputers – small firms and personal users.

As in the case of minicomputers, in the United States new firms entered the industry aiming to serve the new PC market. These prominently included specialized PC design and manufacturing firms (such as Apple, Commodore, Tandy and Compaq). Established mainframe and minicomputer producers were slow in seeing the new market opportunity, and consequently, to address the changing users' needs. When IBM entered the PC market, it relied heavily on external alliances – Microsoft for operating systems software, and Intel for microprocessors. This strategic move, with associated decisions on patent protection and computer design, made it possible for other manufacturers to produce computers that met an "IBM-compatible" standard, which had a major impact on the subsequent evolution of the PC market and the computer market generally. IBM did manage to seize a significant fraction of the PC market for a while, but never was as dominant there as it had been in mainframes. It lost further ground as other firms led the way in the era of networked PCs

(Fransman, 1994). IBM now is out of the PC market entirely, having divested the business to Lenovo in 2005.

A striking characteristic of the firms producing PCs is that they are primarily assemblers, buying most of their components on the open market. Also, most of the software for PCs is developed and supplied by software specialists. This is in sharp contrast with mainframe production, particularly in the early and middle stages of the evolution of the industry. IBM not only designed and produced most of the critical components for its mainframes but also wrote most of the basic software. For a time, IBM also designed and produced a significant fraction of the integrated circuits that were employed in its mainframes. In minicomputers, there was from the beginning more vertical specialization than in mainframe production, with most minicomputer companies buying their integrated circuits, and a number of other key components, on the open market. With the coming of PCs, even more vertical disintegration took place, as will be discussed in Chapter 4.

As noted, the advent of PCs led in the United States to the birth of a number of new firms, several of which turned out to be very successful. Just as in the case of minicomputers, in Europe and Japan, in contrast, few firms entered. And, except where there was heavy government protection or subsidy, American firms came to dominate foreign markets for PCs, until the beginning of the new millennium.

3.2.2   Challenges for history-friendly modeling

One key challenge for history-friendly modeling is to explain what happened to the extent and nature of concentration that occurred in the computer industry as new technologies were introduced and new markets emerged. The evolution of market structure has been marked by the following elements. A dominant firm emerged relatively early in the industry's history and held its market share in the segment it first seized in the face of several "competence destroying" and "architectural" technological innovations (Tushman and Anderson, 1986; Henderson and Clark, 1990; Christensen, 1997). On the other hand, new firms have been the vehicles through which new technologies opened up new market segments. The old established firms have also entered the new market but have been unable to shut the newcomers out.

The verbal histories of the industry provide a sketch of the explanation for why incumbent firms have been able to hold off newcomers with new technology in their traditional markets but have not been able to seize new market opportunities. In the model that follows we present some of the same arguments in stylized form.

3.3 THE MODEL

In this section we lay out the basic model. It is in the nature of complex simulation models that there is a risk of befuddling the reader and obscuring the basic logic of the model by offering too much detail all at once. We begin, therefore, by describing the gist of the model in transparent form. Further detail is provided subsequently.

3.3.1 Overview

In our model we simplify greatly the industry history we have just recounted. The model embraces just two of the historical eras discussed in our stylized history. It begins in the era when mainframe computers come into existence, based on transistors as their key components. Mainframe technology improves over time as the result of the R&D efforts of computer firms, but there are diminishing returns to R&D. Subsequently, the model posits an exogenous change in the form of microprocessor technology; this expands the possibilities for the evolution of mainframes: it also makes possible the design and production of PCs, which are significantly cheaper though less powerful than mainframes. Throughout, potential purchasers of computers value both computer performance and cheapness, but vary in the relative importance they give to these two attributes. Thus, the demand for computers is expressed, following Lancaster (1966), as deriving from a demand for specific product characteristics, that is, performance and cheapness. Some potential computer buyers value

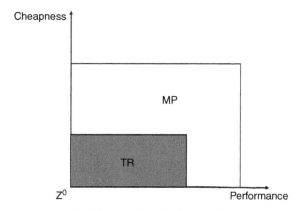

FIGURE 3.1 Attributes and technological limits of computers with transistor and microprocessor technologies.

performance greatly, and are willing to pay a lot for it. These customers make up the market for mainframes. The availability of PCs brings into the computer market a whole new set of customers who value cheapness greatly and are satisfied with more modest computer performance.

For each of the component technologies, there is an implied outer limit for the potential computer designs that can be achieved using them in the two relevant dimensions. For analytic convenience, we treat those technological limits as defining a rectangular box. Thus in Figure 3.1 the two boxes depict the set of technological characteristics that potentially can be achieved in computers designed around transistor and microprocessor technologies as basic components. The use of microprocessors rather than transistors permits the design of better computers, both in terms of performance (Z^{PE}), and of cheapness (Z^{CH}). However, the more dramatic improvement potential lies in the direction of cheapness.

The outer limits of what is feasible under the two technologies are "potentials." The potential is not achievable, however, without significant investment in R&D, and also requires learning from experience. The first efforts of a new firm trying to design a computer using transistors, or (later) microprocessors, will only be able to

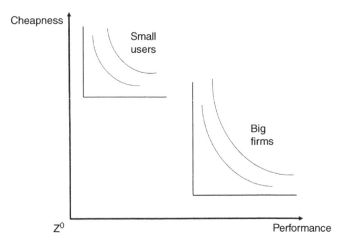

FIGURE 3.2 Preferences and minimum thresholds of attributes requirements for the two user classes.

achieve a design characterized by point Z^0 (for zero experience). Over time, a firm's sustained R&D effort allows it to advance gradually from Z^0 toward $Z_{f,t}$ (where subscript f denotes a specific firm and subscript t refers to a specific period).[2] Later we specify the dynamics of design improvements built into the model.

On the demand side, there are two distinct classes of potential customers. One class, which we will call "large organizations," greatly values "performance" and wants to buy "mainframes." The second class, which we will call "individuals," or "small users," has less need for high performance but values "cheapness" more. It provides a potential market for "personal computers," or PCs.

Each of our two user classes requires minimum levels of performance and cheapness before they can be enticed to buy any computers at all. Once threshold characteristics are reached, the value that customers place on a computer design is an increasing function of its performance and its cheapness. In Figure 3.2 we depict the preferences of large firms and small organizations. The difference in the demand of

2   The point $Z_{f,t}$ is identified by the two coordinates expressing the value of cheapness $(Z_{f,t}^{CH})$ and performance $(Z_{f,t}^{PE})$.

the two user classes is reflected in both the difference in threshold requirements and in the "indifference curves."

If we overlay Figure 3.2 on Figure 3.1, we note that even if computers achieve the outer limits permitted by transistor technology, the threshold requirements of small users will not be met. Thus, the design of computers that can successfully serve the PC market depends on the availability of microprocessors.

The "indifference curves" of Figure 3.2 depict designs of equal value or "merit" in the eyes of the two customer classes. We assume that higher computer merit translates into more computers bought by customers. The details are introduced later on.

The previous discussion suggests the broad outlines of what one would expect to see in a simulated industry history, and also points out some of the issues that need to be addressed in the specification of the dynamics. Assuming that there is some way that firms can obtain funds, computer technology will start out at Z^0. Over time, and with R&D spending, computer designs will improve until ultimately they crack through the threshold requirements of the mainframe market. Then, firms that have achieved threshold-meeting designs will begin to make sales: as computers improve, sales will grow. The introduction of microprocessors will open up the potential to better meet mainframe demand, and to design machines to be sold on the PC market. New firms that try to catch these opportunities need some funding to survive the initial phase, when few sales occur. However, ultimately, one would expect that microprocessor-based computers would take over the mainframe market, and be able to tap the new PC market. We now turn to explicit dynamics.

3.3.2 Innovation dynamics, firms' finance, R&D, advertising and pricing decisions

In our model, firms gradually develop competencies as a result of the R&D investments they make, and the experience they accumulate. Our formulation captures significant elements of the views of firm dynamics put forward by Nelson and Winter (1982a, 1982b), Dosi and Marengo (1993), Teece *et al.* (1992) and Teece (2009).

Firms (indexed by subscript f) are represented by sets of technological and marketing competencies that are accumulated over time, and by rules of action. The focal competencies in the model are design capabilities: by building incrementally on their past achievements and by accumulating experience, firms produce successive generations of computers with superior cost/performance attributes. Other actions reflected in the model of the firm concern the pricing of products, R&D and advertising expenditures, the adoption of new technologies and diversification into new markets. There is no explicit representation of production *per se*, or of investments in capacity. Rather, it is assumed that the requisite production capabilities can be obtained and employed at a cost per computer that reflects the "cheapness" attribute of the design.

As mentioned, our model reflects the fact that, when a firm starts operating in a new technology, a considerable period may pass before it is able to sell any product. At the beginning, some source of funding is required to cover the R&D and other learning costs. For established firms, this funding can come from retained earnings generated by the sale of other products. For new firms, external sources are needed.

At the starting period of our model, with the introduction of transistors, we assume that there are a number of firms (F_{TR}), endowed by "venture capitalists" with an initial budget to spend on R&D, who hope to exploit the new technological opportunities. All firms start with the same initial design capabilities, depicted by Z^0 in Figure 3.1, interpretable as the design characteristics that have been achieved by experimental computers that are in the public domain. Firms start off with different total budgets $(B^0_{f,k})$ dedicated to funding R&D over a period of time.[3] While their initial budgets differ, we assume that all firms have to spend them over the same time period (T^D), and each period they spend a constant fraction of that budget $(1 / T^D)$. If the

---

[3] The mean budget differs between transistor and microprocessor technologies, indexed by k.

funds are exhausted before a marketable design is achieved, firms exit. If a firm achieves a marketable design before funds are exhausted, it uses both the fraction of initial budget and the resources from profits (as explained later) to finance its R&D.

R&D outcomes are influenced by firm-specific strategies represented by choices of search direction in the capabilities space, but also by latent technological opportunities. Firms are born with different, randomly selected directions of search for technological improvement along the two technological dimensions, cheapness and performance. The notion that competencies cannot be changed rapidly and without cost is captured by the (extreme) assumption that the firm-specific parameters governing search do not change. Thus, after the initial period, all firms in the industry are doing different things, achieving computer designs with different characteristics.

As firms spend on R&D, they accumulate technical competencies. Technical progress is represented in the model as a change in computer design along the two technical dimensions, generated by the application of these firm-specific competencies. Technical competencies are represented as a stock that grows over time as a result of R&D expenditures.

Each firm orients its R&D expenditures to improving the computers it produces in a particular direction, that is, along a particular ray in the performance-cheapness space. The improvements period by period in the merit of the computers the firm is able to offer on the market proceed according to the following equations:

$$\Delta Z^{PE}_{f,t} = \beta^{PE} \cdot (R^{PE}_{f,t})^{\beta^R} \cdot (EX_{f,k,t})^{\beta^{EX}} \cdot (\Lambda^{PE}_k - Z^{PE}_{f,t-1})^{\beta^{\Lambda}} \cdot e^{PE}_{f,t} \qquad (1.a)$$

$$\Delta Z^{CH}_{f,t} = \beta^{CH} \cdot (R^{CH}_{f,t})^{\beta^R} \cdot (EX_{f,k,t})^{\beta^{EX}} \cdot (\Lambda^{CH}_k - Z^{CH}_{f,t-1})^{\beta^{\Lambda}} \cdot e^{CH}_{f,t} \qquad (1.b)$$

where Δ represents the difference operator,[4] the superscripts PE and CH refer to performance and cheapness, respectively; the subscript k

4 To be more precise, Δ represents the backward difference operator, that is, $\Delta f_t = f_t - f_{t-1}$.

indicates the technology (transistors or microprocessors); and the subscripts f and t refer to firms and time periods, respectively.

The first variables in the equations ($R_{f,t}^{PE}$ and $R_{f,t}^{CH}$) are a function of the firm's R&D expenditures in the performance and cheapness dimensions.[5] The second element ($EX_{f,k,t}$) represents the experience of the firm in a particular technology k: for each period it increases by one. The third element in the equations is the distance between the maximum level an attribute of a computer can achieve using a technology (Λ_k^{PE} and Λ_k^{CH}) and the currently achieved level of a computer attribute using that technology ($Z_{f,t-1}^{PE}$ and $Z_{f,t-1}^{CH}$). Notice that as a company's computers get better and better, and the room for further improvement using that technology diminishes, the returns to R&D decrease. The last element of the equations is a random component drawn from a normal distribution with mean μ^e and standard deviation σ^e, reflecting the non-deterministic character of technical change.[6]

The company is assumed to orient its research and development spending ($B_{f,t}^{RD}$) so as both to reduce its costs of producing a computer and improve the attributes of the computer it produces, in amounts that preserve the ratio of performance and cheapness that defines its design strategy. Given the value of $Z_{f,t}^{CH}$ it has achieved at a given time, a firm offers its computers to buyers at price $P_{f,t}$ so that

$$P_{f,t} = \frac{v}{Z_{f,t}^{CH}} \tag{2}$$

and:

$$C_{f,t}^{PD} \cdot (1+m) = P_{f,t} \tag{3}$$

Equation 2 just says that the price is the inverse of cheapness, adjusted by a scale factor v. In Equation 3 $C_{f,t}^{PD}$ is the unit cost of

---

[5]   They are obtained by dividing the R&D budget allocated to each attribute by the R&D unit cost (C^{RD}), which is a constant.

[6]   This distribution is truncated at zero in order to avoid negative changes in cheapness and performance.

production of firm f at time t and m is the markup over cost used in pricing. The markup is assumed to be the same for all firms and a constant over time. Thus, progress toward higher "cheapness" is expressed in two tightly linked ways, a lower price to buyers and a lower cost of production.

In turn, the gross profits of a firm $(\Pi_{f,t})$, in the sense of sales revenues minus production costs are:

$$\Pi_{f,t} = (q_{f,t} \cdot P_{f,t}) - (q_{f,t} \cdot C_{f,t}^{PD}) \tag{4.a}$$

where $q_{f,t}$ is the total number of computers sold by the company, explained later in Equation 11. Then, by applying Equation 3, we obtain the following expression for profits:

$$\Pi_{f,t} = q_{f,t} \cdot m \cdot C_{f,t}^{PD} \tag{4.b}$$

Gross profits are used by the firm for several purposes. First, if the firm still has outstanding debt, it allots a fraction φ^{DB} of its gross profit to paying interest and reducing its indebtedness. Second, it spends a fraction φ^{RD} of what remains on R&D,[7] and a fraction φ^A on advertising. The excess gross profits after debt repayment, R&D expenditures and advertising are accumulated in an account $(B_{f,t})$ that yields the interest rate, r, in each period.

Profits also drive exit behavior of the firms. A firm exits when its profits do not guarantee returns higher than the interest rate. More specifically, in each period the variable

$$E_{f,t} = (1 - w^E) \cdot E_{f,t-1} + w^E \cdot Y_{f,t} \tag{5}$$

is computed, where w^E is a parameter that determines the weight of current and past performance in the exit decision. $Y_{f,t}$ takes a positive value if the rate of return of firm f at time t is higher than the interest

---

[7] This fraction is constant in periods of R&D expansion. In periods of R&D shrinkage, R&D expenditures are computed as a fraction $\tilde{\varphi}^{RD}$ of past R&D expenditures, because we assume that R&D expenditures are sticky and cannot be immediately compressed.

rate, and negative otherwise.[8] The value of $E_{f,t}$ is initialized at zero. A firm exits if $E_{f,t}$ is lower than a constant threshold (λ^E).[9] Firms also exit if their profits do not guarantee a minimum level (λ^R) of R&D expenditures (and obviously if they run out of money).

In the model we distinguish between a firm's marketing capabilities and advertising expenditures. Marketing capabilities $(A_{f,t})$ are considered in a very similar way to technological capabilities. Advertising expenditures $(B_{f,t}^A)$ lead to an accumulation of these marketing capabilities over time. Specifically, the model first computes advertising expenditures:

$$B_{f,t}^A = \varphi^A \cdot \pi_{f,t} \cdot (1 - \varphi^{DB}) \tag{6}$$

Advertising expenditures improve marketing capabilities at a decreasing rate:

$$\Delta A_{f,t} = a^0 \cdot (B_{f,t}^A)^{a^1} \tag{7}$$

where $a°$ and a^1 are parameters.

$A_{f,t}$ improves the attractiveness of a computer produced by firm f for the potential customers (see later Equation 9 that determines the propensity of a computer to be purchased by a customer).

3.3.3 Market dynamics

An essential feature of the computer market is the existence of differentiated products and different market segments. We include in the model a stylized account of these features of the demand side of the industry. Computer producers face a market composed of different types of users who have different needs regarding the characteristics of computers. Moreover, demand behavior is influenced by

---

[8] The variable $Y_{f,t}$ is given by the difference between the net worth of firm f at time t $(B_{f,t} - DB_{f,t})$ – where DB is the amount of debt – normalized by the value of initial investment $(B_{f,k}^0)$ accumulated at interest rate r since firm entry, and the same variable at time $t-1$. Simple algebraic manipulations show that $Y_{f,t}$ is positive when the rate of return – the percentage change in the net worth – of firm f is greater than the interest rate, and negative otherwise.

[9] In order to avoid an early exit of the firms, we chose a negative value of λ^E.

informational considerations and by the advertising efforts of producers, as well as by the actual merit of alternatives presented.
"Comparison shopping" is limited. Some customers may purchase
computers that are far from the best in the market at the time, simply
because, viewed in isolation, those computers are worth the asking
price. Finally, "bandwagon" (i.e. imitative behavior relating to brand
preferences) and brand loyalty effects may play an important role in
determining the performance of individual firms.

Each of the two broad markets for computers, one consisting of
large organizations and the other of individuals, in turn is divided into
a set of smaller groups, each associated with a particular potential
computer user or a collection of them. As we will develop in more
detail shortly, the number of computers a user will buy, if it buys any,
is a function of the merit (in its eyes) of the computers it buys.

Early in our simulated histories, many of these potential users
will not have bought any computers yet. As the computers that are
offered get better and cheaper, some of these users will become active
and buy. We assume that a potential user will not necessarily know if a
computer meeting its threshold requirements is actually offered.
Rather we assume that the chances a user will be actively looking at
the available computers are sensitive to the number of firms offering
computers that do meet those requirements. The probability that a
potential user is active increases with the number of computer firms
that are able to offer acceptable computers and it becomes one when
this number reaches a value λ_h^F, a parameter of the model that differs
across the two broad markets, large organizations and individuals
(indexed by h).

Computers in use have a finite life, and for analytic convenience
we assume that all computers bought earlier by a buyer fail at the same
time, which is determined probabilistically.[10] We assume that users

---

[10]   In any period t there is a probability Θ_h that the computers of a user will break down.
This probability is equal for all users and constant over time but differs across user
classes h. The number of breakdowns is determined as the outcome of a number of
binomial trials equal to the number of users.

who have bought computers before, but whose present computers have failed, are definitely in the market for new ones. Thus the total sales of computers at any time by all computer vendors is the sum of sales to potential users that have not bought computers before, and sales to users that had bought before but whose computers have worn out.

We adopt a simple formulation of customer preferences. Consider a particular group of potential buyers of either the "large organization" or "individual" type and a computer produced by firm f at time t with particular characteristics of performance $Z_{f,t}^{PE}$ and cheapness $Z_{f,t}^{CH}$. Then, the merit of this computer for customers within user class h is given by a Cobb-Douglas function with arguments that measure the extent to which threshold requirements have been exceeded rather than the raw values of cheapness and performance themselves:

$$M_{f,h,t} = \gamma_h^M \cdot (Z_{f,t}^{PE} - \lambda_h^{PE})^{\gamma_h^{PE}} \cdot (Z_{f,t}^{CH} - \lambda_h^{CH})^{\gamma_h^{CH}} \tag{8}$$

where γ_h^M is a scale parameter, and λ_h^{PE} and λ_h^{CH} are the threshold levels for acceptable performance and cheapness. If threshold requirements of user class h are not met, then the merit of the computer for that group is equal to 0. The sum of the exponents in Equation 8 operates like a sort of generalized demand elasticity reflecting performance as well as price. Differences in the needs of large organizations and small users are reflected in different values for parameters γ_h^{PE} and γ_h^{CH}.

Let the number of computers of a particular character that potentially would be purchased by a user (if no other competing products were offered in the market) correspond to the level of merit of design $M_{f,h,t}$. In other words, the greater the merit of a machine, the greater the number of machines that will be purchased. Thus, Equation 8 is treated heuristically as a demand curve.

After some time, a pioneering firm in the industry will succeed in achieving a computer design satisfying the minimum thresholds required by customers in the mainframes market and will start selling its product on the market. At the beginning, the market is small, both because the merit of computers is low (the industry is in its infancy and technology has not yet progressed very much) and because many potential buyers may not recognize that these products are available, as described earlier. Also, the PC is not yet feasible technologically. As the quality of computers increases and as more and more firms enter the market, total demand grows as a consequence of both an increase in the number of customers and an increase in the number of computers purchased by each group of customers.

If there is more than one kind of computer that meets threshold requirements, customers are attracted by those with higher merit as it results from the specific mix of performance and cheapness characteristics. However, various informational factors also affect customer behavior. The appreciative story put forth by many scholars of the history of the industry, accounting for the sustained dominance of IBM in the mainframe market, highlighted the role of bandwagon effects, brand loyalty (or lock-in) and advertising. Thus, our formal model needs to respect this analysis, and our treatment of demand includes considerations other than merit. These are captured in a compact formulation by variables representing firms' market shares and advertising capabilities.

For a customer within one of the two big markets h that makes a purchase at time t, the propensity to purchase the computer produced by firm f, is determined as follows:

$$u_{f,h,t} = (M_{f,h,t})^{\delta_h^M} \cdot [max(s_{f,t-1}, \lambda_h^S)]^{\delta_h^{Ss}} \cdot [max(A_{f,t}, \lambda^A)]^{\delta_h^A} \cdot e_{f,t}^u \quad (9)$$

Here, as noted, $M_{f,h,t}$ denotes the "merit" of a computer offered by firm f, $A_{f,t}$ represents the marketing capabilities of the firm, $s_{f,t-1}$ is the market share of the firm's product and $e_{f,t}^u$ is a random component to have a probabilistic rather than a deterministic propensity.[11] The market share variable can be interpreted in terms of a bandwagon effect, according to which buyers are attracted by the products of

---

[11] The random variable $e_{f,t}^u$ is uniformly distributed between 0.9 and 1.1.

firms enjoying larger market shares for reasons such as reputation, network externalities and the like.[12]

The parameter λ_h^S allows us to impute a small positive market share to firms that actually have zero share, thus assuring that firms that have just broken into the market can attract some sales.[13] The parameter λ^A performs a similar role for firms that have just broken into the market and have not yet invested in advertising to create a brand image, $A_{f,t}$.

Then, the probability that a customer will purchase a computer j is computed as follows:

$$U_{f,h,t} = \frac{u_{f,h,t}}{\sum_{f=1}^{F_{h,t}} u_{f,h,t}} \tag{10}$$

where $F_{h,t}$ is the total number of firms offering a product to the user group h at time t. This probability is used as a proxy for the market share of the firm. Therefore, company f will sell its computers to a number of customers indicated by $G_{f,h,t}$, which is obtained as the product between $U_{f,h,t}$ and the number of customers buying a product in user class h at time t. Then the total number of computers sold by company f is given by:

$$q_{f,t} = q_{f,h,t} = M_{f,h,t} \cdot G_{f,h,t} \tag{11}$$

We assume, for the sake of simplicity, that a company can sell its computers either to large organizations or small users, but not both.[14] Hence, we drop the subscript h.

---

[12] The model includes also the possibility of activating lock-ins and brand loyalty effects, whereby customers who had previously bought machines of a particular brand tend to buy again from the same producer. For the sake of simplicity we have not activated this mechanism in the simulations presented in this book.

[13] It differs across mainframes and PCs markets to reflect the different number of potential entrants across the two markets.

[14] The user class to which a firm sells its product is the first one whose minimum thresholds for cheapness and performance are satisfied by the product characteristics. If the requirements of both user classes are satisfied in the same period, the most recent one (individual users) is selected. Later in the chapter we will allow a mainframe company to set up a new division to sell to small users.

Note the following: first, if there is only one computer that meets threshold requirements, each purchasing customer will buy it. Suppose, however, that there is more than one computer that passes the threshold. If δ_h^M is very high, and δ_h^s and δ_h^A are very low, virtually all customers will buy the computer with the highest merit score. On the other hand, if δ_h^M is relatively low, or δ_h^s and δ_h^A are high, a higher merit computer may be "out sold" by a rival computer that has the higher existing market share, or which has been advertised more intensively, or both.

In the absence of the bandwagon effect, or of advertising, the demand module would behave similarly to a standard demand curve. Although a positive probability of survival for inferior computers always remains, demand would largely reflect "best value for the money." Convergence to that result is faster at higher values of the parameter δ_h^M. The consideration of bandwagon and advertising effects potentially changes this picture drastically, introducing inertia and forms of increasing returns.

3.3.4 Competition between technologies

After a number of periods (T_{MP}) have gone by in a simulated history, and after a number of mainframe firms using transistors have successfully entered the mainframe market (called "first-generation mainframe firms"), microprocessors come into existence and are ready to be adopted by current computer firms. Some periods later (T^{AD}), the microprocessor technology is ready to be adopted by computer firms and a number of new firms (F_{MP}) start out at point Z^0 in Figure 3.1, with funding provided by venture capitalists, just as earlier new firms had started out at that point using transistor technology. Some of these firms will fail before they get into a market. Others may succeed. We reflect historical occurrences by assuming that the number of computer firms entering with the microprocessor technology is higher than in the case of the transistor technology $(F_{MP} > F_{TR})$, but they are endowed with a lower initial budget $(B_{f,MP}^0 < B_{f,TR}^0)$.

While existing first-generation mainframe firms do not pose a "barrier to entry" for microprocessor firms who have aimed their trajectory toward the PC market, the presence of such firms in the mainframe market creates a significant barrier to entry there. A microprocessor firm that succeeds in achieving a design that meets threshold requirements in the mainframe market (called "second-generation mainframe firms") still faces competition with existing transistor-based products displaying higher-than-threshold quality levels. Further, the extant transistor-based mainframe producers (i.e. the first-generation mainframe firms) have acquired positive market shares, and are engaged in significant advertising, which further disadvantages a newcomer. In general, therefore, it is an open question whether a second-generation mainframe firm (using microprocessors) can survive in the mainframe market – with the answer depending, in the model, on parameter values. If not, and if extant first-generation mainframe firms cannot switch over from transistors to make mainframes out of microprocessors, the potential of the microprocessor in the production of mainframes will never be realized.

In the actual history, some second-generation mainframe firms using microprocessors entered the mainframe market but did not succeed well there, in part because extant mainframe firms themselves adopted microprocessor technologies. Furthermore, some first-generation mainframe firms, IBM in particular, used microprocessor technology to try to enter the PC market. Thus there are two different kinds of transitional dynamics that need to be built into this model, if it is to be "history friendly." First, we must enable firms that originally are using one technology to switch to another. Second, we must enable firms established in a market to try to diversify into the other.

3.3.5 Transition dynamics

As noted earlier, we seek to capture in our model a number of aspects of the new understanding about dynamic capabilities, and the lock-in of competencies. Firms tend to improve their specific capabilities over time; on the other hand, they often have a good deal of difficulty when they try to implement significantly innovative developments. Tushman and Anderson (1986), Henderson and Clark (1990) and subsequent contributors have documented the difficulty that firms often have in coping when the leading technologies underlying their products change significantly. Quite often, incumbent firms cannot switch over rapidly enough to counter the efforts of new firms using the new technology. Christensen and Rosenbloom (1994a, 1994b) and Christensen (1997) have put a spotlight on similar difficulties that extant firms have had in recognizing new markets when they opened up.

It is fundamental in our model that firm competencies are cumulative, with today's design efforts building on what was achieved yesterday. More radical changes sometimes occur, however. Thus, consistent with the historical experience, we assume that transistor-based mainframe firms (i.e. the first-generation mainframe firms) can switch over to microprocessor technology for use in their mainframe designs, but this may be time-consuming and costly for them. The probability that an extant first-generation mainframe firm will try to switch over is a function of two variables. The first is how far along microprocessor computer designs have been pushed. The second is the closeness of a first-generation mainframe firm to the technological possibility frontier defined by transistor technology. The former clearly is a signal to extant firms that "there is a potentially powerful new technology out there, and we may be in trouble if we don't adopt it." The latter is an indication that "we can't get much further if we keep on pushing along the same road."

If a first-generation mainframe firm decides to switch over, it faces one significant disadvantage, but also has an advantage. The disadvantage is that the experience that got it to the forefront of transistor technology (recall Equation 1) counts for less if it shifts over to microprocessor technology. In general, in its first efforts in microprocessor computer design, the first-generation mainframe firm might be disadvantaged in terms of experience compared to some of the second-generation firms. Further, it must incur a one-time switchover cost in order to start designing, producing and marketing microprocessor based mainframes. However, the first-generation mainframe firm has financial and reputational resources that it can redeploy to working with the new technology.

The specifics of these model mechanisms are as follows. Adoption of the new technology by an incumbent producer takes place in two steps. First, a firm must "perceive" microprocessor technology. The probability that a potential adopter firm f perceives the microprocessor technology at time t ($AD_{f,t}$) depends on its current technological position in relation to the technological frontier in transistors and on the progress realized by the new technology, as specified by the following equation:

$$AD_{f,t} = \left[\frac{(1 - b_{f,t}^{TR}/d^{TR})^{\alpha^{TR}} + (o_t^{MP}/d^{MP})^{\alpha^{MP}}}{2} \right]^{\alpha^{AD}} \tag{12}$$

where d represents the diagonal – the distance from the starting point to its maximum – of a technology, $b_{f,t}^{TR}$ is the distance from the current position of firm f in the technological space to the limits of the transistor technology, and o_t^{MP} is the distance from the starting point to the current position of the best firm using the microprocessor technology. The two exponents α^{TR} and α^{MP} represent the relative weight of the two factors affecting perception (the distance to the current technology frontier and the advancement of the new technology). The parameter α^{AD} measures the general difficulty of perceiving the new technology.

Once firms have perceived the possibility of adoption, they have to invest to acquire the new technology. The total amount of resources to invest for the adoption of the new technology (B_f^{AD}) includes a fixed cost (C^{AD}) equal for all firms, and the payment of a fraction φ^{AD} of firms' current accumulated profits account ($B_{f,t}$), attributable to costs related to the size of the firm. Thus,

$$B_f^{AD} = C^{AD} + \varphi^{AD} \cdot B_{f,t} \tag{13}$$

A firm whose accumulated account does not cover the fixed costs cannot adopt microprocessors. Moreover, the competence-destroying nature of the new technology is captured by the notion that, with the adoption of the new technology, the experience accumulated with transistors can only in part be applied to microprocessors: we assume that the experience after the adoption is equal to a fraction φ_f^{EX} of the experience accumulated with the previous technology.[15] However, firms that have adopted the new technology then have access to the new technological frontier and can innovate faster. They maintain their original strategies regarding the local direction of improvement in the mainframe market. Their trajectories bend, however, in response to the novel potential of microprocessors.

Once the first-generation firm has switched over to microprocessor technology, it has the potential to diversify by designing (and trying to sell) computers on the PC market. The incentive to diversify is a function of the size of the PC market, defined in terms of the number of computers sold, compared to the mainframe market. Specifically, diversification becomes attractive when the ratio between the size of the PC market and the size of the mainframe market is bigger than a threshold value (λ^{DV}), which is a parameter of the model.[16]

Our model assumptions about diversification of mainframe producers into the PC market follow the historical example, in which IBM diversified by setting up an entirely new division. The diversifying company founds a new division, seeking to exploit "public knowledge" in the PC market and to "imitate" PC firms, rather than to apply its own mainframe competencies to the new market. Specifically, the position of the new division in the design space is determined as the average merit of design prevailing in the PC market at the time diversification occurs, and its experience is set to zero. The division's

---

[15]   This fraction differs across firms and is extracted from a uniform distribution between 0.5 and 1.

[16]   The size ratio is units free because we conceive of PC quantities as measured in mainframe-equivalents.

local search direction in the design space is a random draw from the same population characterizing the "de novo" entrants to the PC market. After birth, the new division behaves exactly as a new entrant, with independent products and profits and budget. It does, however, receive some initial resources from the parent company that are a fraction φ^{DV} subtracted from the accumulated profits of the parent. Moreover, the new firm inherits also some of the marketing capabilities, in the form of a costless spillover (ψ^{DV}).[17] Given these favorable initial conditions, the development time required to spend the initial budget (T^{DV}) is shorter than in the case of new entrants.[18]

3.4 HISTORY-REPLICATING AND HISTORY-DIVERGENT SIMULATIONS

3.4.1 *History-replicating simulations*

Generally speaking, this model is able to "replicate" the industry history when endowed with a set of parameter values that reflect the key propositions advanced by economists who have sought to explain the main patterns of the industry history. We call this set of parameter values the "standard set." The patterns that we now identify are typical of simulation runs based on the standard set.

A dominant first-generation (transistor-based) mainframe firm, a simulated counterpart for IBM, emerges relatively quickly in the mainframe market. That firm holds on to its large share of the market, even when new microprocessor firms enter that market and challenge it. Part of the reason the dominant firm holds on is that it shifts over to microprocessor technology in a relatively timely manner. That firm then enters the PC market, and gains a nontrivial, but not a dominant, share. The specific firm that rises to dominance varies from run to run. That is, its dominance does not reflect firm-specific considerations that were introduced ab initio, but rather arises from the interaction of the dynamics of industry evolution with inter-firm differences that

---

[17]   The level of marketing capabilities remains the same in the parent company.

[18]   During this period only a fraction φ^B of initial resources is spent on R&D so to guarantee an adequate level of the budget.

come from random factors. In this sense, the model explains the appearance of dominance but does not aspire to predict which firm will come to be dominant. It thus has something in common with the stochastic theories of the firm-size distribution in the tradition of Gibrat (see Sutton, 1997). In contrast to those theories, however, our model introduces the random effects at specific points in a causal nexus involving many different causal forces.

Economists who have studied the history of the computer industry have tended to identify the following as key factors. First, the early customers of IBM equipment tended to find themselves "locked in" to IBM for upgrades, extensions and renewal of their computer capacity, largely because of specialized software. This made entry of new firms difficult. As expressed in our model, a firm that has a high market share in mainframes will attract a significant share of new purchases – with the deep causes arising from considerations such as those that favored IBM. Second, by the time the new technology came along, computer design under the old technology was reasonably advanced, and the leader, IBM, responded to the availability of new technology quite rapidly. Consistent with that history, our typical model results show that soon after the early second-generation mainframe firms using microprocessors enter the mainframe market, the dominant first-generation firm in that market switches over from transistors to microprocessors. Third, IBM's massive resources enabled IBM to enter the PC market and quickly mount an R&D and advertising effort sufficient to catch up with the earlier entrants into the PC market. However, because the PCs produced by a number of other companies were compatible with the operating software used by IBM PC's, there was no specific lock-in to IBM.[19] And within the class of IBM compatibles, customers were quite sensitive to the merit of the computers being offered, particularly to price. In terms of our model, in the PC market

---

[19] In the actual history, this reflected a critical and much-discussed strategic choice by IBM – the acceptance of a non-exclusive license to the PC operating system software from Microsoft.

the coefficient on quality (merit) was high, and the coefficient on specific market share was low.

3.4.2   History-divergent simulations

After a "history-friendly" replication base case was achieved, we modified the values of the parameters we identified as corresponding to the fundamental causal factors of the observed history, to see if those changes produced quite different patterns of evolution. Here we will focus in particular on parameter changes that, according to the theory we are exploring, should be expected to forestall the rise of a dominant firm in the mainframe market. We then explore parameter settings that should enable the dominant mainframe firm to do particularly well in the PC market.

3.5   THE SIMULATION RUNS

3.5.1   The base case: history-replication

We present here more detail on the set of runs with the parameter values that "replicated" the main features of the historical experience. The model here operated in a way that can be regarded as "history-friendly."

First, we provide in Figures 3.3–3.5 some pictures of a typical run at various stages in the history of the industry. There is an early stage ending around simulation period 30, when a few first-generation mainframe firms were just on the verge of breaking into the mainframe market. The second picture, Figure 3.4, is at period 70, when several first-generation mainframe firms were well established and new second-generation, microprocessor-based firms were entering the PC's segment. The third, at period 130, depicts a time when several of the old first-generation firms had shifted over to microprocessor technology, and a couple had diversified into the PC market. The lines in the figures depict the path of the firms from their start. A gray line signifies that the firm has failed. Breaks in a line indicate a change in the technology used by a firm. The box on the right-hand side of the figures reports market shares of active firms: in black those operating

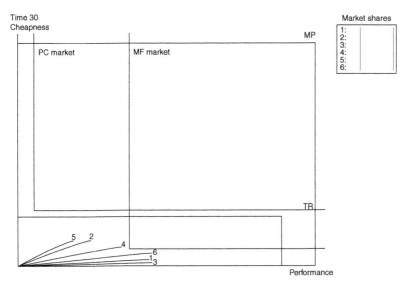

FIGURE 3.3 Simulation time = 30.

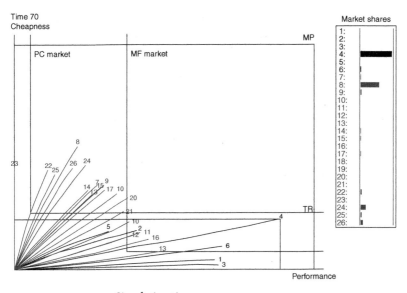

FIGURE 3.4 Simulation time = 70.

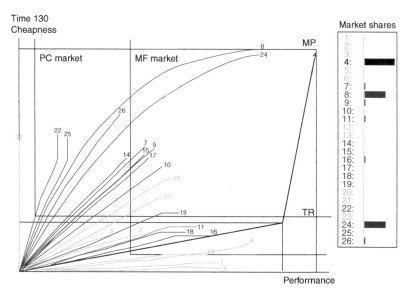

FIGURE 3.5 Simulation time = 130.

in the mainframes market, in gray those operating in the PC market. These figures depict, of course, single runs – but the qualitative patterns are typical, given the parameter settings.[20]

We did 1,000 runs under our standard parameter setting. Figure 3.6 traces the time path of the Herfindahl index of concentration in the mainframe market averaged over those 1,000 runs. Because of the various random elements in our model there was considerable variation from run to run, but most runs told a similar story. Firms using transistor technology began to get into the mainframe market around period 30, and a dominant firm quickly emerged. The dip in the concentration ratio beginning around period 65, and its rise again several periods later, was also quite common in the runs. This pattern reflects first, at the beginning of the dip, the surge of entry into the mainframe market by the second-generation firms using microprocessors, and then the relatively

20   Firm 4 in Figure 3.5 changes trajectory because, while maintaining its local search strategy, with the new microprocessor technology, it becomes more sensitive to the new MP frontier, per Equation 1.

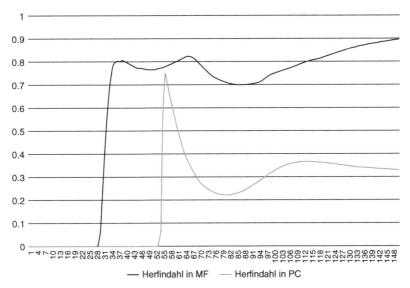

FIGURE 3.6 Herfindahl in PC and mainframe markets (Standard Set).

quick switchover from transistors to microprocessors and recovery of market share by the dominant mainframe firm.

Figure 3.6 also shows the time path of the Herfindahl index in the PC market. As one can see, concentration in that market is much lower than concentration in the mainframe market. That is partially due to the fact that there are more "microprocessor based" start-ups firms, many of which enter the PC market, than earlier there were "transistor based" start-up firms that entered the mainframe market (i.e. the first-generation mainframe firms). That difference was introduced by assumption, reflecting our judgment about the historical size of the potential entrant queues. Historically, technological and financial barriers to entry in PCs were also softer as compared to mainframes. But that clearly is only part of the story. In the model the lower Herfindahl index in the PC market is basically a result of the weaker bandwagon effect.

The new start-ups using microprocessors could enter the mainframe market as well as the PC market. However, in the mainframe

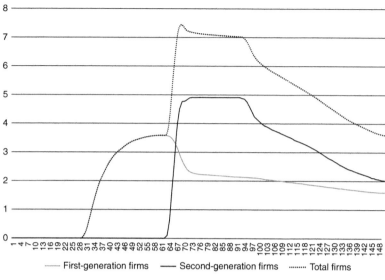

FIGURE 3.7 Number of firms in mainframe market (Standard Set).

market this did not result in sustained effective competition. This fact is depicted in Figure 3.7, which shows the time path of the number of different kinds of firms in the mainframe market. As can be seen, while several new start-ups using microprocessors (second-generation mainframe firms) enter around period 60, on average only two remain in the market for any length of time. Figure 3.8 depicts the number of different kinds of firms in the PC market; it shows that significantly more firms starting out with microprocessor technology survive in the PC market, at least until around period 80 when "IBM" establishes a PC branch.

As shown in Figure 3.8, around period 80 a branch of the dominant mainframe company, which had earlier switched over to microprocessor technology, joins the start-up "microprocessor based" firms in the PC market. In general, this offshoot of "IBM" was quite successful in the PC market, but never achieved the dominance there that the firm held in the mainframe market. All this is depicted in Figure 3.9.

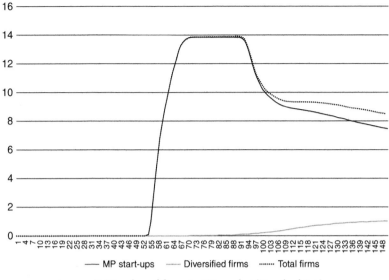

FIGURE 3.8 Number of firms in PC market (Standard Set).

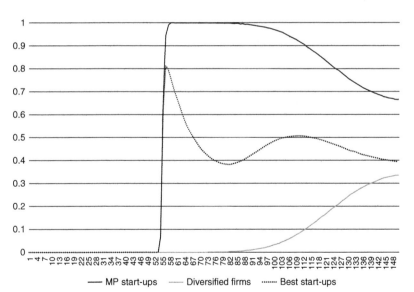

FIGURE 3.9 Market shares in PC market (Standard Set).

The demand equation that generated this "history-replicating" pattern had a relatively high coefficient on "market share" in the mainframe market, and a lower one in the PC market. Thus the first firm that achieved a considerable share in the mainframe market was more advantaged than the first firm that obtained considerable market share in the PC market. Microprocessor technology came into existence only after a large firm had emerged in the mainframe market, and it was not too difficult for that firm to switch over to microprocessors once it was challenged. Its ability to marshal R&D resources and advertising to enter the PC market enabled it to overcome its initial technological lag relatively quickly, but the effectiveness of these investments was not so great as to enable it to come to dominate that market.

3.5.2 Variations: history-divergent runs

As we noted earlier, the sustained dominance of IBM in the mainframe market has been ascribed to two different kinds of factors. One is the importance of bandwagon effects. The other is that IBM achieved dominance in the market before potentially "competence-destroying" new technology emerged, and further, IBM actually was able to take that technology aboard relatively quickly. A reduced level of bandwagon is reflected in the model by a reduced value of the exponent on market share (δ^s_{MF}) in Equation 9. Figure 3.10 shows the time paths of the Herfindahl index in the mainframe market when the exponent on market share is significantly lower (0.6 or 0.4) than in our base case (0.8). All other parameter settings are the same as in the standard set. Notice how the concentration in the market, which largely reflects the share of the leading firm, declines with the reduction in the extent of the bandwagon effect.

The strength of bandwagon effects in our initial setting not only affects the extent to which a dominant firm emerges but also affects the extent to which second-generation firms using microprocessors are able to compete in the mainframe market, and hence the pressure on established mainframe firms to adopt microprocessors. Figure 3.11

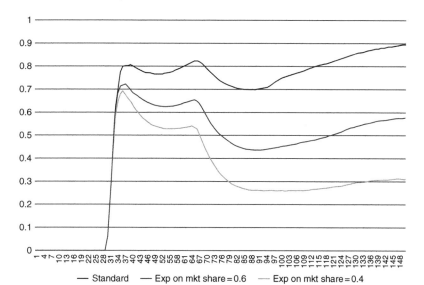

FIGURE 3.10 Herfindahl index in mainframe market with less importance of bandwagon in demand.

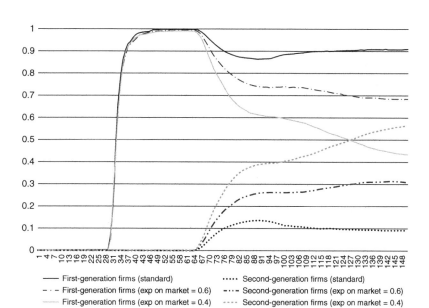

FIGURE 3.11 Share of first-generation (TR) and second-generation (MP) firms in mainframe market.

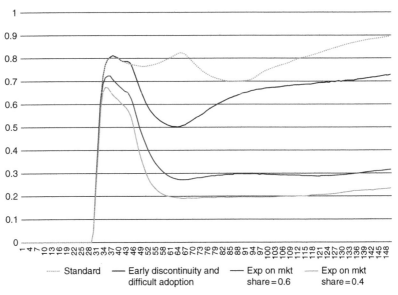

FIGURE 3.12 Herfindahl index in mainframe market: early entry of second-generation (MP) firms and high difficulty of adoption.

depicts the share held by first-generation (initially using transistors and then switching to microprocessors) and second-generation (using microprocessors) mainframe firms in the mainframe market under the standard set and in the cases in which the exponent in the market share in the demand equation is reduced to 0.6 and 04: if the bandwagon effect is not strong, the second-generation mainframe firms can get additional customers and gain market shares in the mainframe market, eventually surpassing the share of the first-generation mainframe firms.

We explore the impact of the introduction time and the characteristics of the new technology in a second set of counterfactual runs. Figure 3.12 depicts the Herfindahl index in the mainframe market for runs in which the second-generation (microprocessor) mainframe start-up firms emerged before "IBM" was able to dominate the mainframe market, and in which the first-generation (transistor based) mainframe firms (including "IBM") had greater difficulty in switching over to microprocessor technology than in the standard case. Specifically, the period of introduction of microprocessors (T^{AD}) is moved up to period 10 (from period 30) and second-generation firms now enter (T_{MP}) at period 15 (instead of period 35). The parameter α^{AD} in Equation 12, which measures the general difficulty of perceiving the new technology, is tripled. In these simulations, the arrival of the second-generation firms reduces temporarily the Herfindahl index, which, however, increases again later on due to the adoption of micro-processors by "IBM." Then we present additional results under two different parameter settings regarding the importance of market share in demand – as we just discussed, the exponent in the market share (δ^{S}_{MF}) in Equation 9 is reduced from 0.8 respectively to 0.6 and 0.4. In both cases the Herfindahl index significantly decreases.

We turn now to the PC market and our attempts at history-divergent modeling of events there. In particular, we explore what might have happened if the conditions in the PC market had been different (in terms of more relevance of R&D for new PC designs and less relevance of early experience in microprocessor technology) and if IBM had a lower cost of diversification and a greater ability to shift large amounts of resources into its PC division.[21] First, we examine a set of runs (set 01) in which the exponent on R&D expenditures (β^{R}) in Equation 1 is higher than in the standard set (from 0.65 to 0.8), the exponent on technological experience (β^{EX}) in Equation 1 is lower than in the standard set (from 0.5 to 0.3), and the exponent on marketing capabilities (δ^{A}_{PC}) in Equation 9 is higher than in the standard set (from 0.1 to 0.3). Second, we try a set in which (in addition to the parameter changes just stated) the cost of diversification for "IBM" is lower (set 02) as the new firm inherits a larger fraction of the marketing capabil-ities (ψ^{DV}) from the parent company (from 0.2 to 0.8). Moreover, we

---

[21]   In Malerba *et al.* (2001, pp. 635–664) we have examined the relative performance of two different diversification strategies by IBM in PCs. The first one is the one dis-cussed in this chapter and is related to the establishment of a totally independent unit in the new market. With the other strategy (named "competence driven") the estab-lished firm uses its existing competencies and follows its technological trajectory also in the new market.

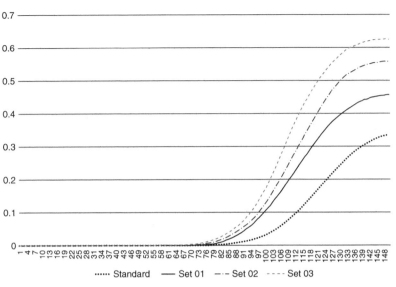

FIGURE 3.13 Share of diversified firms in PC market.

consider a set (set 03) in which the new "IBM" PC division receives
a larger initial budget by the parent company (from 0.3 to 0.5 of the
accumulated profits of the parent). As Figure 3.13 shows, the first
change by itself makes some difference for the structure of the PC
market. However, when IBM is also able to diversify more easily or
more forcefully, it increases its market share significantly.

3.6   CONCLUSIONS

Our history-friendly modeling of the evolution of industry structure in
the computer industry brings to the fore a number of mechanisms and
relationships that are relevant for the study of the evolution of industry
more generally. One is the importance of mechanisms by which products that enjoy larger shares of the market have a higher attractiveness to customers; a strong hold makes entry of new products difficult.
A second is the fact that when a new technology becomes available to
an industry it may not only open the way to improvements in the kinds
of products already being produced but may open the possibility of

products serving new markets. Third, entry may play a powerful role in shaping the evolution of industry structure in a number of dimensions.

The strong incentives that early users of computers had to get the same brand (as consequence of bandwagon effects) played an important role in the ascendancy of IBM to dominance in the expanding market for mainframes. In contrast, early purchasers of PC generally did not have the same kind of bandwagon effects, and this is an important reason why that market has been characterized by turnover of leading firms. We believe that the issue of bandwagon effects deserves more attention in the general literature on the dynamics of industrial organization than it has received to date.

On the other hand, the emergence of a new technology throws up two different kinds of challenges for incumbent firms: one regarding adoption, the other diversification. The first relates to the use and mastery of the new technology by established firms. The second concerns the ability by established firms to see and effectively get into the new markets that the new technology opens up. Consistent with the historical experience in this case, our model represents the second task as more difficult than the first.

More generally, our history-friendly modeling of the evolution of the computer industry highlights the importance of entry conditions. Not only do new firms open up and develop new markets, they also stimulate incumbent firms to adopt and diversify earlier. Because our simulations refer mostly to the US industry, it is fair to say that the US venture capital market played a major role in generating the history that occurred and enabled new firms to enter, move fast and get established in the new market, thus allowing the new market to take off rapidly. As a consequence of this, international industrial leadership remained with US firms, although the identity of those firms changed.

We conclude by noting that these insights, gained from our model, are associated with the explicitly evolutionary nature of that model. As discussed in Chapters 1 and 2, firms try different things, the market selects upon them and selection takes time. The evolution of industry structure is marked by the appearance of some large firms, as a result of the feedback from market success to firm growth. This is a very different theory about firm and industry behavior than the one that presumes that firms always correctly maximize relative to some sharply defined problem, and that the market is always in equilibrium. An essential part of the evolutionary story we have developed here is that firms differed in their level and types of competencies, in their trajectories of advancement and in their ability to see the new market. Another essential part is that entry conditions and financial institutions backing new firms have major impact on the specific evolution of the industry. In short, technological and industrial change must be understood as an evolutionary process.

APPENDIX 3.1   LIST OF VARIABLES AND PARAMETERS

Parameter	Symbol	Value / range
General indices		
Index for firms	f	$\{1, \ldots, F_k\}$
Index for markets (user classes)	h	$\{MF, PC\}$
Index for component technology	k	$\{TR, MP\}$
Index for time periods	t	$\{1, \ldots, T\}$
Industry characteristics		
Scale parameter in Equation 7	a^0	1
Exponent in Equation 7	a^1	0.65
Fixed cost of adoption of the new technology	C^{AD}	2.5
Unit cost of R&D	C^{RD}	0.001
Diagonal – distance from the origin to the frontier of microprocessor technology	d_{MP}	12727.92
Diagonal – distance from the origin to the frontier of transistor technology	d_{TR}	8246.21
Number of firms offering products in market h at time t	$F_{h,t}$	$\mathbb{N}$
Number of potential firms – microprocessor technology	F_{MP}	20
Number of potential firms – transistor technology	F_{TR}	6

Parameter	Symbol	Value / range
Number of groups of potential customers – mainframe market	G_{MF}	2500
Number of groups of potential customers – PC market	G_{PC}	2500
Markup	m	0.1
Distance from the origin to the best microprocessor firm current technological position	o_t^{MP}	$[0, d_{MP}]$
Interest rate	r	0.025
Periods of simulation	T	150
Period of entry of microprocessor-based firms	T_{MP}	35
Period of entry of transistor-based firms	T_{TR}	1
Period from which microprocessors can be adopted by computer firms	T^{AD}	30
Periods to develop a computer project	T^D	35
Periods to develop a computer project – diversifying entrant	T^{DV}	12
Weight of current performance in exit decision	w^E	0.25
Level of design of a computer when a firm has no experience	Z^0	$(0; 0)$
Difficulty in the perception of the new technology in Equation 12	α^{AD}	15
Weight of the advancement of the microprocessor technology in Equation 12	α^{MP}	1
Weight of distance from the transistors technological frontier in Equation 12	α^{TR}	1
Scale parameter in Equation 1.b	β^{CH}	0.0002
Weight of technological experience in Equation 1	β^{EX}	0.5
Scale parameter in Equation 1.a	β^{PE}	0.0002
Weight of R&D investment in Equation 1	β^R	0.65
Weight of distance from the frontier in Equation 1	β^A	1
Weight of cheapness in Equation 8 – mainframe market	γ_{MF}^{CH}	0.2

Parameter	Symbol	Value / range
Weight of cheapness in Equation 8 – PC market	γ_{PC}^{CH}	0.8
Scale parameter in Equation 8 – mainframe market	γ_{MF}^{M}	0.15
Scale parameter in Equation 8 – PC market	γ_{PC}^{M}	0.25
Weight of performance in Equation 8 – mainframe market	γ_{MF}^{PE}	0.8
Weight of performance in Equation 8 – PC market	γ_{PC}^{PE}	0.2
Weight of marketing capabilities in Equation 9 – mainframe market	δ_{MF}^{A}	0.1
Weight of marketing capabilities in Equation 9 – PC market	δ_{PC}^{A}	0.1
Weight of merit of design in Equation 9 – mainframe market	δ_{MF}^{M}	1.5
Weight of merit of design in Equation 9 – PC market	δ_{PC}^{M}	3
Weight of bandwagon in Equation 9 – mainframe market	δ_{MF}^{s}	0.8
Weight of bandwagon in Equation 9 – PC market	δ_{PC}^{s}	0.4
Probability of computer breakdown – mainframe market	Θ_{MF}	0.0416
Probability of computer breakdown – PC market	Θ_{PC}	0.0833
Cheapness technological frontier – microprocessor technology	Λ_{MP}^{CH}	9000
Cheapness technological frontier – transistor technology	Λ_{TR}^{CH}	2000
Performance technological frontier – microprocessor technology	Λ_{MP}^{PE}	9000
Performance technological frontier – transistor technology	Λ_{TR}^{PE}	8000
Minimum level of marketing capabilities in Equation 9	λ^{A}	1

Parameter	Symbol	Value / range
Minimum cheapness threshold – mainframe market	λ_{MF}^{CH}	800
Minimum cheapness threshold – PC market	λ_{PC}^{CH}	2250
Minimum threshold for the diversification in the PC market	λ^{DV}	2
Minimum threshold for exit	λ^{E}	–0.03
Minimum threshold for full market activity	λ_{MF}^{F}	3
Minimum threshold for full market activity	λ_{PC}^{F}	10
Minimum performance threshold – mainframe market	λ_{MF}^{PE}	3600
Minimum performance threshold – PC market	λ_{PC}^{PE}	500
Minimum threshold for R&D to avoid exit	λ^{R}	1
Minimum level of market share in Equation 9 – mainframe market	λ_{MF}^{s}	0.042
Minimum level of market share in Equation 9 – PC market	λ_{PC}^{s}	0.0125
Mean of normal distribution of random factor in Equation 1	μ^{e}	1
Scale parameter in Equation 2	ν	1
Standard deviation of normal distribution of random factor in Equation 1	σ^{e}	0.1
Fraction of profits after debt repayment allocated to advertising expenditures	φ^{A}	0.1
Fraction of accumulated resources allocated to the adoption of the new technology	φ^{AD}	0.2
Fraction of initial budget spent by a diversifying entrant in each period	φ^{B}	0.5
Fraction of profits allocated to debt repayment	φ^{DB}	0.2
Fraction of accumulated resources transferred to the diversifying division	φ^{DV}	0.3
Fraction of profits after debt repayment allocated to R&D expenditure	φ^{RD}	0.1
Spillover of marketing capabilities to the diversifying division	ψ^{DV}	0.2

Parameter	Symbol	Value / range
Firms characteristics		
Marketing capabilities of firm f at time t	$A_{f,t}$	$\mathbb{R}_+$
Probability of adoption of microprocessor technology by firm f at time t	$AD_{f,t}$	$[0, 1]$
Accumulated profits account of firm f at time t	$B_{f,t}$	$\mathbb{R}_+$
Initial budget of firm f – transistor technology	$B^0_{f,TR}$	$[9, 11]$
Initial budget of firm f – microprocessor technology	$B^0_{f,MP}$	$[4.5, 5.5]$
Advertising expenditures of firm f at time t	$B^A_{f,t}$	$\mathbb{R}_+$
Budget for the adoption of the new technology of firm f	B^{AD}_f	$\mathbb{R}_+$
Budget for R&D activities by firm f at time t	$B^{RD}_{f,t}$	$\mathbb{R}_+$
Distance from the current technological position to the frontier of transistor technology	$b^{TR}_{f,t}$	$[0, d_{TR}]$
Unit production cost of firm f at time t	$C^{PD}_{f,t}$	$\mathbb{R}_+$
Debt of firm f at time t	$DB_{f,t}$	$\mathbb{R}_+$
Variable controlling the exit decision of firm f in the current period	$E_{f,t}$	$\mathbb{R}$
Experience in component technology k by firm f at time t	$EX_{f,k,t}$	$\{1, \ldots, T\}$
Random factor of firm f at time t in Equation 1	$e_{f,t}$	$\mathbb{R}$
Random factor of firm f at time t in Equation 9	$e^u_{f,t}$	$[0.9, 1.1]$
Number of groups of customers in market h buying from firm f at time t	$G_{f,h,t}$	$\{1, \ldots, G_h\}$
Merit of design of firm f at time t as perceived by customers in market h	$M_{f,h,t}$	$\mathbb{R}_+$
Price of product j at time t	$P_{f,t}$	$\mathbb{R}_+$
Quantity of firm f sold (in market h) at time t	$q_{f,t}, q_{f,h,t}$	$\mathbb{R}_+$
R&D investment in cheapness by firm f at time t	$R^{CH}_{f,t}$	$\mathbb{N}$
R&D investment in performance by firm f at time t	$R^{PE}_{f,t}$	$\mathbb{N}$
Market share of firm f at time t	$s_{f,t}$	$[0, 1]$

Parameter	Symbol	Value / range
Probability of the product of firm f to be selected by customers in market h at time t	$U_{f,h,t}$	$[0, 1]$
Propensity of the product of firm f to be selected by customers in market h at time t	$u_{f,h,t}$	$\mathbb{R}_+$
Function of rate of return of firm f at time t	$Y_{f,t}$	$\mathbb{R}$
Level of design of firm f at time t	$Z_{f,t}$	$(Z_{f,t}^{PE}; Z_{f,t}^{CH})$
Cheapness of firm f at time t	$Z_{f,t}^{CH}$	$\mathbb{R}_+$
Performance of firm f at time t	$Z_{f,t}^{PE}$	$\mathbb{R}_+$
Profits of firm f at time t	$\Pi_{f,t}$	$\mathbb{R}_+$
Fraction of technological experience transferred to the new technology	φ_f^{EX}	$[0.5, 1]$
Fraction of past R&D expenditure that must be spent in the current period	$\widetilde{\varphi}_{f,t}^{RD}$	$[0.85, 0.95]$

APPENDIX 3.2   SENSITIVITY ANALYSIS

In Chapter 3 we analyzed the outcomes of the model under a set of parameter values (standard set) reflecting the key propositions to explain the main patterns of the industry history. Then we modified the values of the parameters identified as fundamental causal factors of the observed history, to see if those changes produced quite different patterns of evolution (history-divergent runs).

In this section, we study the effects of other parameters that – although necessary to set-up the model – are not recognized as having a peculiar effect on the evolution of the industry. This is the most common form of sensitivity analysis in simulation models (Richiardi et al., 2006; Grazzini et al., 2013).

In our exercise, we exclude three groups of parameters from variation: (1) those parameters explicitly studied in any of the history-divergent runs; (2) those parameters that let variables take values over an extensive range; and (3) those parameters set to specific values that neutralize their role or that keep them to specific ratios with other parameters. The list of parameters included in the analysis is presented in Table A.3.1.

Table A.3.1 *Parameters under sensitivity analysis*

Parameter	Symbol	Value
Exponent in Equation 7	a^1	0.65
Fixed cost of adoption of the new technology	C^{AD}	2.5
Unit cost of R&D	C^{RD}	0.001
Number of potential firms – microprocessor technology	F_{MP}	20
Number of potential firms – transistor technology	F_{TR}	6
Markup	m	0.1
Interest rate	r	0.025
Periods to develop a computer project – diversifying entrant	T^{DV}	12
Scale parameter in Equation 8 – mainframe market	γ^M_{MF}	0.15
Scale parameter in Equation 8 – PC market	γ^M_{PC}	0.25
Weight of merit of design in Equation 9 – mainframe market	δ^M_{MF}	1.5
Weight of merit of design in Equation 9 – PC market	δ^M_{PC}	3
Minimum threshold for the diversification in the PC market	λ^{DV}	2
Minimum threshold for exit	λ^E	−0.03
Fraction of profits after debt repayment allocated to advertising expenditures	φ^A	0.1
Fraction of accumulated resources allocated to the adoption of the new technology	φ^{AD}	0.2
Fraction of initial budget spent by a diversifying entrant in each period	φ^B	0.5
Fraction of accumulated resources transferred to the diversifying division	φ^{DV}	0.3
Fraction of profits after debt repayment allocated to R&D expenditure	φ^{RD}	0.1
Fraction of profits allocated to debt repayment	φ^{DB}	0.2

A sensitivity analysis run is conducted as follows. We extract a value for each parameter included in the analysis within a predefined range: the minimum values of the range is equal to a 10 percent reduction of the standard value of the parameter, the maximum values of the range is equal to a 10 percent increase of the standard value of the parameter. Then, we run 1,000 simulation runs using the extracted set of parameters instead of the standard set.

Our sensitivity analysis is based on 1,000 sensitivity runs: each of these runs can be compared to our history-replicating simulation based on the standard set, since they are obtained by averaging period by period the values of 1,000 simulation runs.

Our analysis focuses on the same aggregate statistics presented in the history-replicating analysis: the Herfindahl index in the main-frame and PC markets, the number and share of different types of firms (transistor, microprocessor startups, diversifying) in both markets. For each of these statistics, we present the average values of five different groups of sensitivity runs: the lowest decile group, the group with values between the 10th and 25th percentile, the group between the 25th and 75th percentile, the group between the 75th and the 90th percentile, and the highest decile group. A sensitivity run is attributed to a group on the basis of the average value across all periods of the simulation. The results are presented in Figures A.3.1–A.3.9.

As it emerges from our results, although the specific values of our statistics are affected by the change in the parameters values, the general dynamics is analogous to what is obtained by our history-replicating simulation even in the most extreme cases. The most relevant parameters in driving the deviation from the standard values are the initial number of firms and the parameters controlling the resources available to firms, such as the parameters in the demand equation, the markup and the R&D costs. A more detailed discussion is required in the case of the Herfindahl index in the PC market (Figure A.3.5), that is apparently not affected by the entry of a strong diversifying firm. This is due to the fact that when concentration is already quite low, the impact of a new entrant is definitely smaller.

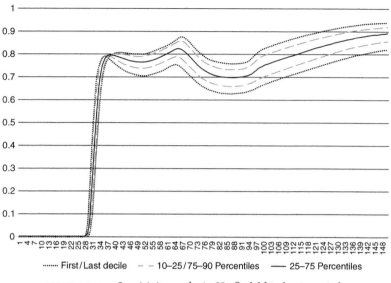

...... First/Last decile   – – 10–25/75–90 Percentiles   —— 25–75 Percentiles

FIGURE A.3.1 Sensitivity analysis: Herfindahl index in mainframes.

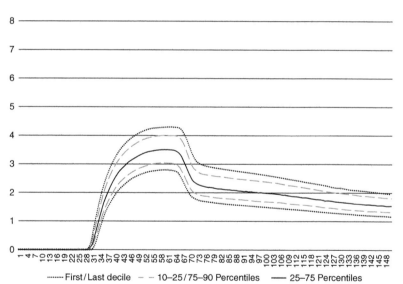

...... First/Last decile   – – 10–25/75–90 Percentiles   —— 25–75 Percentiles

FIGURE A.3.2 Sensitivity analysis: number of TR firms in mainframes.

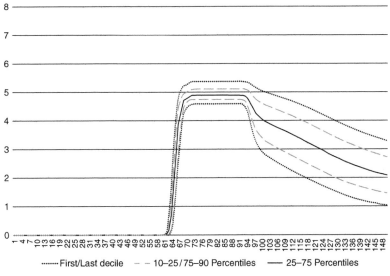

FIGURE A.3.3 Sensitivity analysis: number of MP firms in mainframes.

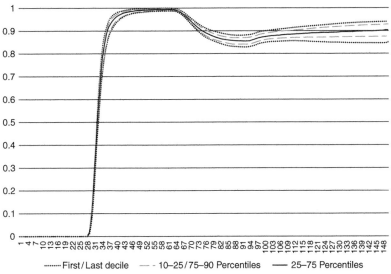

FIGURE A.3.4 Sensitivity analysis: share of TR firms in mainframes.

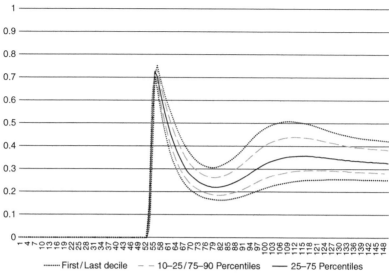

FIGURE A.3.5 Sensitivity analysis: Herfindahl index in PCs.

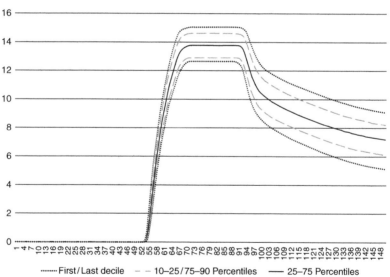

FIGURE A.3.6 Sensitivity analysis: number of MP startups in PCs.

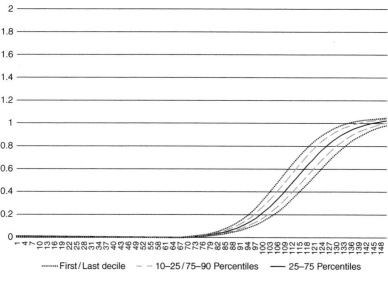

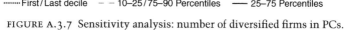

FIGURE A.3.7 Sensitivity analysis: number of diversified firms in PCs.

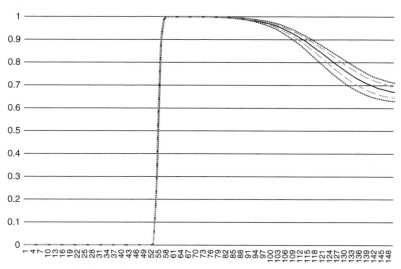

FIGURE A.3.8 Sensitivity analysis: share of MP startups in PCs.

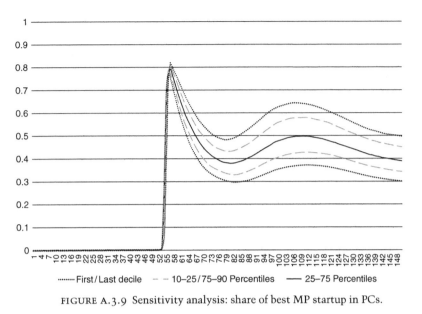

FIGURE A.3.9 Sensitivity analysis: share of best MP startup in PCs.

However, the general dynamics is the same even in this case, as confirmed by the entry pattern of the diversifying firm from the mainframe market (Figure A.3.7) and the evolution of the market share of the best microprocessor startup in the PC market (Figure A.3.9).

4 Vertical integration and dis-integration in the computer industry

4.1 INTRODUCTION

The remarkable increases in computational power and reductions in the costs of computation that have been achieved over the history of the computer industry have been made possible largely by advances in semiconductor technology. At the industry's inception, and more recently, the semiconductors used in computers were designed and produced almost exclusively by independent semiconductor firms. But at times during the industry's history, at least the largest computer firms were vertically integrated and designed and produced the semiconductors they used. This chapter concerns this history of vertical integration and then dis-integration, and the factors shaping that history.

In the following section we describe the history of vertical integration and dis-integration of large computer firms, which we are interested in explaining. Then we consider various theories of vertical integration and lay out the one that seems to provide the best fit to the historical case. Briefly, we build on the "competence-based" approach, and argue that the vertical scope of computer producers was largely determined by the co-evolution across firms of specific capabilities for designing and producing semiconductors, and by the size and nature of markets for semiconductors and computers. Thus, our interpretation departs significantly from standard theories based on transaction costs, and incomplete contracts. Then we develop our history-friendly model, guided by the history and the theory we regard as most persuasive, and present both history-friendly and counter-history runs. We pull the strands together in our concluding section.

This chapter is a major revision of previously published work: Malerba et al. (2008a). The original paper has been improved in the structure, code and technical apparatus.

4.2 THE HISTORY TO BE EXPLAINED

This chapter analyzes the choices computer firms make: of designing and producing semiconductor inputs themselves or buying them from outside vendors. As in Chapter 3, we concentrate on the US computer industry, and we use the same time period we addressed in Chapter 3 to analyze concentration in the industry. As we described there, this period saw a shift in the basic electronic components used in computers from vacuum tubes to transistors, to integrated circuits and then to microprocessors, the advent of which enabled the development of the personal computers (PCs).[1] Our focus will be on the standard electronic components. The large computer companies have always designed and produced customized components in-house; the key decision they faced was whether to make or buy their more standardized components.

As previously discussed, the computer age began with the design and production of mainframe computers used mainly by research organizations and large firms. The first producers – IBM, Burroughs, Univac Rand, NCR, Control Data, Honeywell, GE and RCA – mainly purchased receiving tubes for their computers on the open market. After the introduction of transistors in the early 1950s, some of the largest firms – IBM, RCA and GE among them – became partially or totally vertically integrated into transistors. Meanwhile, the smaller mainframe firms continued to purchase their electronic components, now transistors, on the market.[2] In the industry, IBM began to pull ahead in the mid 1950s, and it came to dominate the world market for computers designed for accounting applications with the introduction of the 1401 in 1960, due to its investments in research and development, production and marketing.

---

[1] For a more detailed description of patterns of vertical integration in computers see Langlois and Robertson (1995), Malerba (1985), Kricks (1995), Bresnahan and Malerba (1999), Langlois and Steinmueller (1999) and Bresnahan and Greenstein (1999).

[2] Transistor technology improved greatly during the 1950s. Transistors were sold both to computer producers and to the military and other markets. Developments in transistors enabled significant improvements in mainframe performance, and some reduction in costs.

The pattern of vertical integration by the leading mainframe firm was reinforced in the early 1960s, in the context of the technological discontinuity marked by the introduction of integrated circuits. IBM vertically integrated into development and production of integrated circuits, first with hybrid integrated circuit technology and then with monolithic devices. Three considerations explain the appeal of integration. First, integrated circuits embedded system elements and thus required close coordination between the system and the component producers in the design and development of both. Second, semiconductor designs became more and more important strategically for system development; therefore their design, development and production were kept in-house to prevent leakage of strategic information. Third, the rapid growth of the mainframe market, and then the minicomputer market in the 1960s and 1970s, led some of the largest computer producers to fear shortages of key semiconductor components. IBM was vertically integrated in the mid 1960s when it launched a new product line, System 360. Its numerous individual products, particularly computers and peripheral equipment, allowed IBM to exploit economies of scale and scope and to maintain its dominance of the world computer market during the 1960s.[3]

Patterns of vertical integration changed again in the 1970s, when the introduction of radically new semiconductor components, microprocessors, opened a fast-expanding market in PCs. IBM soon exited the production of microprocessors because it decided that its capabilities in this area could not keep up with those of Intel, the new leader in the semiconductor industry that had emerged in the rapidly developing component market (see Bresnahan *et al.*, 2012). Intel and the other microprocessor firms could innovate and grow rapidly because they benefited from a very large and increasing demand not

---

[3]   Integrated circuits opened the possibility of designing computers – minicomputers – that had a considerable amount of power, could be produced at a much lower costs than mainframes and could be directed to a different market: medium-size firms and laboratories. In the semiconductor industry, demand coming from computer producers and other markets, as well as the American military and NASA, was satisfied in large part by new merchant specialized producers.

only from computer producers but also from other final markets, such as telecommunications, consumer electronics, military hardware, automobiles and so on. This dis-integration move by IBM was accompanied by an increase in concentration in the semiconductor industry as Intel became dominant.

Moreover, all the new firms that had entered the PC market during the second half of the 1970s – Apple Computer, Radio Shack and Commodore first, followed by a stream of new start-ups – were specialized computer firms. These firms preferred to buy advanced semiconductor devices from large, capable and innovative microprocessor firms, rather than try to vertically integrate. Most of their business went to Intel, confirming its dominant role in the microprocessor market.

An episode that aligns well with our account of the dynamics of integration and specialization was the entry by IBM into PCs. When IBM entered the PC market in the early 1980s, it chose to do so as a non-integrated producer, buying its own semiconductor components – as well as peripherals and software – from outside suppliers. This decision was taken because IBM faced quite capable producers of standard semiconductor components; it needed to speed up PC production and it did not have advanced internal capabilities in this area. So, IBM joined with Intel, the leading producer of semiconductor components. As mentioned in Chapter 3, IBM also made a critically important deal to license its PC operating system from a then-small software firm, Microsoft. Although a leader in the new business of software for PCs, Microsoft was not as plainly qualified in operating systems specifically as Intel was in microprocessors. The two relationships enabled IBM's successful entry into the PC industry, but it did not achieve the dominance there that it had enjoyed in mainframes (Bresnahan and Greenstein, 1999).

4.3   THEORIZING ABOUT VERTICAL INTEGRATION

What kind of theory can explain the patterns of vertical integration and specialization of computer firms presented in the previous section? The currently leading theories are based mainly on some version of the transaction-cost approach. Their focus is on the market failures that may emerge in the exchange of goods and services under particular conditions, and incorporate the view that hierarchical coordination is to be considered as a superior substitute for market transactions in those cases.[4] These issues may be framed in different theoretical settings: for instance, bounded rationality (as in Williamson, 1975, 1979, 1985) or full rationality (as in contract theory). The language of strategic interactions is increasingly used in this context. Choices about integration are considered to be determined by weighing the incentive advantages of markets against the governance advantages of hierarchical organizations.

Without denying the relevance of transaction costs, we simply note here that this approach has a distinctly static flavor and, obviously, considers transactions as the main unit of analysis and exchange as its primary object. Technologies, the properties of the goods and the characteristics of the agents are taken as given, and vertical integration/specialization are commonly examined as a choice at a given moment of time. In our analysis here, on the contrary, capabilities and technology are at the base of our appreciative explanation of vertical integration and specialization. This is presented in a dynamic, evolutionary setting. Following Nelson and Winter (1982) and the capability-based view of the firm (Teece and Pisano, 1994; Teece et al., 1997; Dosi et al., 2000; Teece, 2009; Winter, 1987), we suggest that a central factor explaining the vertical scope of firms is the accumulation of capabilities at the firm and industry levels. Firms accumulate capabilities through a variety of learning processes in specific technological, productive and market domains. Such

---

[4] The classic argument of Williamson, well supported by subsequent research, is that transaction costs arise from transactional hazards that are likely to be pronounced in cases of high asset specificity, asymmetric information and unclear definition of property rights. Under these conditions, limitations on effective writing and/or enforcement of contracts leave room for opportunistic behavior, often leading to suboptimal solutions. See Jacobides and Winter (2012) for references and a view of more recent developments.

competencies tend to be local and specific, and difficult to transfer. Heterogeneity across firms is therefore likely to be a permanent feature of industries, and the actual distribution of capabilities across firms in upstream and downstream industries is likely to exert a fundamental influence on the vertical structure of firms (Jacobides and Winter, 2005, 2012). For example, the decision of an integrated firm to abandon internal production of components is elicited by, and critically depends on, the existence of upstream component suppliers at least as competent as the firm itself.

In this framework, when products are systems with various components and subsystems, a firm's ability to coordinate and integrate its designs internally is an important competence in its own right and may be a significant source of competitive advantage (Langlois and Robertson, 1995). On the other hand, such an advantage can be more than offset by the risk of getting stuck in inferior technological trajectories, especially at times of rapid and uncertain change, or when suppliers can offer significantly superior products.

However, decisions to specialize and to vertically integrate are not symmetrical. A firm that contemplates resorting to external sources for particular components can directly compare its internally produced product with that of the external supplier. In the opposite case, the comparison cannot be so direct and it depends on the expected ability to design and produce in house. Moreover, if a firm decides to discontinue the development and production of certain components, resuming such activities later would in any case require time and effort. Thus, these decisions are not entirely flexible as time goes by.

In addition, the vertical scope of firms has to be analyzed by considering the capabilities of a firm not simply in isolation but in its relationships with the other participants in the relevant industries (Jacobides and Winter, 2005). For example, the degree of heterogeneity and the distribution of capabilities are crucially shaped by market selection, which tends to promote the growth of more efficient firms and of the related organizational arrangements, and to penalize the laggards. Thus, market selection amplifies the impact of differentiated capabilities on the vertical scope of firms. The growth of a competent supplier or of a vibrant supplying industry is likely to induce specialization of the system firms as the supplier becomes able to offer ever better products. In turn, the processes and the *loci* of capability development feed back on the conditions determining the entry of new firms. Thus, vertical integration or dis-integration can profoundly affect the patterns of competition within an industry, creating the conditions for the entry and growth of new competitors who exploit capabilities developed in different contexts.[5]

In sum, the main message of this chapter is that vertical integration and specialization are shaped by the co-evolution of capabilities, the size of markets and the structure of industries. The growth and dynamics of competencies in each of two vertically related industries influence the evolution of the other and shape vertical integration and specialization (Langlois and Robertson, 1995; Jacobides and Winter, 2005).

The previous discussion identifies *capabilities* as a central factor affecting the vertical boundaries of computer firms. In particular, capabilities refer to the accumulation of firms' competencies in specific technological and market realms and to the coordination and integration capabilities relating to components and systems in the development and production of new final products. Within this framework, a set of variables affects the level, type and accumulation of capabilities in various ways. We will concentrate on four of them:

(1) *The size of firms.* Firm size affects the amount of R&D effort and thus the accumulation of competencies (and consequently the quality of systems and components produced). In addition, size fosters vertical integration because very large system firms may need a secure supply of components.

---

[5]   Causation runs in the other direction, too: the process of capability development depends very much on the vertical scope of an industry. Consider the development and production of components, for example. Specialized firms that compete with other specialized firms accumulate knowledge and capabilities differently from vertically integrated firms.

(2) *The size of the market.* A large market allows the entry of new specialized firms and the growth of capable companies. This is the classic Smithian reasoning placed into a capability perspective (cf. Stigler, 1951).

(3) *The market structures of two vertically related industries.* The distribution of capabilities among industry participants may be linked to the structure of the industry: for example, as it might be suggested by the histories of computers and semiconductors, a monopolistic system industry tends to become vertically integrated into components when confronted with a fragmented upstream industry comprising small firms. Contrariwise, a system industry tends to specialize when confronted upstream with an emerging dominant specialist in a concentrated component industry.

(4) *Major technological discontinuities* and the related *competence destruction.* Major discontinuities change the knowledge base and the type of demand and lead to the entry and growth of firms with totally new competencies. Under these conditions, established vertically integrated firms face pressures toward dis-integration.

This discussion and the variables that have been identified can be reprised in terms that highlight the causal mechanisms relative to the specifics of the historical account. To the extent that these mechanisms depend on the quantitative magnitudes of particular effects, we are still relying on the historical record to support the plausibility of the account, and will seek further support from the simulation model.

At the beginning of the computer industry, mainframe firms mostly procured their electronic components from suppliers. A number of factors combined to quickly promote one company to a near-monopolistic position. As transistors replaced vacuum tubes as the basic electronic component of computers, the leading company became vertically integrated; it was large, and it needed a secure supply of components. Once integrated, its large profits in the downstream business funded rapid technological advance in components. Conversely, for the transistor producers, the external market was not so big as to spur a substantial increase in their size relative to the system producers. No dominant company emerged from the group of component producers, and vertical integration of system firms further reduced the growth opportunities of component companies.

When integrated circuits were introduced, the vertically integrated mainframe producers faced pressures toward vertical dis-integration since some of the new component firms could produce better products. However, since the external market for the new types of components was still not large enough, specialized producers remained relatively small (compared to the largest system producer) and did not have massive resources for R&D and innovation. After an initial period of strong technological turbulence, when the new technology began to mature, the leading system company vertically integrated into integrated circuits: vertical integration allowed close coordination between components and systems; components had become more strategic for system development and production, and security of supply considerations became prominent in the logic.

It was the emergence of microprocessors as the electronic base of computers that led even the large computer firms to get out of the component design and production business. At least a few of the specialized producers of components were able to design and supply better products than the integrated computer companies could produce. Moreover, a large, rapidly growing market for microprocessors, not dependent solely on mainframe producers, allowed these new semiconductor firms to invest much more in R&D, grow quickly and produce components of high quality. A leading component company emerged to dominate the industry. Specialization also characterized the new PC producers, because they remained smaller than the leading microprocessor company, which supplied not only the computer industry but also other large markets.

4.4   THE MODEL

4.4.1   An overview

The model we describe in this section is designed to capture, in highly stylized form, the key elements of the foregoing explanation, which we believe accounts persuasively for the observed dynamics of vertical integration and, later, vertical dis-integration in the American computer industry from the early 1950s to the late 1980s. In the formal model, as in the verbal account, the dynamics are shaped by characteristics of the market for computers, the technologies determining computer performance and exogenous developments in semiconductor technology, all of which led to changes over time in firm capabilities and in the incentives computer firms had to integrate vertically.

In several major respects, this model conforms to the one presented in the preceding chapter. A computer produced by a particular company has two attributes that are relevant to its potential purchasers: performance and cheapness. Other things equal, the share of market sales that a particular computer gains is a function of the merit of its design in terms of these two attributes, relative to that of other computers on the market, although sales are also influenced by brand loyalty and inertia of customers. In turn, both of these design attributes are determined by the way the computer is designed as a system, and by the quality of the semiconductor components that go into that system.

Both of these design factors tend to improve over time as a result of R&D done on systems, and on semiconductors. Systems R&D is done by computer producers. R&D on semiconductors is done by semiconductor firms, and also by computer firms that have vertically integrated into the production of their own semiconductors.

Computer firms that sell more computers are more profitable than firms that sell fewer. High profits induce and permit a firm to grow, and as profitable firms expand their sales, they increase their R&D spending. Since on average higher R&D spending enables a firm to make larger improvements in the computers it sells, these assumptions establish a strong potential for a dominant firm to emerge through the dynamics of competition. Diminishing returns to R&D tend to damp this tendency.

The path of semiconductor technology plays a particularly important role in this model. As in our previous discussion, we posit

three distinct eras. In the first, all semiconductors are discrete transistors. In the second era, integrated circuits emerge and in the third,
microprocessors. Within each era, there is continuing improvement
in the basic semiconductors being produced and sold, but with the
advent of a new type of semiconductor the rate of progress speeds
up. Also, before the advent of microprocessors all computers are
mainframes.[6] The development of microprocessors not only permits
improvement in the design merit of mainframes but also enables
the design and production of PCs, which are significantly cheaper
than mainframes, though performing less impressively. These two
products target different classes of buyers, as previously.

The advent of new types of semiconductors is marked by the
entry of new specialized semiconductor firms, which compete with
established producers and each other for sales. Semiconductor firms
sell to other users as well as to computer firms, and the emergence of
integrated circuits and of microprocessors stimulates the development of these other markets as well as the demand from computer
manufacturers. The introduction of PCs, and the resulting opening of
a new market for computers, induces the entry of new computer firms
that specialize in them.

This model is oriented toward explaining whether computer
firms are specialized, buying on the market the semiconductors they
employ in the computers they produce, or whether they are vertically
integrated, designing and producing their own semiconductors. In the
model, all computer firms are born specialized. Once in the computer
business, they can decide to integrate and design and produce their
own semiconductors. Later, they can decide to abandon their semiconductor operations and turn again to the market as their source for
components.

A firm's decision to integrate rests partly on the advantages of
being able to design both the components and the system together. It

---

[6]   In this model we rule out the possibility of having minicomputers as a result of the
       introduction of integrated circuits. We do that in order to keep the model relatively
       simple.

also rests on judgments of the benefit of being able to control the supply of its inputs, and on whether the firm believes it can produce semiconductors at least as efficiently as specialized suppliers.

In general, large computer firms are more likely than small ones to believe they can efficiently design and produce their own semiconductors. This tendency to integrate vertically is enhanced if the industry producing semiconductors for sale is fragmented, and if there is considerable experience with the semiconductors currently in use. On the other hand, vertical integration is deterred if there is a large competent semiconductor supplier who spends a lot on R&D, or when semiconductors of a new kind are just emerging, and the best ways to design and produce them are highly uncertain. In the former case, even a large computer firm may doubt that it can develop semiconductors as good and as efficiently as the dominant specialized supplier. Whether or not large semiconductor suppliers come into existence is a function of the size of the market for semiconductors, including demand from specialized computer firms, government agencies and firms in other industries.

This is the model in broad outline. The description of the important details follows.

4.4.2 Computers

At the beginning of the simulation, firms (numbering F_{MF}) start producing and selling computers. Component technology initially permits only the production of mainframes (MF); later, microprocessor technology emerges and enables the development of PCs, which is undertaken by a new cohort of computer firms (numbering F_{PC}). PCs have lower performance than mainframes, but are cheaper. The two kinds of computers appeal to two kinds of customers.

As a consequence of firms' R&D investment, and the advance of component technology, the characteristics of computers of a given type improve over time. The technical advance of mainframes is movement along a ray in the attribute space corresponding to the mainframe mix of performance and cheapness characteristics. When

PC technology appears, it too advances along a ray, characterized by a higher ratio of cheapness to performance than the mainframe ray has. The distance out along the ray associated with its particular computer type defines the "merit of design" $(Mod)^7$ of a particular computer.

Computers are produced by combining two intermediate inputs, systems (SY) and components (CO).[8] The overall level of Mod reflects the merits of these inputs. Computationally, it is given by a CES function:

$$M_{f,t} = \Phi_\kappa \cdot [\tau_\kappa \cdot (M_{f,t}^{CO})^{-\rho_\kappa} + (1 - \tau_\kappa) \cdot (M_{f,t}^{SY})^{-\rho_\kappa}]^{\left(-\frac{1}{\rho_\kappa}\right)} \qquad (1)$$

with $\Phi_\kappa > 0$, $0 < \tau_\kappa < 1$ and $\rho_\kappa > -1$ (κ = MF, PC). The elasticity of substitution is equal to $1 / (1 + \rho_\kappa)$. The significance of this elasticity derives from the fact that technical progress can occur at different rates in components and systems. The higher the elasticity, the less the advance of the overall Mod is held back by the lagging input. In our parameter settings for the CES function, the weight attributed to the Mod of components (τ_κ) is never lower than the weight on the Mod of systems. PCs have a comparatively higher weight on components as compared to MFs (i.e. $\tau_{PC} > \tau_{MF}$) and the elasticity of substitution is higher in PCs than in MFs (i.e. $\rho_{MF} > \rho_{PC}$). Thus, we assume that improvements in components are reflected more powerfully in PCs than in MFs, and it is easier to substitute components for systems in PCs (realistically, progress in components often involves incorporating system functionality in the component).

Ultimately, overall Mod translates into desired computer attributes in a fixed proportion. The trajectories followed by firms in the space of the characteristics are assumed to be fixed and equal

[7] We use Mod to refer to the variable in the model, M, and its underlying concept. We use "merit" or "merit of design" as terms of general reference to desirable attributes of a computer.

[8] Systems are always produced by computer firms and cannot be sold separately from computers. As this can create some confusion, notice that it is possible to consider mainframes and PCs both as systems technologies (indexed by κ), analogous to component technologies (transistors, integrated circuits and microprocessors, indexed by k), and as computer final products that appeal to different groups of consumers (indexed by h).

among firms producing computers of a given type. Given the level of *Mod* for a computer and the slope of the trajectory it is on (either mainframe or PC), the values of cheapness (Z^{CH}) and performance (Z^{PE}) that appear into the demand function are computed using the appropriate trigonometric formulas: $Z^{CH}_{f,t} = \cos(\vartheta_\kappa) \cdot M_{f,t}$, $Z^{PE}_{f,t} = \sin(\vartheta_\kappa) \cdot M_{f,t}$, where ϑ_κ is an exogenous parameter that differs across MFs and PCs.[9]

The different computer types, either mainframes or PCs, are produced by different companies. We exclude the possibility of diversification in this model; each computer company produces a single type of computer, either mainframe or PC.

4.4.3 Demand for computers

As in the model developed in the preceding chapter, computer customers are characterized by their preferences for the two attributes that define a computer design – performance and cheapness. One buyer class consists of "large organizations" and others who value performance over cheapness, and the other of "individuals and small users" who value cheapness especially and value performance less than do large firms. "Large firms" buy mainframe computers. When microprocessors come into existence and PCs become available, "small users" buy PCs.

Within each buyer class are many buyers.[10] While buyers are identical within each class in terms of the preferences that lead them to one type of computer, they differ in specific behavior because they have different histories, which are partly randomly determined in the model. Buyers respond to the computers offered by different firms according to the relative merit of their products, but also according

---

[9] However, ϑ_κ can be expressed in terms of cheapness and performance: $\vartheta_\kappa = \arctan(Z^{PE}_{f,t}/Z^{CH}_{f,t})$.

[10] To avoid unnecessary computational burdens, we do not scale buyers to a realistic size relative to firms: the model assumptions simply capture the idea that buyers are small and numerous. Optionally, each "buyer" in the formal model could be interpreted as representing a number of buying agents.

to other considerations, which create elements of inertia and path dependence in the success of the sellers. These include reputational effects, technical compatibility issues that create "lock-in" effects and the benefits of standardization across firms (network externalities). The role of these factors is proxied in the model by the share of a computer brand in the overall market for that type at time $t - 1$: the larger the share of the market that a product already holds, the greater the likelihood that a customer will consider that product in period t. We refer to this as the "bandwagon effect." Finally, there is a stochastic element in buyers' choices between different computers.

We represent the market process by characterizing the probability distribution of buyers' choices among the different computers of the desired type. This probability is a re-normalized counterpart of a purchase propensity that depends on the *Mod* and market share of a particular computer.

Formally, the "propensity" $u_{f,h,t}$ for a computer produced by firm f to be sold to a buyer of user class h at time t is given by:

$$u_{f,h,t} = (M_{f,h,t})^{\delta_h^M} \cdot (1 + s_{f,t-1})^{\delta_\kappa^s} \tag{2}$$

where

$$M_{f,h,t} = (Z_{f,t}^{CH})^{\gamma_h} \cdot (Z_{f,t}^{PE})^{1-\gamma_h} \tag{3}$$

$M_{f,h,t}$ is the merit of a computer with *Mod* equal to $M_{f,t}$ as perceived by customers on the basis of their preferences for cheapness and performance; these preferences are expressed through the parameter γ_h which takes different values in the mainframes and PC markets. Finally $s_{f,t-1}$ is the market share of the firm and δ_κ^s is the exponent indicating the bandwagon effect in the computer market for the current technology.[11] The probability $U_{f,h,t}$ of the computer produced by firm f being sold to a buyer of the user class h at time t is given by:

[11] Since the bandwagon effect includes also technological lock-ins and network externalities, we allow for variation across technologies rather than across markets.

$$U_{f,h,t} = \frac{u_{f,h,t}}{\sum_{f=1}^{F_{h,t}} u_{f,h,t}} \qquad (4)$$

where $F_{h,t}$ is the total number of firms offering products to the user class h at time t.

In short, the demand for a computer depends positively on its *Mod* and on its market share in the previous period. The probability that a buyer purchases a computer from a specific firm reflects the "propensity" to buy; propensities are normalized to yield probabilities that sum to one across firms. Then for a computer firm f, the total computers sold are equal to $M_{f,h,t}$ times the number of buyers, that is:

$$q_{f,t} = q_{f,h,t} = M_{f,h,t} \cdot G_{f,h,t} \qquad (5)$$

where $G_{f,h,t}$ is the number of buyers of user class h that buy computers from firm f at time t. We omit the subscript h since by assumption each firm can only sell to one user class.

4.4.4 The market for components

Components are bought by specialized producers of computers and also by customers in other markets (which we refer to collectively as "the external market"). As described earlier, there are three different component technologies k (k = TR, IC, MP), which become available at different times T_k. In this version of the model, the transistor, integrated circuit and microprocessor technologies become available respectively at periods T_{TR} (equal to 1), T_{IC} (equal to 40), and T_{MP} (equal to 120). At the beginning of the simulation, and at the time of each technological discontinuity, a new cohort of firms (numbering F_k) enters the market, producing components with the latest available technology that guarantees at least a *Mod* equal to M_k^{CO}.

The demand faced by component firms comes from two sources:

(i) Demand for components from users other than computer firms. The size of this external market is an exogenous parameter that varies across component technologies (G_k^{CO}). Firms gain a fraction of it with a probability which is a function of their *Mod* and of their previous market share, as in the computer market. This external demand plays a critical role in the model, since it allows component producers to survive and grow in the early stages of development of a new technology and to improve the merit of their components.

(ii) Demand for components from computer firms that have decided to outsource component production (specialized computer firms).

When a specialized computer firm seeks component supplies, it scans the market for potential suppliers. Competition among component producers is modeled in a fashion that parallels the competition of computer producers. A specialized computer producer contracts with a component producer according to a probability function that reflects the relative technical merit of the components offered by different suppliers: the higher the *Mod* of a component, the higher the probability that its producer signs a contract with a computer producer. Moreover, like the demand for computers, the demand for components is influenced by bandwagon effects captured by the previous market share.[12] Formally, this can be described again by Equations 2 and 4, where h represents now the component market, the exponent δ_k^s varies across component technologies and the relevant *Mod* is $M_{f,t}^{CO}$.

A component firm that signs a contract sells a number of components reflecting its customer's computer sales and the number of components required per computer; in the current simulations that parameter is set to 1. After signing the contract the computer firm is tied to the component supplier for a certain number of periods $(T_{f,t}^{CO})$; this number is randomly extracted from an exogenous set of values (between 6 and 10). When this period expires, a new supplier might be selected, using the same procedure, if the firm still decides to buy components on the open market.

---

[12]   Notice that contract stipulation occurs at the beginning of a time period, when the computer firm also considers the possibility of integration. Therefore, the component *Mod* it considers for its decision refers to period $t-1$, that is, before current R&D activities are performed. External buyers evaluate semiconductor products at the end of the period, that is, after current R&D activities are performed.

The external market for components is conceptualized in the same way as the computer market, that is, it comprises a number of heterogeneous buyer groups or submarkets to which component firms may sell. However, the submarkets of the external component market are not modeled explicitly. A firm simply gets a fraction of the buyers in the external market equal to $U_{f,h,t}$. The quantity of components sold on the external market is equal to the number of buyers times the *Mod*, analogously to what happens in the computer market (see Equation 5).

4.4.5   Firms' R&D behavior

We turn now to the treatment of technological progress in the model. Over the course of time treated by the model, technological advance occurs both in the components used in computers and in the systems design of computers. The effect of these advances on the overall *Mod* of a computer is given by Equation 1. The immediate cause of the advances is the R&D activity of component and computer producers, which exploits opportunities presented by an exogenously changing technological environment. The following section lays out the details of the processes by which R&D effort advances system and component *Mod*.

At the beginning of a simulation, firms are endowed with initial *Mod* values (M_κ^{SY} and M_k^{CO}); they begin to compete, make operating profits and invest those operating profits in R&D. Integrated computer firms split their R&D spending between systems and component R&D. Specialized computer companies buy their components on the market and focus all of their R&D on systems design, while specialized component producers do R&D on components only. The details of these model mechanisms follow. We begin with the determinants of profits and R&D spending, and then turn to the specific mechanisms of technical progress in the next section.

Operating profits of a computer firm f ($\Pi_{f,t}$) are calculated in each period t as:

$$\Pi_{f,t} = (q_{f,t} \cdot P_{f,t}) - (q_{f,t} \cdot C_{f,t}^{PD}) \tag{6}$$

where $q_{f,t}$ is the number of units sold by the firm, $P_{f,t}$ is the price and $C_{f,t}^{PD}$ is the unit production cost of a computer. Conceptually, price is conceived as unit production cost plus a markup:

$$P_{f,t} = C_{f,t}^{PD} \cdot (1 + m) \tag{7}$$

We make the simple assumption that the markup is constant across firms and over time. These relations also apply to component firms and products, by simply substituting the corresponding value of the unit production cost of a component $(C_{f,t}^{CO})$.

As highlighted by the use of different symbols, the unit production cost is not determined in the same way for computers and components, although in both cases the *Mod* plays an important role. Moreover, some specificities related to the firm type (computer specialist, component specialist, integrated producer) must also be taken into account.

In the case of computer products, unit production cost is calculated from the cheapness element of the firm's computer *Mod*[13] at the given time, on the basis that cost is price divided by the markup factor (from Equation 7) and price is inversely related to cheapness:

$$P_{f,t} = \frac{v_\kappa}{Z_{f,t}^{CH}} \tag{8}$$

where v_κ is a proportionality factor that differs across the two system technologies that define the computer product types (mainframes and PCs). By combining Equations 7 and 8, we get the following expression for unit production cost:

$$C_{f,t}^{PD} = \frac{v_\kappa}{Z_{f,t}^{CH} \cdot (1 + m)} \tag{9}$$

---

[13]   Recall that the computer *Mod* is a function of the system *Mod* and the component *Mod* per Equation 1.

The unit production cost of a computer includes all the costs to produce a computer, and in particular the cost of the component – both in the case of integrated computer firms and in the case of specialized computer firms that buy the components from external suppliers. We assume that the computer *Mod* of a specialized producer depends on the *Mod* of a purchased component just as it would if the component were produced in-house. Therefore we disregard various things that might conceivably happen as a direct consequence of getting components from an inter-firm rather than intra-firm transaction.[14] On these assumptions, the unit production cost of a specialized computer producer and an integrated firm are closely matched if they have the same values for system and component *Mod*. They have the same overall *Mod*, by Equation 1, and hence the same implicit unit cost as implied by the cheapness element of that *Mod*. There is a difference, though, between the two types of firms: the computer specialist actually pays an amount in the form of the markup charged by the component producer, that is not due by the integrated firm; therefore, the profit equation for a computer specialist must be rewritten as follows:

$$\Pi_{f,t} = (q_{f,t} \cdot P_{f,t}) - (q_{f,t} \cdot C_{f,t}^{PD}) - (q_{f,t} \cdot m \cdot C_{f,t}^{CO}) \tag{10}$$

Notice, however, that the outsourcing relieves the buyer of component R&D investment costs that are borne by the integrated producer. Thus, the full cost relationships between the two vertical structures inevitably involve the costs and benefits of R&D expenditures.

In the case of a component product, we do not distinguish between performance and cheapness attributes: we simply assume that components with higher *Mod* have also lower production costs, that is:

---

[14] An example of such a consequence might be a "holdup" by the component supplier, an attempt to impose different terms than those agreed in the transaction. This possibility is, of course, central to the Williamsonian assessment of the advantages of vertical integration.

$$C_{f,t}^{CO} = \frac{v_k}{M_{f,t}^{CO}} \qquad (11)$$

where v_k is a proportionality factor[15] that differs across the three component technologies (transistors, integrated circuits, microprocessors). Here the same rules apply to both the component specialist and the integrated firm.

On the expenditure side, our general assumption is that R&D expenditures are determined by plausible rules of thumb. A constant fraction of operating profits (φ^{RD}) is invested in R&D in each period, and in the present work we assume that the fraction is 100 percent. We assume that component producers devote their operating profits to component R&D, while specialist computer firms devote them entirely to system R&D. Integrated computer producers present the interesting case, and its treatment is critical to the overall assessment of the different vertical structures.

We assume that the amount an integrated firm allocates to component R&D corresponds to the markup that an independent component producer would charge on components of the same *Mod*, which is (in the short run) exactly the cost that the firm avoids by being integrated. The remainder of the integrated firm's gross profits is devoted to system R&D.[16]

When the integrated firm and the computer specialist have the same values for system and component *Mod*, the foregoing assumptions create a close match between the two vertical structures, when considered per unit of output. The two computer producers offer

---

[15]   These proportionality factors, as well as those required to calculate the computer production cost, are set to values that guarantee that the cost of a component is always lower than the cost of the computer that uses that component. To get this result we also specify the technological limits for the *Mod* of a system (Λ_k^{SY}) depending on the component technology with which it is combined. These limits are rarely binding and have no impact on the results in the current set of parameters.

[16]   In the transition period from specialization to integration (see Section 4.4.7) the newly integrated firm has to fund its R&D expenditures with the profits of a specialized firm. Therefore it spends on component R&D an amount up to (and not necessarily equal to) what a hypothetical supplier would spend. The remainder, if any, is spent on system R&D.

products of the same merit and charge the same price. The computer specialist spends on system R&D the amount of its operating profit. The component supplier of the specialized firm charges a markup over its production cost, and allocates that profit to component R&D. That investment is exactly matched by the integrated firm, which by assumption spends the same amount on component R&D that is spent by any producer of components of the same Mod. The remainder of the R&D expenditure of the integrated firm goes to systems R&D, and in that it mimics what the specialist computer firm spends.

If the integrated computer firm and the specialist not only had identical system and component *Mods* but also sold the same quantity of computers, then the two structures would be perfectly matched both in their short-term results and in their absolute allocations of R&D expenditures to the improvement of systems and component technology. Of course, even if this hypothetical match were to arise in the course of a simulation run, it would not be expected to persist: for one thing, R&D outcomes are uncertain, and the asymmetry created by chance events will quickly be amplified by feedback effects. Beyond that, however, our assumptions allow for a systematic asymmetry relating to the benefit side of R&D investments, which we now describe.

Our model allows that integrated firms may benefit from coordination advantages in conducting their R&D. They can produce components tailored to their systems – thus enhancing the benefits from their R&D efforts on components. To represent this effect in the model, we assume that the component R&D expenditures of integrated firms are costlessly augmented by a factor called "spillover" (ψ^{CO}), whose effect depends on the level of system R&D investment. Thus, the effective level of component R&D of an integrated computer producer is:

$$B_{f,t}^{CO} = q_{f,t} \cdot m \cdot C_{f,t}^{CO} + \psi^{CO} \cdot B_{f,t}^{SY} \tag{12}$$

The first term reflects the assumption, previously stated, that the integrated firm spends on component R&D an amount that corresponds to the markup on purchased components of the same production cost. It is a cash outlay. The second term in Equation 12 is not a cash outlay but a proxy for the effect of the coordination advantages of integration. This formulation implies that the integrated structure is equivalent to the specialized form in terms of R&D efficiency when the spillover, ψ^{CO}, is equal to zero, but is superior if ψ^{CO} is positive.

Taken as a whole, the foregoing constellation of assumptions is helpful in allowing us to explore the implications of assuming that the choice between integration and specialization does not turn fundamentally on short-run questions of relative production cost. Rather, it turns in the short run on the implications of the historically determined heterogeneity of capabilities that prevails at a point of time, and in the longer run on the merits of the alternative ways of organizing the quest for progress that are implicit in the different vertical structures.

As just described, our assumptions make the burden of R&D expenditures per unit the same for firms that are matched in *Mod*. This implies that, in absolute terms, a larger producer will do more R&D than a smaller one, and thus tend to pull ahead in the long run. In the dynamics of the overall model, the external market for components therefore plays a key role: the larger it is, the more rapidly the technology of specialized component producers will advance – other things equal.[17] While a large external market for components favors the specialized structure, the competitive strength of the integrated structure is enhanced by the spillover effect in component R&D. That effect also shapes the dynamics in a cumulative, scale-related way, since its power depends on the fraction of component R&D conducted by a single integrated firm.

Overall, the model frames the evolutionary struggle between integrated and specialized firms as being shaped by two exogenous forces. A large external market opens the possibility that economies of scale in R&D will favor the specialized firms. A large spillover

---

[17] The "other things" include particularly the influence of industry structure, which of course is endogenous in our model.

enhances the R&D productivity of integrated firms. How these forces play out depends on the evolution of industry structure, which is endogenous. Finally, the course of that evolution may change when the underlying component technology changes, and it is specialized component firms that pioneer the new technologies.

4.4.6 Technical progress

By investing in R&D, firms buy themselves a chance at technical progress, that is, an increase in their *Mod* values. We now explain the model's representation of this process.

Technical progress is modeled as a random process that is conditioned, in each time period, on the firm's R&D spending and on its prevailing *Mod*.[18] There are separate processes for components and systems, which differ only as to the means and variances of the normal distributions involved. Thus, integrated firms have two technical progress functions, while specialized computer firms and component firms have only one technical progress function, respectively for systems and for components. According to these schemes, in each period firms draw possible values of the natural logarithm of *Mod* from a normal distribution. The number of draws[19] that any firm can take to improve its systems $(N_{f,t}^{SY})$ and components $(N_{f,t}^{CO})$ is proportional to its R&D spending for systems $(B_{f,t}^{SY})$ and components $(B_{f,t}^{CO})$ in that time period; the parameters of proportionality C_{κ}^{RD} and C_{k}^{RD} are the costs of a draw for system technology κ (κ = MF, PC) and component technology k (k = TR, IC, MP), respectively:

$$N_{f,t}^{SY} = \frac{B_{f,t}^{SY}}{C_{\kappa}^{RD}} \tag{13.a}$$

---

[18] The detailed modeling here follows that in Nelson and Winter (1982a), chapters 13–15.

[19] When the resulting number of draws is not an integer value, a random choice is made between the adjacent integer values in such a manner as to make the expected number of draws equal to the result of the calculation in Equation 13. For example, a result of 2.75 translates into 3 draws with probability 0.75 and 2 draws with probability 0.25.

$$N_{f,t}^{CO} = \frac{B_{f,t}^{CO}}{C_k^{RD}} \qquad (13.b)$$

The natural logarithm of the firm's current value of *Mod* is compared with the results of any draws it makes, and the best value among these determines, via exponentiation, the value of the firm's *Mod* for the following period.

The distribution of the outcomes of draws (potential new *Mod* values) has a higher mean when the current value is higher. Thus, technological change is represented as partly cumulative at the firm level. The mean also becomes more favorable with time, because it reflects the influence of "public knowledge" – a variable exogenous to the industry and conceived as representing the level of knowledge available in published academic research, specialized journals, or techniques that have become widely known. The details of these assumptions follow.

Public knowledge advances according to a trend that is specific to each system and component technology. The two system technologies (mainframe and personal computer) evolve along independent trajectories. This is not the case for component technologies. When a new component technology is introduced, its corresponding level of public knowledge is lower than that reached by current technology, but then it grows faster and surpasses the public knowledge of the older technology. Entry of new component firms occurs exactly in the period (T_k) in which the public knowledge of the new technology is equal to the public knowledge of the old technology. The rate of growth of public knowledge approaches a constant value characteristic of the technology, which is to say that the asymptotic trend is one of exponential growth. Later technologies show more rapid growth than earlier ones. An integrated computer firm is assumed to adopt the new component technology – meaning that its R&D results subsequently reflect the public knowledge of the new technology – when the level of the public knowledge of the new technology surpasses the mean of its own distribution for component draws. Thus, a firm that has managed to achieve technical results beyond the public knowledge level of the old component technology is hypothesized to be a late adopter of the new ones, while lagging firms tend to switch earlier.

As noted earlier, the values of the *Mod* obtained through the firms' draws are compared with the previous value of *Mod*, and the highest among these values is kept. Thus, higher R&D spending gives a firm more draws, and more draws increase the chances of getting a higher *Mod* for the following period – but do not make it a certainty. Specifically, the result of an individual draw is determined initially as a value drawn from a normal distribution for the natural logarithm of the *Mod* value. The mean of this distribution is a weighted average of the natural logarithm of the *Mod* of the product of firm *f* at time *t* – 1 and of the natural logarithm of the level of publicly available knowledge at time *t*:

$$\mu_{f,t}^{SY} = w^K \cdot \ln\left(M_{f,t-1}^{SY}\right) + \left(1 - w^K\right) \cdot \ln K_{\kappa,t}^{SY} \tag{14.a}$$

$$\mu_{f,t}^{CO} = w^K \cdot \ln\left(M_{f,t-1}^{CO}\right) + \left(1 - w^K\right) \cdot \ln K_{k,t}^{CO} \tag{14.b}$$

The standard deviations of the distributions are exogenous parameters that potentially differ across technologies for systems (σ_κ^{RD}) and components (σ_k^{RD}). Exponentiation of the result of the individual draw yields the value to be compared with the previous *Mod* (and other draw results, if any).

By setting the parameter w^K close to zero or one, the model is capable of representing extreme cases where progress in the industry is, respectively, "science-based" or "cumulative." In the former case, firm R&D expenditures are not the ultimate drivers of progress, they essentially cover the cost of commercializing innovative possibilities created outside the industry. In the latter case, firms are creating the effective technology, in a step-by-step cumulative process. Since accumulation is firm-specific, whereas public knowledge is a shared resource, it is clear that firm *Mod* values should be expected to diverge from each other to a greater extent when w^K is high than when it is low.[20]

The current level of the public knowledge of a technology is obtained from the following equations:

$$K_\kappa^{SY} = I_\kappa^0 \cdot exp(l_\kappa^1 \cdot t) \cdot \left[1 - \frac{1}{I_\kappa^2 \cdot \left(t - (T_\kappa - T^{SY}) \right)} \right] \qquad (15.a)$$

$$K_k^{CO} = I_k^0 \cdot exp(l_k^1 \cdot t) \cdot \left[1 - \frac{1}{I_k^2 \cdot \left(t - (T_k - T^{CO}) \right)} \right] \qquad (15.b)$$

where I^0, I^1, and I^2 are technology-specific parameters, T_κ is the entry time of firms using system technology κ (κ = MF, PC), T_k is the entry time of firms using component technology k (k = TR, IC, MP) and T^{SY} and T^{CO} represent delay time between technology emergence and entry of new firms, for system and component technologies, respectively. A higher value of I^0 yields a higher track for the public knowledge trajectory,[21] and a higher value of I^2 means that the asymptotic growth rate I^1 is approached more quickly. With I^2 set to a high value a new technology appears and then improves rather abruptly to quickly surpass the prevailing one (in terms of public knowledge).

4.4.7 Decisions on vertical integration and specialization

When a contract with a supplier expires, specialized computer producers may decide to vertically integrate into semiconductors, if they think that they can design and produce components that are

---

[20]   In the current parameterization of the model, the value of w has been set to 0.75 for all types of firms: that is to say that technical progress is highly cumulative. Experiments with lower values of the cumulativeness parameter yield as expected lower degrees of concentration and a stronger tendency toward vertical disintegration. However, these effects are weaker as compared to changes in the other parameters on which we have focused our attention in this chapter. Clearly, systematic exploration of different combinations of the values of the cumulativeness parameter for the three types of firms is on the agenda for future work.

[21]   The parameter I_{TR}^0 is set exogenously at 2; the parameter I_{IC}^0 is set to a value that guarantees that $K_{IC}^{CO} = K_{TR}^{CO}$ in period T_{IC}; the parameter I_{MP}^0 is set to a value that guarantees that $K_{MP}^{CO} = K_{IC}^{CO}$ in period T_{MP}. Both I_{MF}^0 and I_{PC}^0 are set exogenously at 2.

comparable in merit to those offered by specialist suppliers. As noted previously, this is more likely to be the case if computer producers are significantly larger than extant suppliers and can spend substantially more on R&D. We propose that the decision to vertically integrate also depends on the age of the component technology.

These considerations are reflected in the following formulation of the probability to integrate. Consider a computer firm f that at time $t - 1$ has been buying the components it uses. It now contemplates producing them in-house. We define the propensity to integrate as:

$$i_{f,t} = \left[min\left(\frac{t - T_k}{\chi^0}, 1 \right) \right]^{\chi^1} \cdot \left[\frac{q_{f,t}}{q_t^{CO}} \right]^{\chi^2} \tag{16}$$

where T_k is the entry time of firms using technology k (k = TR, IC, MP); $q_{f,t}$ is the number of computers sold by firm f; q_t^{CO} is the number of components sold by the largest component producer, χ^0 is a scale parameter for the technological age, and the exponents χ^1 and χ^2 determine the weight of technological age and size effects.

The probability of integration is then given by:

$$I_{f,t} = \frac{\xi^I \cdot i_{f,t}}{1 + \xi^I \cdot i_{f,t}} \tag{17}$$

where ξ^I is a parameter.[22] The initial value of the component Mod ($M_{f,t}^{CO}$) of a firm switching to integrated production is equal to a fraction φ^I of the Mod of its previous supplier. We also assume that the decision to integrate is not reversible in the short run: a recently integrated firm cannot switch back to specialization until a given number of time periods (T^I) has passed.

As noted previously, the decision to specialize is not symmetrical to the decision to vertically integrate, because its information base is significantly different. The decision is modeled as depending on a comparison between the Mod of the component produced

---

22 This formulation corresponds to the assumption that the odds favoring integration ($I / (1 - I)$) are proportional to i. Since i is not necessarily below one, it cannot directly serve as a probability.

internally and the *Mod* of the best component available on the market. The details of the formulation, however, are analogous to those for the integration decision.

Specifically, the propensity of an integrated firm to switch to buying rather than making its components is given by:

$$\varsigma_{f,t} = max\left(\frac{M_t^{CO} - M_{f,t}^{CO}}{M_{f,t}^{CO}}, 0\right) \tag{18}$$

where M_t^{CO} is the highest component *Mod* available on the market at time t. Then, the probability to switch to buying components from the market is:

$$S_{f,t} = \frac{\xi^S \cdot \varsigma_{f,t}}{1 + \xi^S \cdot \varsigma_{f,t}} \tag{19}$$

which implies that the odds favoring specialization are proportional to $\varsigma_{f,t}$.

A specialized computer firm may also decide to change its supplier, if a better producer has emerged in the market. The procedure for changing supplier follows the same rule for the specialization process. That is to say, whenever its contract with the supplier expires, a specialized firm checks if a better supplier than the current one exists. If this is the case, a new supplier is chosen using the rating mechanism described in the discussion of the demand module (Section 4.4.4).

4.4.8   Exit

Both computer firms and component suppliers exit the market when they are doing very little business.

For computer firms, the exit rule depends as follows on a market share threshold. For each computer firm and in each period, the variable

$$E_{f,t} = (1 - w^E) \cdot E_{f,t-1} + w^E \cdot s_{f,t} \tag{20}$$

is computed, where $s_{f,t}$ is the market share of firm f at time t and w^E is a parameter that determines the weight of current and past performance in the exit decision. A small value of w^E has the effect of allowing a lot of time for firms to recover from temporary competitive setbacks.[23] If $E_{f,t}$ is lower than a constant threshold λ^E, the firm exits.[24]

The rule governing the exit of the component producers is different and simpler. The probability of exit for a firm is an increasing function of the number of consecutive periods in which it does not sell to a computer producer. So the rule is defined as follows:

$$E_{f,t}^{CO} = \left(\frac{T_{f,t}^E}{T^E}\right)^2 \tag{21}$$

where $T_{f,t}^E$ is the number of consecutive periods, up to t, in which firm f does not sell to a computer producer, and T^E is a parameter representing the maximum number of consecutive periods without sales that any component firm can sustain. Then $E_{f,t}^{CO}$ is the probability of exit, and the specific result is determined by a draw from the uniform distribution. The quadratic formulation reflects an assumption that the effect on the probability of exit of an increase in the time without a sale is weaker for short periods of time.

4.5 THE SIMULATION RUNS

4.5.1 The history-friendly simulation

The history-friendly simulation is the result of setting model parameters to values that reflect the processes that have historically driven industrial evolution, vertical integration and specialization, according to the accounts and the interpretive framework discussed

---

[23] As is well known, Equation 20 generates the $E_{f,t}$ series as a geometric distributed lag function of the $s_{f,t}$ series, with weights decreasing into the past like $(1 - w^E)^t$.

[24] To guarantee the viability of the industry the exit threshold must not be higher than $(1 / F_\kappa)$, where F_κ is the initial number of firms in the market. Here the initial value of $E_{f,t}$ is set exactly at this value $(1 / F_\kappa)$ and $\lambda^E = 2 / (3 \cdot F_\kappa)$, which implies that firms exit if they operate long enough at less than two-thirds of their initial market share.

earlier. It is based on the following assumptions regarding the relevant variables and parameter values.

- The size of the external market for components is relatively small in the case of transistors and integrated circuits and significantly larger for microprocessors ($G_{MP}^{CO} > G_{TR}^{CO}$ and $G_{MP}^{CO} > G_{IC}^{CO}$);
- The weight on components relative to systems is higher in determining the *Mod* values for PCs as compared to mainframes ($\tau_{PC} > \tau_{MF}$);
- PCs are cheaper than mainframes ($\vartheta_{MF} > \vartheta_{PC}$), so that a new class of customers, who attribute more value to cheapness than to performance, buy PCs, and that market grows rapidly;
- Bandwagon effects are very important for mainframes and much less so for PCs ($\delta_{MF}^s > \delta_{PC}^s$);
- In the demand for semiconductors, bandwagon effects are much stronger for microprocessors than for transistors and integrated circuits ($\delta_{MP}^s > \delta_{TR}^s$ and $\delta_{MP}^s > \delta_{IC}^s$);
- The technological discontinuity related to microprocessors allows much greater improvements in component designs, and thus it is modeled as: (a) a higher change of trend than the previous one related to integrated circuits ($l_{MP}^1 > l_{IC}^1$) (see Equation 15) and (b) a larger difference between the initial values of the *Mod* of component products at entry when the technological discontinuities occur ($M_{MP}^{CO} - M_{IC}^{CO} > M_{IC}^{CO} - M_{TR}^{CO}$), as defined in Section 4.4.4.

Under this parameterization, the simulation replicates the key aspects of the history recounted at the beginning of this chapter. Our results in this and the following exercises refer to averages over 1,000 runs. Figures 4.1.a and 4.1.b report the Herfindahl index and the ratio of integrated firms to total of firms in the industry, termed the integration ratio.

In the first era the computer industry undergoes a sharp increase in concentration, as shown in 4.1.a. There is no comparable increase in concentration in semiconductors, where bandwagon effects are weaker, and of course the transistor technology is aging. Figure 4.1.b shows the resulting multi-decade drift toward full integration of the dominant mainframe firm, reflecting the logic of Equation 16.

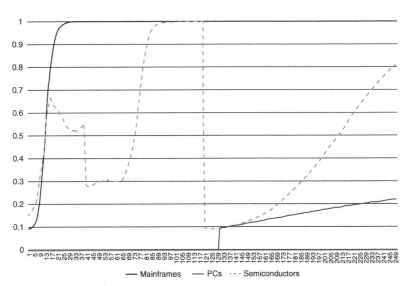

FIGURE 4.1.A Herfindahl index (Standard Set).

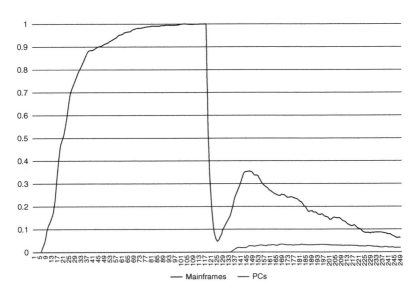

FIGURE 4.1.B Integration ratio (Standard Set).

Integration is sustained because the monopolistic mainframe produ-cer finances large R&D investments out of its profits, and thereby maintains technological leadership in components. Concentration tendencies in the semiconductor industry are weak not only because of the absence of bandwagon effects but also because external demand is small, and vertical integration by the mainframe leader further reduces the demand faced by the specialist component producers.

At period 40, integrated circuits are introduced and we have assumed that they are introduced by new firms, a new generation of semiconductor companies. As shown in 4.1.a, the result is an abrupt decline in concentration in semiconductors. In a fraction of the runs, the dominant mainframe firm dis-integrates temporarily in response to the novelty of the technology; these moves account for the pause in the rise of the integration index in the cross-run averages shown in Figure 4.1.b. They are soon reversed, however, as the mainframe producer continues to be very large compared to the new semiconduc-tor producers. As of period 90, integration prevails across virtually all runs. Competition induces a sharp shakeout in semiconductors, and concentration increases (around period 65). When vertical integration is complete in the computer market, the semiconductor producers are left with very little demand and exit the market. Exit produces an increase in concentration until no firm is left in the market. In parti-cular, from around period 75 on, the number of simulations in which no semiconductor company survives increases rapidly, reaching over 80 percent of the total runs after period 90 and 95 percent after period 100. When there are no firms in an industry, the Herfindahl index, H, is undefined. In those cases, for computational reasons, we attribute a value equal to 1 to the H index. That is to say, we approximate the H index in the zero firms case to the value that the index takes in the period immediately before the last exit – typically with one firm alive. Thus, in Figure 4.1.a, the H index for the semiconductor industry becomes close or equal to one between period 90 and 120. Figure 4.1.c reports the average number of firms, illustrating that in that period there are no firms in the market.

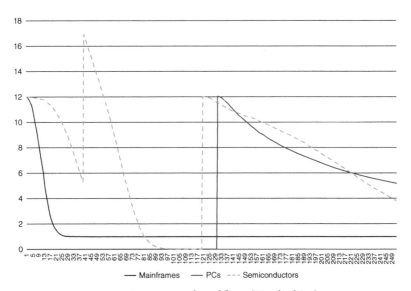

FIGURE 4.1.C Average number of firms (Standard Set).

The advent of microprocessors (period 120) sets in motion a different story. This technological discontinuity involves a major improvement in component technology relative to integrated circuits. The appearance of strong demand from outside the computer industry is represented by a parameter change – a drastic increase in the size of the external market. The model represents the endogenous response to this change, which includes large investments in R&D and growth of the new semiconductor firms. Similarly, a parameter change captures our judgment that bandwagon effects in the demand for components, both in the computer market and in the external market, were much stronger for microprocessors than they were in the earlier phases. The combined and interrelated effects of these changes appear in the relevant time period in Figures 4.1.a and 4.1.b. Note the abrupt dis-integration in response to the superior *Mod* of components from the external supplier (see Equation 18). This adds further to the demand facing the component industry, which produces feedback effects including additional R&D spending. There is a brief period of rising integration, which ends about period 155. After that, integration trends downward, while concentration in the components industry marches slowly upward to the end of the run. The leading microprocessor companies continue to prosper by producing components of greater merit.

In the PC market, most producers remain small relative to the largest microprocessor supplier, which emerges before any of the new producers of PCs became very large. The growth of concentration is gradual and the industry structure remains quite competitive by ordinary standards. Recall that we have assumed that bandwagon effects for PCs are smaller than for mainframes. Under these circumstances, no PC producer can establish and maintain sales large enough to make vertical integration reasonable as the bottom track in Figure 4.1.b shows. The establishment of a near-monopoly in the supply of components serves, however, to maintain competition in the PC market, since most firms get their microprocessors from the same source.

4.5.2 Testing the model: counterfactual simulations

To check the model's consistency with our historical interpretation and the validity of our causal explanations, we conducted a series of counterfactual simulations. Specifically, we changed the values of the parameters that, according to our assumptions, account for the success of the attempt to be history-friendly, and try to answer the following questions:

(a) Would the absence of an external market for components lead to more vertical integration of computer firms?
(b) Would the absence of bandwagon effects in the mainframe market diminish concentration there and lead to more specialization?
(c) Would the absence of such effects in the semiconductor market lead to more vertical integration of computer firms?
(d) Would a smaller technological discontinuity attending the appearance of microprocessors lead to more vertical integration of computer firms?

We did a set of runs for each question, changing parameter values appropriately.

4.5.2a The absence of an external market for components induces more vertical integration

First, we focus on the size of the external market for components (G_k^{CO}). In the history-friendly simulation, a large external market for microprocessors allowed new semiconductor firms to quickly develop high-quality components and to grow large, thereby inducing specialization of computer producers. In this first counterfactual simulation, we eliminate external sales for component firms ($G_k^{CO} = 0$ for all k). Figures 4.2.a and 4.2.b shows the result. Overall, they confirm the strong causal role of the external market.

In the transistor period, the main difference observed in comparison with the standard case is the strong decline in concentration in the semiconductor market: the absence of an external market limits

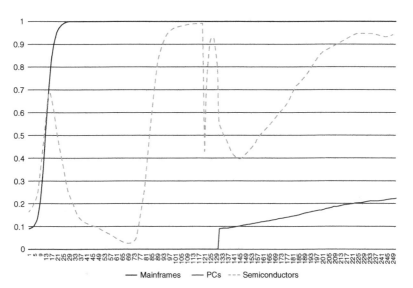

FIGURE 4.2.A Herfindahl index (No external market for semiconductor firms).

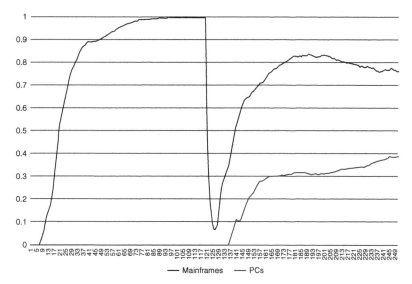

FIGURE 4.2.B Integration ratio (No external market for semiconductor firms).

the growth of successful firms, thus preventing the emergence of leaders in the industry. After the introduction of integrated circuits, vertical integration by the dominant mainframe firm occurs earlier in most runs. This process, coupled with the absence of an external market for semiconductors, accelerates the exit of component firms: the Herfindahl index grows rapidly and sharply, until no firm is left in the market.

The technological discontinuity associated with microprocessors (period 120) shows a sharper contrast with the history-friendly case. A short period of vertical dis-integration again occurs. In most individual runs, the signing of a contract between the dominant mainframe firm and a component producer initiates a period of near-monopoly in the semiconductor market. When the contract expires, the dominant mainframe firm vertically integrates again so that most of the demand facing the leading semiconductor producer disappears. This firm loses its dominance in the market for microprocessors and concentration falls. This tendency soon disappears, however. Competition among surviving semiconductor producers for the business of PC firms induces selection, and high concentration reappears, earlier than in the standard simulation (around period 180 and after). Moreover, both mainframe and PC producers show a faster and stronger drive toward vertical integration: The growth of semiconductor companies and of the quality of their components is limited by the absence of an external market. At the end of the simulation, concentration in all markets is not much different from that in the history-friendly simulation, but the dominant mainframe firm is typically integrated, and there is much more vertical integration in PCs as well.

4.5.2b The absence of bandwagon effects in mainframe demand reduces concentration there and leads to more specialization
In these counterfactual simulations, we decrease the exponent δ^S_{MF} in Equation 2 from 6 to 2. Results are shown in Figures 4.3.a and 4.3.b,

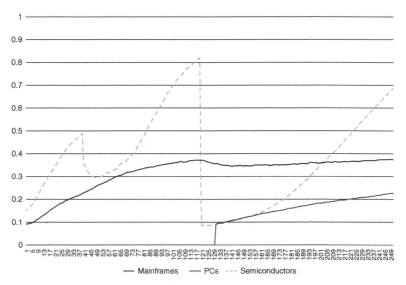

FIGURE 4.3.A Herfindahl index (Low bandwagon for mainframe firms).

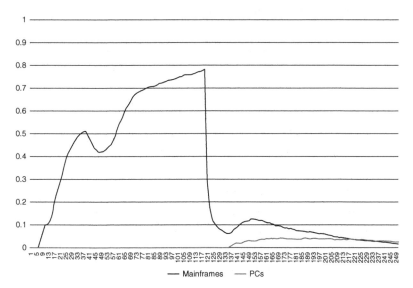

FIGURE 4.3.B Integration ratio (Low bandwagon for mainframe firms).

and they are quite dramatic. The rapid transition to near-monopoly in mainframes is replaced by a leisurely but systematic drift toward higher concentration. By end of the run, the Herfindahl index has risen to about 0.4 from an initial value of 0.1. Thus, in our model, bandwagon effects in the demand for mainframes are crucial in producing concentration in the mainframe industry. Concentration begets vertical integration by way of the relative size effect (Equation 16). In this counterfactual, both concentration and vertical integration grow slowly in the first two eras, the transistor and integrated circuits periods. The microprocessor discontinuity in semiconductors has no effect on concentration in mainframes, except for a minor blip that may reflect adoption lags. Vertical integration, however, plunges even more dramatically than in the history-friendly case, and concentration in the semiconductor industry plunges with it. After the discontinuity, vertical integration recovers feebly but generally remains very low. Concentration grows steadily in the component market, however. On the average, it reaches a marginally lower level by the end of these simulations as compared to the history-friendly simulations.

In sum, the absence of strong bandwagon effects in the demand for mainframes removes the tendency toward quick monopolization of this market. A drift toward concentration remains, but it is a reflection of the divergence of technological capabilities – differences in *Mod* are the sole carrier of path dependence in market shares.[25] In the semiconductor industry, the drift toward concentration is stronger, but it is subject to reset in times of technological discontinuities – as is dramatically illustrated by the abrupt decline of concentration at the time of the microprocessor discontinuities. The strong drift toward concentration reappears after that break. Thanks to the combined effects of the lower concentration on integration and the technological discontinuities on *dis*-integration, there is typically a lower frequency of integration in this counterfactual than in the history-friendly case.

4.5.2c   The absence of bandwagon effects in semiconductor demand does not necessarily lead to more vertical integration

In these counterfactual runs, bandwagon effects in the semiconductor market are eliminated by setting to zero the market share exponent δ_k^s in Equation 2.[26] Figures 4.4.a and 4.4.b show the results. In sharp contrast to the previous case, this change produces only modest effects. It produces no visible effects in the transistor and integrated circuits eras, where vertical integration of computer firms implies a very small demand for components and hence little room for the bandwagon effect to have an impact. As expected, however, concentration in the microprocessors market is decreased significantly compared with the history-friendly simulation. The vertical scope of computer firms is not affected, which is unsurprising given that

---

[25]   In particular, firms in our model do not have a persistent "size" attribute that would introduce a Gibrat-style mechanism for the increase of concentration.

[26]   Adapted to the component market, as pointed out in Section 4.4.4.

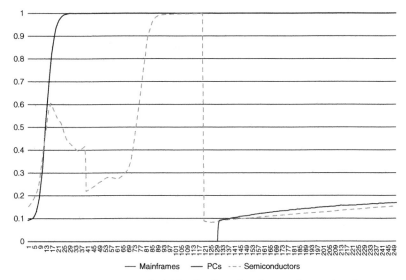

FIGURE 4.4.A Herfindahl index (Low bandwagon for semiconductor firms).

FIGURE 4.4.B Integration ratio (Low bandwagon for semiconductor firms).

specialization occurred also in the history-friendly run. This exercise contributes further corroboration of our claim that the external market for semiconductors and the technological turbulence associated with the major discontinuity of microprocessors were key factors in the evolution of vertical structure in this historical case. These causes lay behind the low frequency of vertical integration of mainframe producers and the pattern of complete specialization by PC producers.

4.5.2d If there is only a minor technological discontinuity in microprocessors, and no external market, vertical integration is increased

In the history-friendly simulation, the introduction of microprocessors implied a significant increase in the merit of design of components compared to the previous types of semiconductors. Now in this counterfactual exercise the magnitude of this discontinuity is reduced by decreasing by 50 percent the value of the initial *Mod* for microprocessors (M_{MP}^{CO}) and by eliminating the external market for them $(G_{MP}^{CO} = 0)$. The consequences are dramatic, as one can see from Figures 4.5.a and 4.5.b.

After the discontinuity, the mainframe producer continues to be vertically integrated in most runs, most of the time. Only quite late does specialization start occurring, reflecting the emergence of a leader firm in the semiconductor industry. PC firms also tend to vertically integrate, though to a lesser extent. The PC market becomes more concentrated because the vertically integrated PC firms grow, while some specialized PC firms that did not choose advanced microprocessor producers exit the market. The exit of specialized PC firms reduces the demand for components and increases concentration in the semiconductor industry.

4.6 CONCLUSIONS

The model is able to reproduce the main stylized facts of the patterns of competition and vertical integration in the computer and semiconductor industries. In addition, counterfactual experiments show that

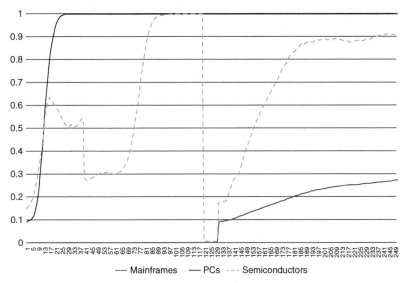

FIGURE 4.5.A Herfindahl index (Minor discontinuity).

FIGURE 4.5.B Integration ratio (Minor discontinuity).

the model responds to changes in the key parameters in ways that are consistent with the hypotheses and reasoning that are at its core.

The model illustrates, first of all, how the patterns of vertical integration and specialization in the computer industry change as a function of the evolving levels and distribution of firms' capabilities. In this respect, the model incorporates and develops the basic insights of the capabilities approach to the theory of the firm. Other considerations, such as transaction costs and the design of optimal contracts allocating residual property rights, or "double marginalization" considerations are consciously left in the background. These variables may indeed exert important influence on the vertical scope of firms. In fact, there have been recent efforts to reflect both transaction-cost and capabilities-based considerations, and to analyze their co-evolution (Williamson, 1999; Jacobides and Winter, 2005, 2012). Indeed, one key point of that analysis is embodied in our modeling of the decision of a computer firm to specialize: Acquiring components from "the market" is a realistic option only when there are capable transacting partners on the other side of that market. As to the long-run patterns of integration and specialization, we believe that in our historical case those were largely driven by the accumulation of competencies, which defined the basic structural conditions for decisions to specialize or integrate. We also argue that novel contexts associated with technological discontinuities, and with innovative entry by new firms, presented distinctive pressures on such decisions.

Second, the model shows how the vertical scope of upstream and downstream firms co-evolves over time as a result of R&D investments, learning processes and market selection. The decision to specialize or to integrate at a particular point in industry history depends on the prevailing capabilities of other firms in both sectors of the industry, and on how those are reflected, via selection processes, in performance outcomes such as market shares and growth.

Third, the model emphasizes three conditions – the size of the external market, the magnitude of the technological discontinuities and the extent of bandwagon effects in demand. It demonstrates how these conditions engender, in the course of time, critical effects and feedbacks on market structure and on the vertical scope of firms in the computer and semiconductor industries.

The analysis of a single industry does not, of course, provide a sufficient basis for drawing broader generalizations. Indeed, we do not claim that this chapter embodies a new, fully-fledged theory of the vertical scope of firms. In other industries, other factors might have played a more prominent role. And, most likely, the development and analysis of a formal model of a different industry would involve different modeling strategies. However, over the past twenty years, the competence-based theory of the firm has provided such important contributions in fields as different as strategic management, organization theory and industrial dynamics, that in our view it now offers a legitimate, serious and vibrant alternative to more mainstream approaches.

APPENDIX 4.1   LIST OF VARIABLES AND PARAMETERS

Parameter	Symbol	Value / range
General indices		
Index for firms	f	$\mathbb{N}$
Index for markets (user classes)	h	{MF, PC, CO}
Index for component technologies	k	{TR, IC, MP}
Index for time periods	t	{1, ..., T}
Index for system technologies	κ	{MF, PC}
Computer industry and technology characteristics		
Unit cost of R&D – mainframe technology	C_{MF}^{RD}	250
Unit cost of R&D – PC technology	C_{PC}^{RD}	250
Number of entering firms – mainframe market	F_{MF}	12
Number of entering firms – PC market	F_{PC}	12
Number of groups of potential customers – mainframe market	G_{MF}	100
Number of groups of potential customers – PC market	G_{PC}	100

Parameter	Symbol	Value / range
Level of public knowledge for system technology κ at time t	$K_{\kappa,t}^{SY}$	$\mathbb{R}_+$
Scale parameter in Equation 15 – mainframe technology	l_{MF}^0	2
Scale parameter in Equation 15 – PC technology	l_{PC}^0	2
Growth rate in Equation 15 – mainframe technology	l_{MF}^1	0.01
Growth rate in Equation 15 – PC technology	l_{PC}^1	0.01
Multiplier of technology age in Equation 15 – mainframe technology	l_{MF}^2	1
Multiplier of technology age in Equation 15 – PC technology	l_{PC}^2	1
Mod of computer products at entry – mainframe technology	M_{MF}^{SY}	1
Mod of computer products at entry – PC technology	M_{PC}^{SY}	4
Period of introduction – Mainframe technology	T_{MF}	1
Period of introduction – PC technology	T_{PC}	130
Delay between system technology introduction and new firms entry	T^{SY}	1
Weight of current market share in Equation 20	w^E	0.3
Weight of cheapness in Equation 3 – mainframe market	γ_{MF}	0.3
Weight of cheapness in Equation 3 – PC market	γ_{PC}	0.7
Weight of *Mod* in Equation 2 – mainframe market	δ_{MF}^M	1
Weight of *Mod* in Equation 2 – PC market	δ_{PC}^M	1
Weight of bandwagon in Equation 2 – mainframe technology	δ_{MF}^s	6
Weight of bandwagon in Equation 2 – PC technology	δ_{PC}^s	1
Trajectory angle (in radians) – mainframe technology	ϑ_{MF}	$\pi/3$

Parameter	Symbol	Value / range
Trajectory angle (in radians) – PC Technology	ϑ_{PC}	$\pi/6$
System *Mod* technological frontier – integrated circuit technology	$\varLambda_{IC}^{SY}$	20
System *Mod* technological frontier – microprocessor technology	$\varLambda_{MP}^{SY}$	60
System *Mod* technological frontier – transistor technology	$\varLambda_{TR}^{SY}$	10
Exit threshold for computer firms	λ^E	0.055
Scale parameter in Equations 8 and 9 – mainframe technology	ν_{MF}	60
Scale parameter in Equations 8 and 9 – PC technology	ν_{PC}	100
Elasticity-related parameter in Equation 1 – mainframe technology	ρ_{MF}	1
Elasticity-related parameter in Equation 1 – PC technology	ρ_{PC}	−0.5
Standard deviation of technical progress normal distribution for system technology κ	σ_κ^{RD}	0.0144
Weight of component in Equation 1 – mainframe technology	τ_{MF}	0.5
Weight of component in Equation 1 – PC technology	τ_{PC}	0.75
Scale parameter in Equation 1 – mainframe technology	$\varPhi_{MF}$	1
Scale parameter in Equation 1 – PC technology	$\varPhi_{PC}$	1
Spillover of system R&D to component R&D in integrated firms	ψ^{CO}	0.1
Component industry and technology characteristics		
Unit cost of R&D – integrated circuit technology	C_{IC}^{RD}	250
Unit cost of R&D – microprocessor technology	C_{MP}^{RD}	500
Unit cost of R&D – transistor technology	C_{TR}^{RD}	200

Parameter	Symbol	Value / range
Number of firms entering components market when technology k is introduced	F_k	12
Number of external markets for components – integrated circuit technology	G_{IC}^{CO}	8
Number of external markets for components – microprocessor technology	G_{MP}^{CO}	1050
Number of external markets for components – transistor technology	G_{TR}^{CO}	8
Level of public knowledge for component technology k at time t	$K_{k,t}^{CO}$	$\mathbb{R}_+$
Scale parameter in Equation 15 – integrated circuit technology	I_{IC}^0	1.782
Scale parameter in Equation 15 – microprocessor technology	I_{MP}^0	1.075
Scale parameter in Equation 15 – transistor technology	I_{TR}^0	2
Growth rate in Equation 15 – integrated circuit technology	I_{IC}^1	0.15
Growth rate in Equation 15 – microprocessor technology	I_{MP}^1	0.2
Growth rate in Equation 15 – transistor technology	I_{TR}^1	0.1
Multiplier of technology age in Equation 15 – integrated circuit technology	I_{IC}^2	1
Multiplier of technology age in Equation 15 – microprocessor technology	I_{MP}^2	1
Multiplier of technology age in Equation 15 – transistor technology	I_{TR}^2	1
Mod of component products at entry – integrated circuit technology	M_{IC}^{CO}	2
Mod of component products at entry – microprocessor technology	M_{MP}^{CO}	25
Mod of component products at entry – transistor technology	M_{TR}^{CO}	1
New firms entry time – integrated circuit technology	T_{IC}	40

Parameter	Symbol	Value / range
New firms entry time – microprocessor technology	T_{MP}	120
New firms entry time – transistor technology	T_{TR}	1
Delay between component technology introduction and new firms entry	T^{CO}	10
Maximum number of consecutive periods without sales before exit	T^{E}	100
Weight of Mod in Equation 2 – components market	δ_{CO}^{M}	1
Weight of bandwagon in Equation 2 – integrated circuit technology	δ_{IC}^{s}	2
Weight of bandwagon in Equation 2 – microprocessor technology	δ_{MP}^{s}	4
Weight of bandwagon in Equation 2 – transistor technology	δ_{TR}^{s}	2
Scale parameter in Equation 11 – integrated circuit technology	v_{IC}	50
Scale parameter in Equation 11 – microprocessor technology	v_{MP}	50
Scale parameter in Equation 11 – transistor technology	v_{TR}	50
Standard deviation of technical progress normal distribution for component technology k	σ_{k}^{RD}	0.0144
Common industry characteristics		
Number of firms selling in market h at time t	$F_{h,t}$	$\mathbb{N}$
Markup	m	0.1
Periods of simulation	T	250
Weight of product Mod in Equation 14	w^{K}	0.75
Fraction of profits invested in R&D	φ^{RD}	1
Computer firms characteristics		
Budget for component R&D by firm f at time t	$B_{f,t}^{CO}$	$\mathbb{R}_{+}$
Budget for system R&D by firm f at time t	$B_{f,t}^{SY}$	$\mathbb{R}_{+}$
Unit production cost of a computer produced by firm f at time t	$C_{f,t}^{PD}$	$\mathbb{R}_{+}$

Parameter	Symbol	Value / range
Inverse exit propensity of computer firm f at time t	$E_{f,t}$	$[0, 1]$
Mod of computer of firm f at time t	$M_{f,t}$	$\mathbb{R}_+$
Mod of system of firm f at time t	$M_{f,t}^{SY}$	$\mathbb{R}_+$
Number of new potential system $Mods$ drawn by firm f at time t	$N_{f,t}^{SY}$	$\mathbb{N}$
Cheapness of computer of firm f at time t	$Z_{f,t}^{CH}$	$\mathbb{R}_+$
Performance of computer of firm f at time t	$Z_{f,t}^{PE}$	$\mathbb{R}_+$
Mean of technical progress normal distribution for system of firm f at time t	$\mu_{f,t}^{SY}$	$\mathbb{R}_+$
Component firms characteristics		
Exit probability of component firm f at time t	$E_{f,t}^{CO}$	$[0, 1]$
Consecutive periods up to t with zero sales to computer firms by component firm f	$T_{f,t}^{E}$	$\{1, \ldots, T\}$
Common firms characteristics		
Unit production cost of a component produced by firm f at time t	$C_{f,t}^{CO}$	$\mathbb{R}_+$
Number of groups of customers in market h buying a product from firm f at time t	$G_{f,h,t}$	$\{1, \ldots, G_h\}$
Mod of computer of firm f at time t as perceived by customers in market h	$M_{f,h,t}$	$\mathbb{R}_+$
Mod of component of firm f at time t	$M_{f,t}^{CO}$	$\mathbb{R}_+$
Number of new potential component $Mods$ drawn by firm f at time t	$N_{f,t}^{CO}$	$\mathbb{N}$
Price of firm f at time t	$P_{f,t}$	$\mathbb{R}_+$
Quantity sold by firm f (in market h) at time t	$q_{f,t}, q_{f,h,t}$	$\mathbb{R}_+$
Market share of firm f at time t	$s_{f,t}$	$[0, 1]$
Duration of a contract between a specialized computer firm and a component supplier	$T_{f,t}^{CO}$	$\{6, \ldots, 10\}$
Probability of product of firm f to be selected by customers in market h at time t	$U_{f,h,t}$	$[0, 1]$
Propensity of product of firm f to be selected by customer in market h at time t	$u_{f,h,t}$	$\mathbb{R}_+$
Mean of technical progress normal distribution for component of firm f at time t	$\mu_{f,t}^{CO}$	$\mathbb{R}_+$
Profits of firm f at time t	$\Pi_{f,t}$	$\mathbb{R}_+$

Parameter	Symbol	Value / range
Integration and specialization		
Probability to integrate of firm f at time t	$I_{f,t}$	[0, 1]
Propensity to integrate of firm f at time t	$i_{f,t}$	$\mathbb{R}_+$
Mod of the best component available on the market at time t	M_t^{CO}	$\mathbb{R}_+$
Quantity sold by the largest component producer at time t	q_t^{CO}	$\mathbb{R}_+$
Probability to specialize of firm f at time t	$S_{f,t}$	[0, 1]
Minimum duration of integration	T^I	16
Parameter in Equation 17	ζ^I	1
Parameter in Equation 19	ζ^S	1
Propensity to specialize of firm f at time t	$\varsigma_{f,t}$	$\mathbb{R}_+$
Fraction of last supplier *Mod* inherited by a newly integrated firm	φ^I	0.8
Multiplier of technology age in Equation 16	χ^0	20
Weight of technology age in Equation 16	χ^1	1
Weight of size effect in Equation 16	χ^2	1

APPENDIX 4.2   SENSITIVITY ANALYSIS

We follow here the same approach to sensitivity analysis employed in the previous model: we study the effects of those parameters that – although necessary to set up the model – are not recognized as having a peculiar effect on the evolution of the industry.

In our exercise, we exclude three groups of parameters from variation: (1) those parameters explicitly studied in any of the history-divergent runs; (2) those parameters that let variables take values over an extensive range; (3) those parameters set to specific values that neutralize their role or that keep them to specific ratios with other parameters. The list of parameters included in the analysis is presented in Table A.4.1.

A sensitivity analysis run is conducted as follows. We extract a value for each parameter included in the analysis within a predefined range: the minimum value of the range is equal to a 10 percent reduction of the standard value of the parameter, the maximum values of

Table A.4.1 *Parameters under sensitivity analysis*

Parameter	Symbol	Value
Unit cost of R&D – integrated circuit technology	C_{IC}^{RD}	250
Unit cost of R&D – mainframe technology	C_{MF}^{RD}	250
Unit cost of R&D – microprocessor technology	C_{MP}^{RD}	500
Unit cost of R&D – PC technology	C_{PC}^{RD}	250
Unit cost of R&D – transistor technology	C_{TR}^{RD}	200
Number of entering firms – mainframe market	F_{MF}	12
Number of entering firms – PCs market	F_{PC}	12
Number of firms entering components market when technology k is introduced	F_k	12
Markup	m	0.1
Maximum number of consecutive periods without sales before exit	T^E	100
Minimum duration of integration	T^I	16
Weight of current market share in Equation 20	w^E	0.3
Standard deviation of technical progress normal distribution for component technology k	σ_k^{RD}	0.0144
Standard deviation of technical progress normal distribution for system technology κ	σ_κ^{RD}	0.0144
Fraction of last supplier *Mod* inherited by a newly integrated firm	φ^I	0.8
Multiplier of technology age in Equation 16	χ^0	20
Spillover of system R&D to component R&D in integrated firms	ψ^{CO}	0.1

the range is equal to a 10 percent increase of the standard value of the parameter. Then, we run 1,000 simulation runs using the extracted set of parameters instead of the standard set.

Our sensitivity analysis is based on 1,000 sensitivity runs: each of these runs can be compared to our history-replicating simulation based on the standard set, since they are obtained by averaging period by period the values of 1,000 simulation runs.

Our analysis focuses on the same aggregate statistics presented in the history-replicating analysis: the Herfindahl index in the main-frame, PC and semiconductor markets, the total number of firms in the mainframe, PC and semiconductor markets, and the integration ratio in the mainframe and PC markets. For each of these statistics, we present the average values of five different groups of sensitivity runs: the lowest decile group, the group with values between the 10th and 25th percentile, the group between the 25th and 75th percentile, the group between the 75th and the 90th percentile, and the highest decile group. A sensitivity run is attributed to a group on the basis of the average value across all periods of the simulation. The results are presented in Figures A.4.1–A.4.8.

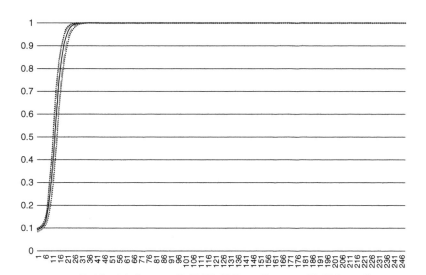

FIGURE A.4.1 Sensitivity analysis: Herfindahl index in mainframes.

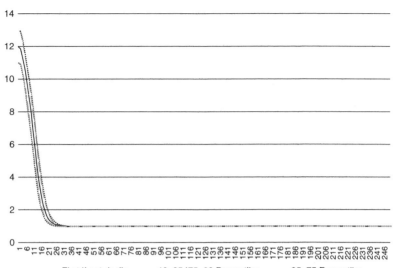

FIGURE A.4.2 Sensitivity analysis: average number of firms in mainframes.

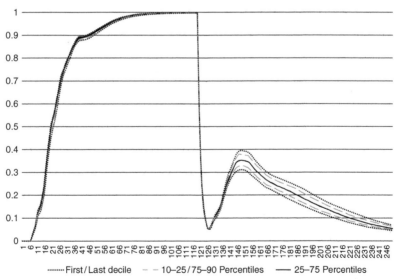

FIGURE A.4.3 Sensitivity analysis: integration ratio in mainframes.

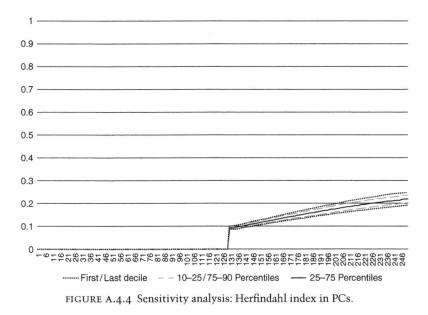

FIGURE A.4.4 Sensitivity analysis: Herfindahl index in PCs.

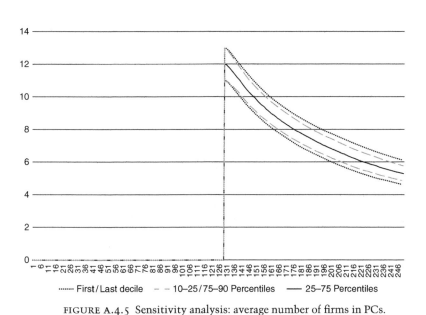

FIGURE A.4.5 Sensitivity analysis: average number of firms in PCs.

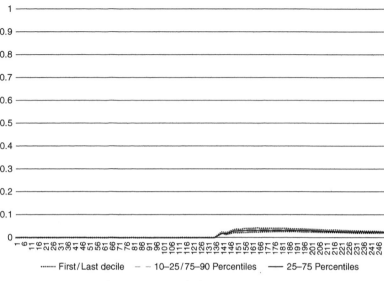

FIGURE A.4.6 Sensitivity analysis: integration ratio in PCs.

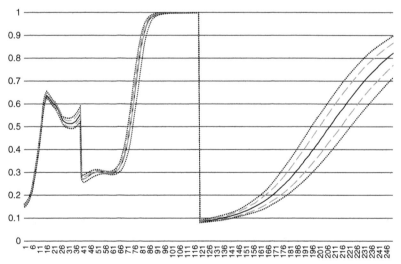

FIGURE A.4.7 Sensitivity analysis: Herfindahl index in semiconductors.

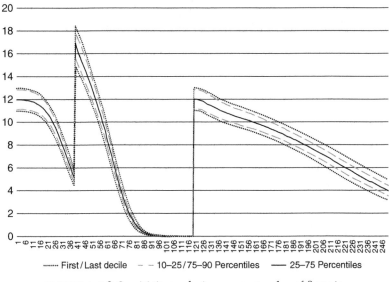

FIGURE A.4.8 Sensitivity analysis: average number of firms in semiconductors.

Again, from our results it emerges that, although the specific values of our statistics are affected by the change in the parameters values, the general dynamics is analogous to what is obtained by our history-replicating simulation even in the most extreme cases. The most relevant parameters in driving the deviation from the standard values are the initial number of firms and the parameters controlling the exit conditions.

5 The pharmaceutical industry and the role of demand

5.1 INTRODUCTION

This chapter presents a "history-friendly" model of the evolution of the pharmaceutical industry, and in particular of the so-called golden age. This industry is an ideal subject for such an analysis, especially because it has characteristics and problems that provide both contrasts and similarities with the computer industry. Like computers, the pharmaceutical industry has traditionally been a highly R&D and marketing-intensive sector and it has undergone a series of radical technological and institutional "shocks." However, despite these shocks, the core of the leading innovative firms and countries has remained stable for a very long period of time. Entry by new firms has been a rather rare occurrence until the advent of biotechnology. However, while the evolution of computers coincides largely with the history of very few firms, that of pharmaceuticals involves at least a couple of dozens of companies. Further, the degree of concentration has been consistently low at the aggregate level and the industry has never experienced a shakeout of producers.

We argue that the observed patterns of the evolutionary dynamics were shaped by three main factors, related both to the nature of the relevant technological regime and the structure of demand:

(1) The nature of the process of drug discovery, in terms of the properties of the space of technological opportunities and of the search procedures by which firms explore it. Specifically, innovation processes were characterized for a long time by "quasi-random" search procedures (random screening), with little positive spillovers from one discovery to the next (low cumulativeness).

This chapter is a major revision of previously published work: Garavaglia *et al.* (2012).The original paper has been improved in the structure, code and technical apparatus.

150

(2) The type of competition and the role of patents and imitation in shaping gains from innovation. Patents gave temporary monopoly power to the innovator, but competition remained strong nevertheless, sustained by processes of "inventing around" and – after a patent expires – by imitation.

(3) The fragmented nature of the relevant markets. The industry comprises many independent submarkets, which correspond broadly to different therapeutic classes.[1] For example, cardiovascular products do not compete with antidepressants. And, given the quasi-random nature of the innovative process, innovation in one therapeutic class typically does little to enhance innovation opportunities in other markets.

These features have been reflected in dynamic paths of evolution that are quite distinct from those seen in computers.

5.2 THE EVOLUTION OF THE PHARMACEUTICAL INDUSTRY: A STYLIZED HISTORY

The historical evolution of the pharmaceutical industry is customarily divided into three eras.[2] The industry was born in the late nineteenth century as part of the nascent chemical sector. The pioneers

---

[1] Therapeutic classes are a way of classifying medical drugs according to their functions, i.e., according to the organ or system on which they act and/or their therapeutic and chemical characteristics. Each therapeutic class is a group of similar medications classified together because they are intended to treat the same medical conditions. Therapeutic classes are used by doctors and pharmacists when selecting appropriate treatments for patients. Commonly used therapeutic classes include analgesics, antibiotics, anticonvulsants, etc. The Anatomical Therapeutic Chemical (ATC) Classification System classifies each drug in a series of class, starting with a group of fourteen classes organizing drugs according to the system of the body that the medication is meant to affect, such as the nervous system, immune system or respiratory system. Drugs are then classified into broad therapeutic groups according to their function, e.g., analgesics or antipsychotics. A drug can belong to more than one group, but we abstract from this complication in our model: a drug belongs only to a single therapeutic class.

[2] For a detailed discussion of the evolution of the pharmaceutical sector see, among others, Pisano (1996), Henderson et al. (1999), Malerba and Orsenigo (2002), Sutton (1998), Pammolli (1996), Grabowski and Vernon (1977, 1994a), Chandler (1990, 2005a), Galambos and Sewell (1996), Galambos and Sturchio (1996), Gambardella (1995).

were mainly Swiss and German firms, such as Bayer, Hoechst, Ciba and Sandoz, which first entered the industry exploiting the competencies and knowledge they had accumulated in the related areas of organic chemicals and dyestuffs. In the United States, the industry developed later as the outcome of the growth of firms such as Eli Lilly, Abbott, Smith Kline, Upjohn, Squibb, Parke Davis (later merged with Warner-Lambert), Burroughs-Wellcome, and Wyeth (i.e. American Home Products). These companies were involved in processing, packaging, marketing and distributing a variety of drugs. Until World War I, US companies relied on the technologies provided by the European firms and specialized in two distinct trajectories. A first group engaged mainly in the production and marketing of their existing drugs, based largely on natural substances, which were patented and sold over the counter. The second group developed new, chemically based prescription or "ethical" drugs and marketed them through pharmacists and doctors (Chandler, 2005a).

Until World War II, the industry did not engage in intensive R&D. Few new drugs were introduced into the market, the most important innovations being the introduction of alkaloids, coal tar derivatives and sulfa drugs between 1938 and 1943 (Sutton, 1998). These drugs were, however, of limited effectiveness and had correspondingly only limited commercial success.

The modern pharmaceutical industry emerged in the second era, "the golden age," (after the 1940s) largely as a fallout of the wartime crash programs in penicillin and sulfa drugs. Participation in such programs helped firms (particularly in the United States and in the United Kingdom) to develop new capabilities in finance, technology and organization; it also opened innovative opportunities, initially in antibiotics and then in many other therapeutic areas. Scientific medical knowledge also expanded in the immediate postwar years. Nearly every government in the developed world began to support health-related research; in the United States, public funding of biomedical research increased dramatically. The National Institutes of Health (NIH) became a major actor in the field, both conducting its own research and funding external projects. A large fraction of the latter supported basic or fundamental science in universities, the results of which were widely disseminated through publications in refereed academic journals.

Despite these advances, knowledge about the causes of diseases and the ways drugs worked remained limited. Firms sought to discover drugs through "random screening," looking at thousands of compounds for potential therapeutic activity. Unsurprisingly, only a very small fraction of them showed promising potential, and discovery was frequently serendipitous. When a promising molecule was identified that might prove effective in a drug for a particular disease – often in the search for a cure for a different disease – it was then developed into a potential drug through painstaking processes of chemical synthesis, to optimize safety and efficacy characteristics and reduce the side effects.

Another pillar of the industry's development was the rapid growth of demand. On the one hand, few effective drugs existed and the space for new treatments and cures for most diseases was immense. Further, the spread of health insurance in the United States and of the welfare state in most European countries offered a large, rich and organized market for drugs. In the United States, demand was strengthened by the sheer size of the domestic market, and the industry benefited from the absence of price regulation for its products. Patent protection allowed (temporary) monopolistic pricing. Most European countries, however, allowed patents only on drug production processes, not on the drug products themselves. The United Kingdom was the major exception.

A major turning point occurred in 1946, when the US Patent Office granted a patent on streptomycin, overturning decisions that had previously denied patentability to antibiotics on the ground that they were naturally occurring substances rather than inventions. The scope of the patent law was further expanded in 1980, when the US Supreme Court upheld the patenting of living organisms – specifically, a genetically modified bacterium – in the case *Diamond v. Chakrabarty.* Other pro-patent developments occurred around the same time. The general US patent regime has become increasingly protective of patent holders, despite recurring debates and controversies.[3] In addition, imitation and hence price competition was hampered by legislation concerning generic versions of the original product. Until the Hatch-Waxman Act was passed in the United States in 1984, generic versions of drugs that had gone off patent had to undergo extensive human clinical trials before they could be sold in the US market, so that it might be years before a generic version appeared after a key patent expired. In 1980, generics held only 2 percent of the US drug market.

Moreover, in the United States drug prices were not subject to governmental regulation, as they were in Japan and most European countries (with the notable exceptions of Germany and the Netherlands). Neither did insurance companies provide a major source of countervailing leverage on pricing. The fragmented structure of health care markets and the consequent low bargaining power of buyers further protected pharmaceutical companies' rents. High pricing flexibility supported high returns and profitability, fueling further investments in R&D.

As a consequence, the basis was laid for the transformation of the industry into a highly R&D-intensive and innovative sector. Many firms, especially those active in the ethical segment, started to set up large, formalized in-house R&D programs. In the United States, companies like Merck and Pfizer, previously important suppliers of fine chemicals, entered the drug market in earnest through innovation-based strategies.

Despite the "blind" nature of drug discovery based on random screening, the industry's commitment to R&D started to soar: the ratio of R&D to sales rose from 3.7 percent in 1951 to around 10 percent in

---

[3]   A modest step away from this trend took place very recently in the *Myriad Genetics* case (2013). The Supreme Court essentially held that human genes, as such, are not patentable.

the 1960s, and 15–20 percent in the 1980s and afterward (Chetley, 1990; Balance 1992, cited in Sutton).

In the following two decades, hundreds of therapeutically active molecules and several important classes of drugs were discovered and introduced, ranging from antibiotics to antidepressants to diuretics. Correspondingly, the number of new chemical entities (NCEs) approved by the Food and Drug Administration (FDA) rose from 25 in 1940–49 to 154 in the 1950s, then to 171 in the 1960s and reaching 264 in the 1970s (Lichtenberg, 2006).

The industry began also to invest heavily in sales efforts and marketing. Until the 1930s, the industry's products were primarily patented medicines that were advertised and sold directly to patients. But prescription drugs were growing in importance, and by 1929 they accounted for 32 percent of consumer expenditures. In the 1930s a number of laws were passed in the United States that formalized a distinction between drugs that could be sold directly to consumers and those that required a doctor's prescription (Sutton, 1998). By 1949 the share of the latter had increased to 57 percent and pharmaceutical companies increasingly directed their promotional efforts to prescribing physicians, building vast and sophisticated marketing forces. The proportion of prescription drugs in consumer drug expenditures increased further, to 83 percent by 1969 (Chandler, 2005a, p. 179).

Until the 1970s, the R&D-intensive core and the advertising-intensive segment of the industry were reasonably distinct. The two trajectories began to converge afterward, mainly through entry in the ethical drugs market by the latter (advertising-intensive firms) via mergers with the former (R&D-intensive firms). In this period the industry also became truly international. The high weight of sunk costs in R&D and marketing encouraged expansion into new markets to reduce average costs. Access to foreign markets was, however, often conditioned on compliance with local regulation. It was thus not surprising that it was the largest, highly R&D-intensive German, Swiss and American companies that proceeded more decisively in their international expansion, establishing not only their own presence but also networks of relations with local firms through licensing and commercialization agreements.

Within this favorable context, the industry produced high rates of innovation, growth and profitability. Rates of sales growth averaged well over 10 percent a year from the 1950s until the 1980s. The reported after-tax rates of return were so high, on the order of 21–22 percent, that the Kefauver Committee of the US Senate investigated them (Comanor, 1986). The economic and financial performance of the industry was spectacular until the 1980s and even since then it has remained remarkable.

The investigations of the Kefauver Committee signaled a changing political climate for the industry, which is inherently controversial in nature and extremely sensitive to public and political perceptions. Also the thalidomide scandal triggered additional debate about the behavior and performance of pharmaceutical companies.[4]

Following the scandal and the investigations of the Kefauver Committee (and analogous public initiatives in Europe), most countries tightened their regulatory processes for new drugs. In the United States, the Food and Drug Administration had been established in 1938 to confirm the safety of all food and drug products, after a newly introduced sulfa drug, elixir sulfonamide, led to 107 deaths (Boslaugh, 2008, p. 395). The 1962 Kefauver-Harris Amendments changed the Food and Drug Agency's mandate so that it was now charged with monitoring the efficacy as well as the safety of new drug products (Peltzman, 1973). The Amendments introduced a proof of efficacy requirement for approval of new drugs and established controls over the clinical (human) testing of new drug candidates. After that, the size,

---

[4]   Thalidomide was a drug introduced, first in Germany, in the late 1950s. It was prescribed as a sedative or hypnotic, but it became also used against nausea and morning sickness in pregnant women. At that time, controls and tests for potential harmful effects to the fetus were very loose. Following standard procedures, the drug had only been tested on mice. Soon after its introduction, evidence became available that thalidomide caused phocomelia and other extreme deficiencies in infants. Around 10,000 cases were reported all over the world and only 50 percent of those babies survived. An outraged public opinion and press campaign led to the withdrawal of the drug (Heaton, 1994, p. 40).

costs and stringency of these trials increased – at least until the mid nineties – and failures at the clinical trial stage produced high attrition rates for proposed new drugs. Although the effects of the Amendments on innovative activities and market structure have been the subject of considerable debate (see for instance Chien, 1979; Peltzman, 1973 and Comanor, 1986), they certainly led to large increases in R&D costs and in the costs of obtaining approvals for new drugs; longer development periods for NCEs; and stronger barriers to imitation, even after patent expiration, thereby penalizing the less innovative firms.

The 1970s led to the third era in the evolution of the industry. Progress in pharmacology, physiology, enzymology and biology generally led to a deeper understanding of the mechanisms of action of drugs as well as of diseases. In turn, these advances opened the way for new drug discovery methods, called "guided search" and "rational drug design." These made it possible – in principle – for researchers to screen and design compounds with specific therapeutic effects in view. Further, revolutionary advances in DNA technologies and molecular genetics produced a profound transformation of the knowledge base of the industry. The required competencies for drug discovery and development were profoundly affected by these changes, and the firms had to adapt by mastering molecular biology and related techniques while maintaining their traditional competencies in chemistry.[5]

The incumbent firms largely managed to accomplish the radical transformation of their competencies required by the "biotechnology revolution." At the same time, a significant level of entry of new start-up firms occurred for the first time since World War II. The new entrants did not, however, displace the incumbents. Rather, with only a couple of exceptions like Genentech and Amgen, they functioned essentially as suppliers of new specialized techniques and promising molecules to the established firms of the industry – ultimately giving rise to a dense web of collaborative relationships as a market for technology developed among those incumbents and the

---

[5] We do not attempt in this chapter to model the advent of biotechnology: a preliminary effort in this direction can be found in Malerba and Orsenigo (2002).

new biotechnology companies.[6] In these years the American pharmaceutical industry became the world leader, and almost all of the traditional Swiss, German and British giants started to make significant R&D investments in the United States, trying to gain advantage from the large and rich public and private research base.

5.3   CHALLENGES FOR HISTORY-FRIENDLY MODELING: THE PATTERNS OF COMPETITION AND THE EVOLUTION OF MARKET STRUCTURE

Throughout its history, the pharmaceutical industry has been characterized by relatively low overall concentration, especially when compared to other R&D and marketing-intensive industries. The central question in this chapter is this: Why have pharmaceuticals never been highly concentrated? And why is this sector dominated by a handful of large firms that entered early in the history of the sector and have maintained their leadership for decades?

Until the mid nineties, no firm had a share of the world market larger than 4.5 percent. In fact the world market shares of a firm in the top twenty ranged in 1996 from 1.3 to 4.5 percent (Garavaglia *et al.*, 2012). In the United States the fraction of sales accounted for by the top four firms (CR4 index) was 28 percent in 1947, 24 percent in 1967 and 22 percent in 1987 (Sutton, 1998). More recently, concentration has been increasing, largely as a consequence of mergers and acquisitions, and despite the entry of the new biotechnology firms and the expansion of the generic segment of the industry. Yet, in 2004, the largest pharmaceutical firm held a world market share close to 10 percent and the CR4 concentration ratio was around 33 percent in the United States and in the European Union, still denoting relatively low concentration.

These concentration numbers summarize a persistent market structure involving a core of leading firms and a large fringe of smaller ones. Among the ten–twenty largest firms in the world, competition is

---

6   For detailed accounts of the emergence and development of the biotechnology industry, see Orsenigo (1989), Gambardella (1995), Pisano (1996), Henderson *et al.* (1999).

intense. The leaders change but despite this turnover at the top, the core of major firms has been remarkably stable (Pammolli, 1996). Similarly, entry was not a significant phenomenon until the biotechnology revolution.

The "oligopolistic core" of the industry consisted of – and to a considerable extent is still composed by – the early innovative Swiss and German firms, joined after World War II by American and British companies. Virtually all of these companies maintained over time an innovation-oriented strategy. Firms have temporary monopolies in individual product markets through patents. Indeed, pharmaceuticals has historically been one of the few industries where patents provide strong protection against imitation (Levin et al., 1987).[7] Innovative drugs arrive quite rarely, but after arrival they experience extremely high rates of market growth. In turn, this entails a highly skewed distribution of the returns on innovation and of product market sizes, as well as of the intra-firm distribution of sales across products. Typically, a few "blockbuster" drugs dominate the product ranges of all major firms (Sutton, 1998; Matraves, 1999, p. 180), but such dominance is transitory because patents expire. In the global market as a whole, no dominant positions developed.

The picture is somewhat different, however, at the level of the individual submarkets like cardiovascular and diuretic drugs, and tranquilizers. The pharmaceutical industry as a whole addresses a fragmented market involving a number of nearly independent submarkets. The largest firms of the industry hold dominant positions in individual therapeutic classes (TCs). In some TCs, the CR4 index was over 80 percent in 1995,[8] and in many others only two or three drugs account for more than 50 percent of the market sales (Chong et al.,

---

[7] Note, however, that the scope and efficacy of patent protection has varied significantly across countries. While the United States has provided relatively strong patent protection in pharmaceuticals, many other European countries did not offer protection for pharmaceutical products: only process technologies could be patented. France introduced product patents in 1960, Germany 1968, Japan 1976, Switzerland 1977, Italy and Sweden in 1978.

[8] In antiviral products, for example, the CR4 was 86 percent in 1995.

2003). These firms also represent the most active firms in terms of innovative output (measured by the introduction of NCEs in the market). Yet, even in submarkets, dominant positions are quite often temporary and contestable.

Thus, the overall pattern we seek to explain involves low degrees of concentration in the aggregate, coexisting with persistence of a large core of industry leaders, with greater dynamism and market power in individual submarkets. Our analysis in this chapter is informed by the long-running debate in industrial economics concerning the link between concentration and innovative performance. This discussion is frequently deemed inconclusive and fragile (Cohen and Levin, 1989), as neither empirical evidence nor the theory provide robust conclusions. Nevertheless, the literature is almost unanimous in suggesting three factors that may explain the patterns observed in pharmaceuticals.

The variable force of imitation. Imitation and the complex obstacles to it play a crucial role in the patterns of the pharmaceutical industry. Without question, the large innovative firms have enjoyed strong "isolating mechanisms" shielding them from direct imitation in the submarkets they dominate, and this shielding has protected their profits. Among such mechanisms, patents were crucial for preventing direct imitation within the limited terms of the individual patents. Beyond that, the organizational capabilities developed by the larger pharmaceutical firms have acted as a further mechanism supporting the appropriability of rents from innovation. For example, as discussed by Pisano (1996), the process of random screening was anything but random as an organizational process. Over time, major incumbents developed highly sophisticated processes for carrying out mass screening programs – processes that were very systematic in every respect but one, the absence of a sharp *ex ante* definition of the target of the research. These capabilities also required rigorous handling of large databases. Since random screening capabilities were based on organizational processes and tacit skills internal to the firm, they were difficult for potential entrants to imitate and thus they provided first-mover advantages. In addition, under the random screening paradigm, spillovers of knowledge between firms were relatively small, so that an incumbent having an advantage relative to potential entrants could maintain it over time. Moreover, large incumbents could better control the risks inherent in quasi-random search by relying on the law of large numbers and on their ability to carry on parallel projects (Nelson, 1961). Thus, while relatively little could be learned from competitors, much could be learned from large-scale screening in-house – and that tended to sustain the advantages of incumbents (Pisano, 1996; Henderson *et al.*, 1999).

Yet, the competitive story in pharmaceuticals is not exclusively about the contest between innovation and imitation in the domain of *really* new drugs. Firm strategies included efforts to "invent around" the patents on existing molecules,[9] or to introduce new combinations among them, or new ways of delivering them. Together, these efforts have constituted a major component of firms' innovative activities, broadly defined. Thus, while the center of the competitive stage was legitimately held by the introduction of highly innovative products, firms also competed through incremental refinements of existing drugs, as well as through imitation after (and sometimes even before) patent protection had expired. Also, a large "fringe" of firms could thrive through commodity production and marketing of licensed products; price competition in this segment has always been intense.

Indeed, many firms that did not innovate themselves coexisted with innovators: They did not specialize in R&D and innovation, but rather in the production and marketing of products invented elsewhere. Large companies like Bristol-Myers, Warner-Lambert, Plough, and American Home Products were in this group, but also many

---

[9] To "invent around" a patent is to create an alternative to a patented product by making maximum use of the knowledge that is embodied in that product or expressed in its patent, while not actually infringing the patent. Metaphorically, it is a matter of cutting close, but not too close, to the patent.

smaller producers, and almost all of the firms in countries like France, Italy, Spain and Japan. Finally, generic competition after patent expiration has become increasingly strong. The Hatch-Waxman Act in 1984 significantly lightened the safety and efficacy regulation for generic drugs considered "chemically- and bio-equivalent" to branded products,[10] and allowed pharmacists to sell "equivalent" generics instead of branded products prescribed by doctors. The market for generics was then opened and – despite strong differences across countries – it has been growing rapidly ever since. Today generics are estimated to account for more than 50 percent of drugs prescribed (in volume) and around 10 percent in terms of value. A generic producer is now among the ten largest pharmaceutical companies worldwide. Several large producers of brand-name drugs have diversified into generics (according to FDA estimates, brand-name firms now produce 50 percent of generics) giving strategic expression to the adage "if you can't beat them, join them."

The properties of the innovation process. The second factor underlying the patterns in this industry is the innovative process, characterized by rich opportunities, extreme uncertainty and the difficulty of leveraging the results of past innovative efforts into new products (i.e. limited economies of scope and cumulativeness of technological capabilities). Hence, innovative firms have only small room for establishing dominant positions. Market leadership can be easily contested by new innovators.

Concentration can nevertheless arise through success-breeds-success processes: an innovative firm enjoying high profits has more resources to invest in R&D and therefore has better chances to innovate again as compared to non-innovators. However, to the extent that the probability of success of any one project is independent from past history, the tendency toward concentration is weakened.

---

[10]   "Chemical and bio-equivalence" are established through testing programs by manufacturers that are much less extensive (and expensive) than the clinical trials required for pioneer drugs.

The "random screening" approach to drug discovery is at the base of the extreme uncertainty of pharmaceutical research. The process of discovery and development of a drug closely resembled a lottery, because success is a chance event and big wins are rare (Sutton, 1998). Successful development of a NCE was indeed a rare event: estimates suggest that, out of all new compounds that were explored, only one over 5,000 reached the market (Koenig, 1983, cited in Sutton p. 204). Despite this, as observed in the previous pages, random screening was an extremely successful strategy, which led to the discovery and introduction of a staggering variety of new important classes of drugs and NCEs.

The biotechnology and genomic revolutions have not yet substantially modified the intrinsically uncertain nature of the process of drug discovery and development. Despite the spectacular scientific advances, our understanding of the causes of diseases and of the mechanisms of action of drugs remains poor and innovative success still has a large random component. If anything, the productivity of research has been falling in recent years: R&D costs have been soaring but the number of new drugs introduced in the market is stagnating.

While the decline in pharmaceutical R&D productivity is well documented, there is considerable disagreement about its causes. Some interpretations emphasize the strong cyclical components that characterize the production of new drugs, implying that the current downswing might be considered only as a temporary phenomenon. Regulation is also often blamed for rising costs and dwindling productivity. Another interpretation suggests that the decline in productivity could be the outcome of an intrinsic difficulty in discovering new drugs for increasingly complex pathologies: The low hanging fruits have already been picked and now the challenge becomes harder (Pammolli et al., 2011). In a different but related way, it is suggested that drug firms find enormous difficulties in keeping pace with the increased intrinsic complexity of the biochemical problems that innovative search is addressing. Huge bottlenecks remain between the explosive growth of available experimental information made possible by the scientific revolution and the ability to use that knowledge for developing new drugs, especially at the target validation stage (Orsenigo *et al.*, 2001; Nightingale and Martin, 2004; Nightingale and Mahdi, 2006).

Market fragmentation. A third crucial factor limiting concentration is the fragmented nature of the pharmaceutical market. As observed previously, the pharmaceutical market comprises many independent submarkets – corresponding to different therapeutic classes – with little or no substitution between products. Given a large number of submarkets and their small share of the aggregate market, monopoly conditions in individual submarkets do not translate directly into aggregate concentration; it matters how the submarket monopolies are distributed among firms. As the number of submarkets increases, it becomes more difficult for any one firm to dominate a larger, fragmented market. The point is in principle quite simple. If a market of size 100 is homogeneous, the assets needed to gain market shares are relatively undifferentiated. Economies of scale and learning processes then might enable one firm to obtain an aggregate competitive advantage. However, if the same market of 100 is divided into 10 submarkets of size 10, if different assets are important in each submarket and if knowledge transfer among submarkets is difficult, then the probability that different firms will be competitively superior in the different niches is higher. And, compared to the case of homogeneous final products, it is less likely that a single firm will cover the entire market.

5.4   THE MODEL

5.4.1   *Overview*

Imitation, market fragmentation and an innovative process characterized by low cumulativeness set a competitive context in pharmaceuticals that is quite different from the case of computers, which we examined in Chapters 3 and 4. The question to be addressed in this chapter is whether these factors together can explain the persistent patterns in the industry's history: (i) low aggregate concentration; (ii) higher concentration in individual submarkets; (iii) stability in industry leadership, both at the aggregate level and, though less so, in submarkets; and finally (iv) dominance by early entrants. In the model of this chapter we seek to answer this question only for the "random screening" period. We do not attempt to represent or analyze the era following the biotech revolution, when scientific knowledge (from molecular biology) provided significant guidance for search.

Given this background, we propose a model with the following elements. A number of firms compete to discover, develop and market new drugs for a large variety of diseases. They face a space of opportunities that, at the beginning, is largely unexplored. That is, we assume a context corresponding to the early "golden age," when formal R&D capabilities in the industry were in their infancy. We represent R&D activity as having two stages, the first being the discovery of promising molecules and the second the attempt to develop the molecules discovered into drugs. In the first stage, firms explore randomly in the "space of molecules." Some molecules have chemical properties that can be exploited in order to develop a drug, but most are useless – in our model terminology, they have "zero quality." There is little scientific knowledge guiding search, and success is a random event. When a firm finds a molecule that might become a useful drug, the firm patents it. The patent provides protection from imitation for a certain amount of time and over a range of "similar" molecules.

After a discovery, a firm engages in the development of the drug, which requires time and resources. The firm does not know how difficult, time consuming and costly the process will be, or what the quality of the new drug will be. Development projects sometimes fail, because the quality of the drug does not meet minimum requirements for sale in the marketplace; these requirements are a model representation of the regulatory process (for example, the US FDA). While the drug is under development, a firm puts aside marketing resources: after development is completed, the firm uses these resources to launch the product in the marketplace. Sales are influenced by the quality of the drug, by the firm's marketing efforts and by the price that is charged.

Firms are represented as strategically heterogeneous, displaying differing propensities toward innovation, on the one hand, and imitation and marketing, on the other. The first successful drug offered for treatment of a particular disease faces no competition, and the firm may experience a burst of growth. But after some time, other firms may discover and develop a competing drug. Moreover, after patent expiration, imitation may occur. As a consequence of the competition from competing or imitative products, the market share and revenue of the original innovator will be eroded away by competitors and imitators.

A key concept in the model is that of a "therapeutic class" (TC). As noted previously, this term refers to a group of drugs that are related in the sense that they address similar or related disease conditions. In our model, a therapeutic class is associated with a patient population, which has a certain size. In addition, a therapeutic class is identified with a collection of molecules that have therapeutic potential for the disease conditions of that class. In our model, therapeutic classes are anonymous as well as abstract; that is, they do not have names that correspond to real-world therapeutic classes.

The discovery of a drug based on a molecule in a particular therapeutic class does not increase the probability that a firm can discover another drug in a different class, given the firm's level of innovative effort. Diversification into different therapeutic classes is treated as purely random: firms are always searching everywhere in the space of molecules. In addition, the therapeutic classes are treated as fully independent submarkets. A firm's growth will then depend on the number of drugs discovered and commercialized, the size and the growth of the submarkets they are present in, the number of competitors and the relative quality and price of the drugs.

A firm can choose to invest simultaneously in several parallel projects of research for developing different drugs. This choice is influenced by the firm's budget constraint, the economic value of the market (i.e. the value of the actual or potential revenues in the targeted therapeutic class); and the degree of appropriability (i.e. the residual length of patent protection). As it discovers and develops new products, a firm will progressively diversify into new TCs. Profits coming from the sales of drugs are reinvested in R&D and marketing. Firms' resources come from the commercialized drugs that assure the flows of revenues needed to invest in new projects. As time passes in the simulated history, there is a broad tendency to diminishing returns to R&D that is attributable to the fact that the space of untapped opportunities is getting depleted by the ongoing discovery process – but the complex details of this evolution are determined endogenously. In the following sections we describe in more detail the formal structure of the model.

5.4.2 The formal model

Technological and market environment
The environment facing pharmaceutical firms is characterized by the set of therapeutic classes, numbering H. Each TC has a different number of potential patients who need treatment for a specific disease. This determines the potential demand for drugs in that submarket. This potential demand is represented by a number (q_h) set at the beginning of each simulation drawing from a normal distribution with mean μ^q and standard deviation σ^q, truncated at 0 to avoid negative values. Firms are perfectly informed about the size of potential demand. Patients in each TC are grouped according to their willingness to buy drugs characterized by different qualities. Some of them, for example, may be unwilling to buy low-quality drugs at the current price because of the presence of side effects.

Associated with a TC h there is a certain number of molecules X_h that can be effective for use in this class. Each of these molecules has a certain quality Q_x (see Figure 5.1). The probability of finding a "zero quality" molecule is equal to z. On the other side, the complementary probability of finding a promising molecule x with $Q_x > 0$ is

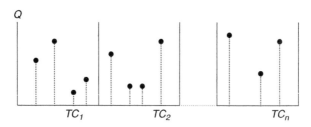

FIGURE 5.1 Therapeutic classes (TC) and molecules.

$(1 - z)$; the quality values for these molecules are drawn from a normal distribution[11] with mean μ^Q and standard deviation σ^Q.

When a molecule is discovered a patent is granted, and it is stored in a firm-specific portfolio of molecules available for future development projects. Patents have a specific duration, T^{PT}, and width, W^{PT}. The "width" is the model representation of the fact that a patent prevents competitors from developing molecules that are highly similar to the patented one (spatial location along the horizontal axis represents the similarity). Once the patent expires, the molecule goes into a public portfolio where it is available for development by any firm.

Firms

The industry is populated by F potential firms that may enter the market. Parameter F is exogenous: it is calibrated in relation to the number of TCs (H) and the duration of the simulation (T) in order to preserve the internal consistency of the model (see Appendix 5.2). Each potential entrant is endowed with an initial budget B^0, equal for all firms. Over time, firms' budget levels evolve due to R&D and marketing expenditures and the profits obtained from the sale of drugs.

Each firm f is characterized by a different "strategy," or propensity, to devote available resources to research and marketing activities. This propensity is quantitatively represented by a firm-specific parameter, φ_f^{RD}, with a value drawn from a uniform distribution.

[11]   This distribution is truncated at zero and this adds something to the probability of a zero quality molecule. With our parameter settings, this effect is trivial (0.2%).

Specifically, φ_f^{RD} represents the share of the budget allocated to R&D expenditure, with the complementary share going to marketing. A second parameter, φ_f^{SR}, represents the share of the R&D budget going to search, as distinguished from development. Thus, a firm's budget is divided each period among search, development and marketing activities as follows:

$$B_{f,t}^{SR} = \varphi_f^{RD} \cdot \varphi_f^{SR} \cdot B_{f,t} \qquad (1.a)$$

$$B_{f,t}^{D} = \varphi_f^{RD} \cdot (1 - \varphi_f^{SR}) \cdot B_{f,t} \qquad (1.b)$$

$$B_{f,t}^{A} = (1 - \varphi_f^{RD}) \cdot B_{f,t} \qquad (1.c)$$

where φ_f^{RD} and φ_f^{SR} are firm-specific and time-invariant.

Innovators and imitators

Firms are heterogeneous in another respect: they can behave as innovators or imitators. Innovators look for new molecules by randomly screening the possible molecules and incur a search cost. Imitators select among the molecules whose patent has expired, thus avoiding the cost of search. From period to period, a particular firm conducts a variable mix of innovative and imitation activities. In each period, a firm's propensity to R&D activities (φ_f^{RD}) represents also the probability of being temporarily an innovator, whereas the probability of being temporarily an imitator is given by $1 - \varphi_f^{RD}$. Therefore, firms with a very low propensity to research will most of the time be imitators. The opposite holds for innovators. However it may happen that no molecule is available for imitation because all discovered molecules are covered by patent protection. In this case imitators are forced to behave as innovators.

Innovative activities

Innovators look for new molecules by investing in a search process. Search involves the payment of a fixed cost (C^{SR}) in order to draw a molecule from the space of available molecules. Thus, the number of molecules $(N_{f,t}^X)$ drawn by a firm in each period is determined by the ratio between the fraction of the budget allocated to search $B_{f,t}^{SR}$ and the cost C^{SR}:

$$N_{f,t}^X = \frac{B_{f,t}^{SR}}{C^{SR}} \tag{2}$$

Firms do not know the "height" (quality) Q_x of a molecule x that they have drawn: they only know whether Q_x is greater than zero or not. If the molecule has a non-zero value and it has not been patented by others, then a patent for that molecule is obtained. The patented molecules become part of an individual "portfolio" that each firm maintains for potential drug development. However, as we shall discuss later, a fraction of the patented molecules will not be actually developed and commercialized, because either their quality does not satisfy the minimum requirements set by public health agencies or they are not sufficiently economically attractive.

Imitative activities

Imitative firms have access to the public portfolio of already discovered molecules whose patent has expired, without incurring any cost for doing so. Thus, their search process is not random. This portfolio includes not only the molecules from which other firms generated a drug but also those molecules that have not been developed because the firms owning them have failed or because those molecules were not economically attractive. We now explain in more detail the rules guiding the selection of the molecules to be developed.

Development activities

Both innovators and imitators develop products from molecules by engaging in drug development activities. If the molecule x is potentially interesting (i.e. it has a quality Q_x greater than zero), the firm starts a development project, using the budget allocated to this kind of activity, $B_{f,t}^D$ to pay for the cost of development. The time and the cost necessary to complete a development project are assumed – for sake of simplicity – to be fixed and equal for all molecules and firms, the only difference being that both the per-period cost (C_ι^D) and the time spent (T_ι^D) for innovation $(\iota = in)$ are larger than that for imitation[12] $(\iota = im)$: in other words $C_{in}^D > C_{im}^D$ and $T_{in}^D > T_{im}^D$. Thus, the total cost of development of an innovative molecule is given by $C_{in}^D \cdot T_{in}^D$ and the total cost of development of an imitative product is given by $C_{im}^D \cdot T_{im}^D$. If the cost of development is larger than the available development budget, $B_{f,t}^D$, the molecule remains stored in the firm's portfolio and the firm waits to accumulate enough financial resources to start the development project. Once a development project starts, all necessary resources are removed from the available development budget, $B_{f,t}^D$, and stored in a separate account that yields interests at rate r. When the project ends, the quality of the molecule (the new drug) is revealed.

Products must have a minimum quality, indicated with λ^Q, in order to be sold in the marketplace. In other words, products are subject to a "quality check" by an external agency (e.g. the FDA). In the simulations, the minimum quality threshold, λ^Q, is set equal to the mean of the random distribution generating the quality of the molecules $(\lambda^Q = \mu^Q)$. Below this value, the drug cannot be commercialized and the project fails.[13]

Parallel projects and project selection
In every simulation period, firms – both innovators and imitators – choose how many development projects to start and which of the most promising molecules to develop. In other words, firms run parallel projects. The choice of how many development projects to be conducted simultaneously and of the molecules to be developed is governed by some rules described later in the chapter. Firms determine the number of new projects to be started in each period t after they

---

[12]   Imitators are characterized by faster and cheaper development processes. More precisely, an imitative firm spends 1/3 of the money that an innovative firm pays for the drug development process, which takes half as long.

[13]   Recall here that a large proportion of searches fails entirely, returning molecules of zero quality with probability z.

choose whether to behave as innovators or imitators in the current period. The number of new development projects of a firm f is determined by the following equation:

$$N^D_{f,t} = \left\lfloor \frac{B^D_{f,t}}{C^D_i \cdot T^D_i} \right\rfloor \tag{3}$$

where $\lfloor \cdot \rfloor$ is the floor function. A firm can start as many as $N^D_{f,t}$ of new projects at time t only if the budget available for development activities $B^D_{f,t}$ covers $N^D_{f,t}$ times the total costs of the development process $(C^D_i \cdot T^D_i)$, which depend on the innovation or imitation strategy adopted by the firm at time t. Of course, a firm may have only few – and even no – molecules in its portfolio, so that the budget constraint might not be binding.

The next step is the selection of the candidates for the development stage. Innovative firms select their projects from the available molecules in the firm's portfolio. They consider two features of the molecules in order to choose the more promising ones. First, they look at the economic value of the TC h, to which the molecule x belongs. Other things being equal, a TC having a large number of patients tends to be more attractive for firms. The economic value of a TC h is calculated in period t in terms of the revenues provided by the products sold in that TC in period $t\text{-}1$, $(V_{h,t-1})$. Thus, the economic value of the TC depends on the number of patients and, other things being equal, a TC having a large number of patients tends to be more attractive for firms. But, even if the number of patients is exogenously given, the economic value of the TC changes over time according to the monopolistic power stemming from patents and the degree of competition among firms. In the case of a newly opened TC the revenues are computed on the basis of the number of patients in that TC (which is known by the firms) and fixing the highest price allowed, according to the pricing behavior described later. Second, innovative firms also consider the residual length of the molecule's patent protection $(T^{PT}_{x,t})$, that is, the time left for gaining monopolistic profits from the molecule while it is under patent protection.

Then, each innovative firm ranks its molecules according to their attractiveness $(v_{x,t})$, that takes into account both the economic value of the TC and the residual length of the molecule's patent protection:

$$v_{x,t} = V_{h,t-1} \cdot T_{x,t}^{PT} \tag{4}$$

Imitative firms choose from the public portfolio of already discovered molecules. By definition the patents of molecules in the public portfolio are already expired: therefore, imitative firms consider only the economic value of the TC to build the attractiveness ranking of molecules.

Once the number $N_{f,t}^D$ is calculated, both innovative and imitative firms choose the top-ranked molecules and start the selected development projects.

Pricing and marketing activities

After development is completed, and if the revealed quality of the product thus obtained meets the minimum "legal" quality requirements set by the external agency, firms start to produce the drug and launch it on the marketplace.

In the model, we assume that the unit cost of manufacturing (C^{PD}) is constant and equal for all drugs. Firms set a price $(P_{j,t})$ according to a markup rule, as follows:

$$P_{j,t} = C^{PD} \cdot (1 + m_{j,t}) \tag{5}$$

where $m_{j,t}$ is the markup charged by firms. The markup is structured in order to take into account the competitive pressure in the therapeutic class:

$$m_{j,t} = (1 - \omega) \cdot m_{j,t-1} + \omega \cdot \left(\frac{s_{f,h,t-1}}{\varepsilon - s_{f,h,t-1}} \right) \tag{6}$$

where $s_{f,h,t-1}$ is the market share of the firm in terms of patients in TC h at time t, ε is the perceived price elasticity of demand[14] and ω is a weight that captures the ability of market leaders to exploit their market power in terms of prices.

When a drug is launched in the market, companies invest also in marketing activities, which yield a level of "product image" perceived by the consumers. During the development of the product a firm accumulates the resources needed for later marketing investments by putting aside a share of the total resources allocated to marketing $(B_{f,t}^A)$. These resources are accumulated in a separate account that yields interests at rate r. This "saving" process begins when (and if) the drug under development achieves a quality equal to the minimum threshold set by the regulatory authorities (λ^Q). Although firms do not discover the real quality Q_x of the molecule x until the end of the development process, they receive this early indirect indication – that is, the drug satisfies the minimum regulatory requirement – of the quality of the molecule during the development process. The total budget devoted to marketing is split among the ongoing projects according to the ranking of therapeutic classes in terms of economic value $(V_{h,t-1})$.

Marketing expenditures for product j (B_j^A) are made entirely at the launch of the drug at time T_j. They affect demand by creating a favorable product image $(A_{j,t})$ in the eyes of consumers:

$$A_{j,T_j} = a^0 \cdot (B_j^A)^{a^1} \tag{7}$$

where a° and a^1 are parameters. This level of "image" is eroded with time at a rate equal to η according to:

$$A_{j,t} = A_{j,t-1} \cdot (1 - \eta) \tag{8}$$

---

[14]   The elasticity ε bears no necessary connection to the actual responsiveness of demand to price. This formulation gives us a simple way to parameterize pricing behavior in a way that is theoretically understandable. It is derived from the Lerner index of market power and relates the actual markup to the one that a notional firm with that market share would have in an asymmetric Cournot equilibrium: the markup is constant when it is equal to that notional equilibrium value.

Demand and sales

Drugs are bought on the marketplace by groups of heterogeneous consumers. Each patient buys – by assumption – one unit of the drug. The propensity of an individual patient in a TC h to buy a drug j is represented by $u_{h,j,t}$, provided that the drug satisfies the minimum quality threshold of the patient (otherwise her propensity to buy is equal to zero). This propensity is determined by quality, price and marketing image, as formally expressed by the following equation:

$$u_{h,j,t} = (Q_j)^{\delta_h^Q} \cdot \left(\frac{v}{P_{j,t}}\right)^{\delta_h^P} \cdot (A_{j,t})^{\delta_h^A} \tag{9}$$

where Q_j is the quality of the drug j, $P_{j,t}$ is the price of drug j at time t, v is a scale parameter for the price, and $A_{j,t}$ is the "image" in the eyes of consumers created by marketing expenditures. The exponents δ_h^Q, δ_h^P, and δ_h^A are specific to each TC h.[15] So, in general, higher quality, lower price and higher product image increase the attractiveness of the drug as compared to competing products.

However, quality affects demand also in another way, by determining the number of potential patients that a drug can reach. Drugs of different quality reach different shares of potential patients because they have different minimum quality requirements. Low quality drugs appeal only to a fraction of potential patients (because of problems of negative side-effects, tolerability, efficacy and so on). Higher quality drugs can instead satisfy a larger number of patients. Only high quality drugs are able to satisfy all the potential demand; if only low quality drugs are offered in a TC, a portion of the demand remains unsatisfied. As higher quality products are introduced in a TC, the number of potential patients who actually buy the drug increases. When drugs having different qualities are available in a TC, the low quality products will compete with the higher quality drugs only for a fraction of potential patients, whereas the higher quality

---

[15] To create some heterogeneity across TCs, the exponents are drawn from distributions that produce moderate dispersion, percentagewise, around the mean values (see Appendix 5.1).

products can also reach other consumers. Thus the higher the quality of a drug, the larger is its potential market, the higher will be the firm's sales and market share and consequently the higher the markup and price.

Specifically, we assume that patients within a TC h (q_h) are divided into four groups g, ordered from the less demanding ($g = 1$) to the most demanding ($g = 4$). Each group is characterized by a minimum quality threshold λ_g^Q. Patients in any given group buy the drug (one unit per patient, as mentioned previously) only if the drug's quality is higher than the relevant threshold of that group. The size of a group g in the therapeutic class h, $q_{g,h}$, is equal to one-fourth of the total number of potential patients in that TC: $q_{g,h} = q_h / 4$.

The threshold for the "low quality" group (λ_1^Q) is set equal to the quality check of the health agency (e.g. the FDA), λ^Q, and it has access to ¼ of potential patients. A product whose quality is lower than this threshold cannot be sold on the market. A product with quality λ_2^Q has access to ½ of the patients in that TC; a product with a quality λ_3^Q may sell to ¾ of potential patients; a product characterized by a quality higher than the threshold defined for more "quality conscious" patients (λ_4^Q), has access to all the potential patients in that TC. This structure is exogenously fixed and is the same for all the therapeutic classes.

At any point in time, in a TC drugs of different quality may be available. For example, suppose the highest quality drug offered in a TC h at a particular time is such that its quality exceeds λ_3^Q but not λ_4^Q. In that case, patients in group 4 of TC h will not purchase a drug in that period, because there is no drug on offer that meets their quality requirements. In general, let $G_{h,t}$ denote the number of groups of patients buying a drug in TC h in period t. Then, the total number of patients buying a drug in the TC in that period is given by:

$$q_{h,t} = \sum_{g=1}^{G_{h,t}} q_{g,h} \tag{10}$$

Given these assumptions, this number turns out to be ¼, ½, ¾ or all of the patients in the TC. When in a given TC more than one drug is available at time t, consumers choose among the competing drugs according to Equation 9: a drug will attract a number of patients that is proportional to its merit $u_{h,j,t}$ as compared to those of competing products for the share of patients that the drug is able to reach.

Hence, the number of actual consumers of drug j at time t is given by:

$$q_{j,t} = \sum_{g=1}^{G_{h,j}} \frac{u_{h,j,t}}{\sum_{j\in\mathfrak{I}_{g,h}} u_{h,j,t}} \cdot q_{g,h} \qquad (11)$$

where $G_{h,j}$ is the number of groups of patients in TC h that could buy drug j, h is the TC to which drug j is related and $\mathfrak{I}_{g,h}$ includes all drugs related to TC h with a quality higher than the threshold of group g.

A firm may sell more than one product in a given TC: the consumers served by firm f in a TC h at time t $(q_{f,h,t})$ are computed by summing the consumers of all products sold by the firm in the TC. Finally, the share of patients held by a firm in a TC $(s_{f,h,t})$ is the ratio between the number of patients of that TC served by the firm $(q_{f,h,t})$ and the total number of patients in that TC that actually are buying a drug $(q_{h,t})$. This variable affects the determination of the markup charged by the firm (see Equation 6).

Budget and accounting
Profits of firm f given by product j at time t are indicated by $\Pi_{j,t}$. Because a firm f may have more than one product, a firm's total profits $(\Pi_{f,t})$ are given by the sum of profits obtained from all of its products:

$$\Pi_{f,t} = \sum_{j=1}^{J_{f,t}} \Pi_{j,t} = \sum_{j=1}^{J_{f,t}} (P_{j,t} - C^{PD}) \cdot q_{h,j,t} \qquad (12)$$

where $J_{f,t}$ is the number of drugs produced by firm f at time t. In each period, the firm reinvests all profits to finance R&D and marketing activities, without paying dividends to shareholders. We do not attempt to model stock market responses.

Exit rules

Given that firms start new projects only if they have a budget large enough to complete the process of product development, it is not possible for firms to have a negative balance in their accounts. However, firms may exit the market for various different reasons. The model includes three exit rules.

First, a firm exits if it has no sales revenue and the budget is lower than the minimum needed to complete one project. Second, exit occurs if an innovative firm fails to draw a promising molecule in its search process for more than T^E periods, where T^E is an exogenous parameter. This rule is meant to capture the notion that innovative firms leave the market if they are consistently unable to discover new potential drugs. Third, a firm exits when its total market share is lower than a minimum threshold, λ^E. This implicitly reflects a managerial judgment that a very marginal position of a firm in the market is ultimately untenable. The model includes also an exit rule at the product level: a firm withdraws a product from the market if it is purchased by less than a fraction λ^J of current consumers in the TC.

5.5   THE SIMULATION RUNS: "HISTORY-FRIENDLY" RESULTS

The simulation runs discussed here (1,000 runs) for each parameter setting have basically two aims. First, we try to replicate some basic stylized features of the history of the pharmaceutical industry in the era of random screening, in particular industry concentration and patterns of competition. Second, we develop some theoretically driven counterfactual exercises. We investigate whether history could have been different had the value of some key parameters taken alternative values.

The parameterization used for our "history-friendly" simulations (see Appendix 5.1), henceforth called the Standard Set, reflects both some fundamental theoretical hypotheses and, in a highly qualitative way, some empirical evidence. The specification of the value of the parameters of the model includes also some strongly simplifying assumptions and inevitably reflects our ignorance about the "true" values of some key parameters. The Standard Set provides also a benchmark case on the basis of which counterfactual simulations can be run in order to check the robustness of the appreciative model and the logical consistency of the formal model.

The calibration of the model is the result of repeated changes in the parameters and methods of the model in order to obtain a satisfactory specification.[16] Some parameters are selected on the basis of the knowledge we have about their meanings and values as shown by the empirical literature and the evidence provided by the industry's specialists (for example as it regards the time necessary to bring a drug to the market, patent duration, etc.). The value of other parameters has been selected to preserve coherence between the relative orders of magnitude of the variables, concerning for example R&D and marketing intensity, the interest rate, the markup, etc. In many cases, however, the values assigned to key parameters of the model are largely *ad hoc*: we do not know the actual distributions of the opportunities for discovery, and we have only generic knowledge about the economic value of the drugs that have been developed.

In the Standard Set, the landscape explored by firms is sufficiently rich in terms of opportunities for discovery to allow for the survival of the industry and the introduction of a large number of new drugs. However, search remains a very risky and most of the

---

[16] As remarked previously (p. 16, chapter 2), there is a common belief that the mere presence of a large number of model parameters suffices to make it possible for the model to match given data, and perhaps makes it "easier" to do so. The argument is logically flawed, because the supposed "free parameters" are actually not free at all; hence the argument is essentially irrelevant to the simulation modeling of the kind pursued here.

time unsuccessful activity: the parameter describing the probability of finding a "zero quality" molecule (z) is set equal to 0.97. Moreover, the distribution of the quality value of the molecules is highly skewed. Search, development and marketing activities are expensive and take time. Broadly in line with the empirical evidence, we set the development time of a drug $(T_{in}^D$ and $T_{im}^D)$ equal to eight and four periods (with one period corresponding roughly to one year) respectively for innovative and imitative products. Patent duration (T^{PT}) is set equal to twenty periods. The relative costs of search, development and marketing broadly reflect the proportions currently observed in the industry (Di Masi *et al.*, 2003). The number of TCs (H) is high (200). Marketing expenditures have an important role in accessing a large number of customers and the sensitivity of demand to price (exponent δ_h^P in Equation 9) is rather low. In the Standard Set there are no economies of scale and scope and no processes of mergers and acquisitions.

5.5.1 The standard set

Concentration, entry and exit
The results of the simulations based on the Standard Set replicate the basic stylized facts about the industry. In each TC, concentration – measured by the Herfindahl index (HI) – tends to decrease quickly after an initial upsurge (Figure 5.2). As time goes by this decline slows down and concentration reaches on average a value of 0.3 at the end of the simulation runs. This pattern reflects the monopoly power of early entrants in each TC, and the subsequent introduction of competitive innovative and imitative products. Thus, the degree of competition in an individual TC gradually rises and concentration decreases. Two main events are clearly observable in Figure 5.2. The first products enter the market after eight periods of development. These products are the initial leaders of the TC, facing no competition. Second, after twenty-four periods imitative products enter the market (patent duration lasts for twenty periods and four periods is the minimum time span needed to develop an imitation).

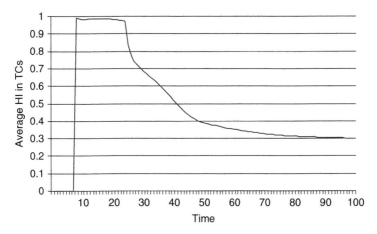

FIGURE 5.2 Average Herfindahl index in TCs.

Concentration is always much lower in the aggregate market than it is in individual therapeutic classes (Figure 5.3). It increases, however, after period fifty as bigger firms – exploiting their larger financial resources and hence a larger number of draws – enter new submarkets by finding and developing new products and imitating existing ones. Moreover, as drug discoveries accumulate with the passage of time, the remaining technological opportunities are less numerous. They are also less attractive, since firms development efforts favor the more attractive TCs, per Equation 4. Note, finally, that the model contains no mechanisms by which the fund of opportunities becomes enriched or renewed after the start of the simulation.[17] Thus, as time goes by, the discovery of new products and the opening of new submarkets become increasingly difficult. Concentration increases as success-breeds-success processes sustain initially lucky firms. This tendency is countered, however, by the intrinsic randomness of innovation and by imitation. Thus, aggregate concentration as measured by the Herfindahl index, remains

[17]   In the actual history of the industry, the biotech revolution was arguably such an enrichment episode. As noted previously, we have not attempted to model the biotech revolution.

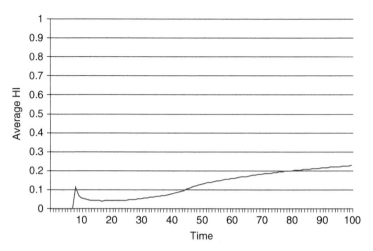

FIGURE 5.3 Herfindahl index in the aggregate market.

relatively low, reaching a value of 0.23 at the end of the simulation. Furthermore, since innovation is not cumulative and firms always have a positive, if small, probability of discovering a blockbuster product, the leadership of the industry changes frequently. On average, the industry leader changes every seven periods and the leader is always an innovator.

Selection is particularly intense in the first half of the simulation. Around thirty-five firms out of fifty potential entrants succeed in developing a drug good enough to be sold in the market. After period thirty a shake out occurs and approximately fifteen firms exit because they have inadequate success in continuing to discover promising molecules or they are unable to complete the development process for the molecules they do discover or their market share becomes too small (Figure 5.4). The ultimate explanation for such outcomes lies, of course, in the fact that search and development are costly and uncertain processes, and initial budgets are limited. The brief upsurge in the number of active firms around period twenty-five reflects the entry of some imitative firms, after the first patents have expired. As time goes by, though, the industry becomes more stable: both entry and exit

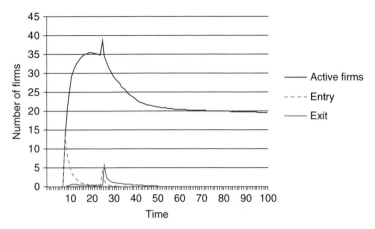

FIGURE 5.4 Number of active firms in the aggregate market, entry and exit.

decrease and most of the firms that have survived tend to remain alive until the end of the simulation. Such firms typically own a portfolio of products, and even though their market shares in individual submarkets tend to decline – causing them to withdraw some products – they continue to receive profits stemming from drugs in other TCs.

Innovation, imitation and firms' diversification

These broad dynamic trends result from significant heterogeneity across TCs. In a few TCs there are no firms, while in others several are present. Firms compete simultaneously through processes of innovation, imitation and diversification into new submarkets.

In the early periods of the simulation, all products in the market are innovative, and patented. After twenty periods, the patents of the first set of innovative products begin to expire and imitation starts to take place. The absolute numbers of both innovative and imitative products rise, but as imitation occurs the share of imitative products increases continuously, also because even innovation-oriented firms engage in parallel research projects and develop imitative drugs (Figure 5.5). However, innovative products are much more profitable

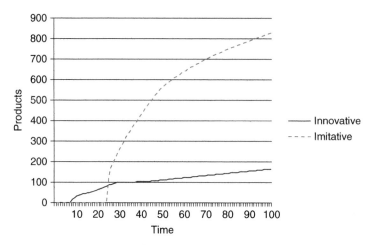

FIGURE 5.5 Number of innovative and imitative products.

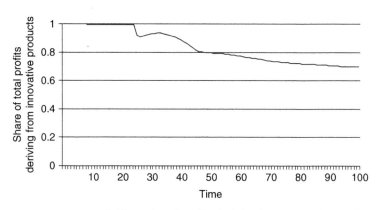

FIGURE 5.6 Share of total profits deriving from innovative products.

than imitative ones: at the end of the simulation, the share of profits of innovative products accounts for around 70 percent of the profits of all products in the market (Figure 5.6).

Firms increasingly diversify into new TCs: the rate of discovery of new therapeutic classes is quite high in the first part of the runs,

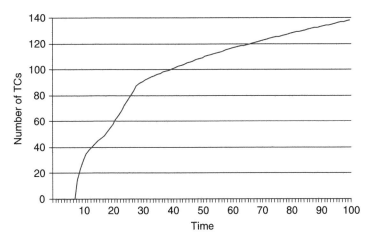

FIGURE 5.7 Number of discovered TCs.

but then it slows down, as fewer new markets remain untapped[18] (Figure 5.7). In each TC there is an increasing number of products and firms (at first only innovators, then also imitators). At period fifty, there is at least one product on the market in more than 110 of the existing 200 TCs. This number then grows to 140 at period 100 as the number of unexplored therapeutic classes declines and as firms tend to crowd in the richest therapeutic class. The decreasing rate of discovery is also correlated to the higher competitive pressure of the imitative products on the innovative ones: Firms tend to select imitative drugs in large submarkets rather than developing new products in small therapeutic areas. At the end of the simulation runs, there are on average seven firms offering products in a TC. However, the

---

[18] The number of draws that firms make varies drastically across firms and over time. On average, a firm has around 10 draws per period, with a maximum of 60 halfway during the simulation. These numbers are lower in the earlier and later stages of the simulation and they refer only to firms actually making at least one draw, i.e., excluding imitators and firms who do not have the resources to search for new molecules. Of course, the number of successful draws (molecules with positive quality) is then determined also by the parameter z (probability of finding a zero quality molecule). Moreover, many of these successful draws do not translate into drugs because they will not satisfy the quality check.

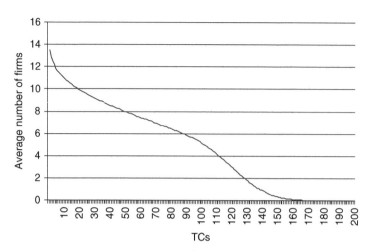

FIGURE 5.8 Number of firms in each TC.

distribution of the number of firms (and products) in the TCs is quite skewed (Figure 5.8).[19]

As a consequence of the processes of innovation, imitation and diversification, firms grow quickly and enjoy high levels of profitability. A skewed firm size distribution emerges (Figure 5.9) with some larger firms (mainly innovators) who are present in a high number of TCs, and many smaller companies (mainly imitators),[20] a result that is in line with the empirical evidence (Cabral and Mata, 2003).

Prices

The price of drugs generally declines over the course of the simulation (Figure 5.10). Innovative products under patent protection face

[19]   The number of firms active in each TC, as displayed in Figure 5.8, is computed as the average over 1,000 simulations of the number of active firms in each TC at the end of the simulation. Specifically, for each simulation we rank TCs according to the firm counts. Then, we compute the average number of firms in each TC, as identified in that ranking, over the 100 simulations. That is to say, we pool together the most crowded TCs in each run and compute the average number of active firms. Next, we pool the second ranked TCs and calculate the average firm count; and so on.

[20]   We have run standard tests of Gibrat Law on the growth of firms (not reported here), which do not reject the null hypothesis that firm's growth is erratic (see Bottazzi et al., 2001, for empirical results very similar to those we found). A thorough analysis of the properties of firm's growth in the model as compared to real data is the object of further research.

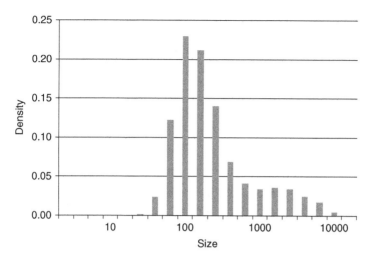

FIGURE 5.9 Firm-size distribution.

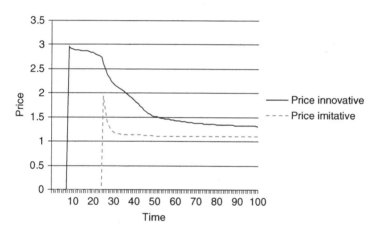

FIGURE 5.10 Average price of products.

stronger competition over time through the entry of competing innovative products in each TC. In the model, such competition affects
prices via the market share effects in the pricing rules. Thus, firms
introducing new products in an already occupied TC are prevented
from charging very high prices. The decline in prices of products
whose patent has expired is even more pronounced because of the

fiercer competition they suffer from imitation. Prices of imitative products, after an initial peak due to cases of duopoly between the first innovative incumbent and the second entrant, fall sharply thereafter. Thus, further imitative entry is discouraged and then prices remain stable over time.

5.6 THE SIMULATION RUNS: COUNTERFACTUALS

The Standard Set does a relatively good job in reproducing some of the stylized facts of the pharmaceutical industry: low and relatively stable concentration, strong competition between innovators and imitators, skewed size distribution of firms, declining productivity of R&D as time goes by.

In this section we report counterfactual experiments. We modify the model parameter settings with the aim of answering the following basic questions: Which factors contribute to shape industry structure in pharmaceuticals? In particular, under what conditions could the pharmaceutical industry have become more concentrated than observed both in the baseline simulations and in reality?

Following our discussion in Section 5.3, we focus on three main sets of variables. First, we explore the role of imitation, focusing on the degree of patent protection. Next, we examine the properties of the innovation process, focusing on opportunity conditions and on the degree of cumulativeness. Jointly, appropriability conditions, the nature of the opportunity space and the degree of cumulativeness define the properties of the technological regime underlying the innovation process in pharmaceuticals (Malerba and Orsenigo, 1995, Breschi *et al.*, 2000). Third, we consider characteristics of demand, particularly the degree of fragmentation of the market.

5.6.1 Imitation and patent protection

It is widely recognized that pharmaceuticals are one among the few industries in which patent protection is demonstrably important for preventing imitation and stimulating innovation. Nevertheless, imitation remains a distinctive feature of the industry acting as a strong countervailing force to concentration. Thus, we examine the effects on market structure of alternative regimes of patent protection and imitation. We address this issue by analyzing two changes to the parameter settings. First, we consider a simulation in which patent protection (T^{PT}) is granted for forty periods (as compared to twenty in the Standard Set). Next, as an extreme case, we investigate the effects of protection of only one period.

It is worth noting, first of all, that the industry does "survive" even with extremely low patent protection: More firms survive, but they remain smaller, especially the innovators. Indeed, both concentration in each TC and aggregate concentration are lower as compared with the Standard Set. In the case of longer patent protection, however, the results are somewhat surprising. Firms enjoy of course more durable market power in each TC after introducing a new drug. Thus, concentration increases in individual TCs (Figure 5.11a), although over time it tends to converge to the Standard Set value. Yet, aggregate concentration decreases and it remains lower as compared with the Standard Set (Figure 5.11b).

These results are the outcome of some interesting dynamics. To begin with, the number of innovative products increases with the

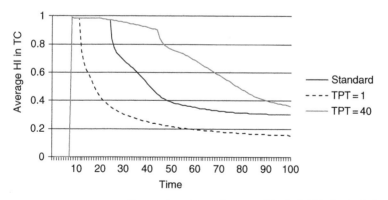

FIGURE 5.11A Patent duration and average Herfindahl index in TCs.

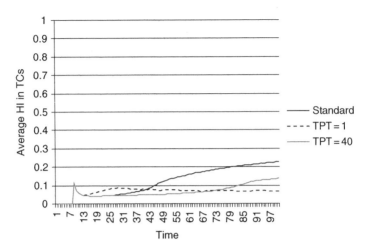

FIGURE 5.11B Patent duration and aggregate Herfindahl index.

length of patent duration (about 70 percent) although non linearly. The number of imitative products increases too (around 25 percent), starting twenty periods later (Figures 5.12a and 5.12b).

Thus, longer patent protection does indeed induce higher rates of innovation in the model. However, two effects occur. A stronger patent regime indirectly benefits imitating firms too, simply because there are more products to imitate. Moreover, innovative firms – enjoying higher profits – are able to explore more TCs (by about 30 percent). Aggregate concentration declines because more firms are active in more submarkets. For the same reason, concentration in individual TCs ultimately tends to decline, and the decline becomes rapid after period forty as imitation starts to bite and the rate of discovery of new TCs declines. More innovation implies faster exhaustion of opportunities to discover new TCs and molecules and an earlier onset of the tendencies characteristic of static (rather than dynamic) competition. Conversely, with short-lived patent protection the number of explored TC is reduced almost to one-third, and the number of products in the market to one-half, of the values realized in the standard simulation (Figures 5.12a and 5.12b).

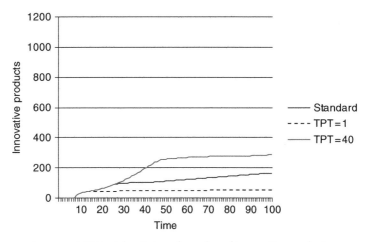

FIGURE 5.12A Patent duration and number of innovative products.

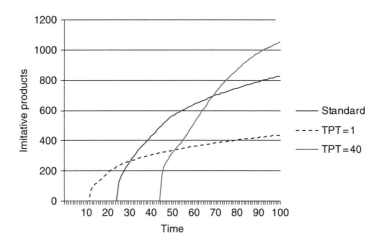

FIGURE 5.12B Patent duration and number of imitative products.

These causal mechanisms are reflected in the behavior of prices. With short patent protection, prices are significantly lower and the prices of innovative products are only slightly higher than the prices of imitative products (Figures 5.13a, 5.13b and 5.13c). With long patent protection, the price of innovative products is significantly higher

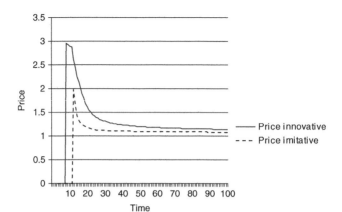

FIGURE 5.13A Patent duration and prices, $T^{PT} = 1$.

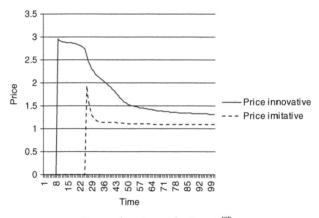

FIGURE 5.13B Patent duration and prices, $T^{PT} = 20$.

than the price of imitative drugs. It remains also higher for a longer period of time, as compared to the Standard Set, although it eventually converges at very similar values. In this respect, the model reproduces the classic tradeoff: lower patent protection leads to lower prices but also to less innovation and vice-versa. However, a further effect should be highlighted. Higher innovation leads to more imitative products and more TCs discovered – as just noted – but also to more innovative

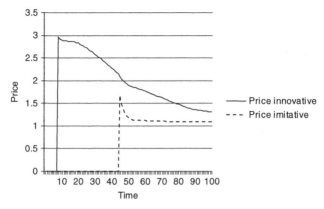

FIGURE 5.13C Patent duration and prices, $T^{PT} = 40$.

products within each TC (and therefore fiercer competition among them). This effect moderates price increases.

In sum, our results suggest some important qualifications to the standard hypotheses regarding the relationships between innovation, concentration, prices on the one hand and the strength of patent protection on the other. In the model, stronger patent protection promotes concentration and higher prices in individual TCs, but these effects are partially lessened by the higher opportunities to imitate and to diversify into new submarkets and by stronger competition among innovative products. These results suggest two further observations. First, the patterns of industry evolution appear to be heavily influenced by the complex ecology of innovators and imitators. Second, these findings depend crucially on a set of conditions and parameters values that have been fixed in these simulations. For example, the decline of aggregate concentration and prices seems to be affected by sufficiently rich opportunities for innovation, large number of TCs and submarkets, and a strong aggregate demand for drugs.[21]

[21] Garavaglia et al. (2012, 2013) provide a systematic exploration of the interactions between different values of opportunity and appropriability conditions, cumulativeness and demand conditions.

5.6.2 The properties of the innovative process

We turn now to the second set of factors that is considered to explain the observed low levels of concentration in pharmaceuticals, the nature of the R&D process and the space of search (Gambardella, 1995; Sutton, 1998). We focus on two important dimensions of the innovative process. First, the richness of the opportunities for innovation. Second, the absence of cumulativeness in the innovative process (the fact that the knowledge accumulated in discovering and developing one drug does not confer significant advantages in the search for new products in different TCs and in the future). These two considerations imply that the degree of serial correlation in the introduction of successful innovations by a firm is small. As previously noted, a "lottery model" seems to be a valid representation of innovation in the pharmaceutical industry (Sutton, 1998).

Innovative opportunities

How would market structure and innovation evolve in "richer" and "poorer" environments in terms of innovative opportunities? The effects of these changes are ex-ante uncertain: on the one hand, higher opportunities might reduce concentration, making it easier for firms to find molecules and to introduce new products; imitation would become easier too. On the other hand, higher opportunities might increase concentration, to the extent that success-breeds-success processes favor the growth of the larger firms, even in the absence of cumulativeness in the search process (Nelson and Winter, 1982 and 1982b).

To investigate this question, we focus on the properties of the search space. We explore the simulation results with different settings of the distribution of opportunities. We run simulations with different probabilities of finding a promising molecule in the search process, comparing the Standard Set (where the probability of finding a "zero quality" molecule is $z = 0.97$) with a simulation in which opportunities are richer ($z = 0.90$) and with one where opportunities are poorer ($z = 0.99$).

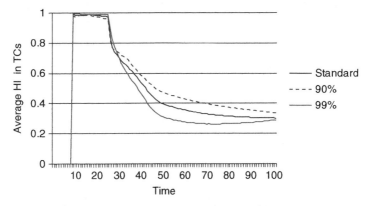

FIGURE 5.14A Opportunities and average Herfindahl index in individual TCs.

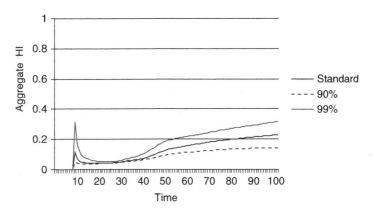

FIGURE 5.14B Opportunities and aggregate Herfindahl index.

The results show that a higher probability of finding promising molecules implies slightly higher concentration in each TC, but a lower aggregate concentration (from HI = 0.23 in the standard set to HI = 0.13 when $z = 0.90$ and to HI = 0.30 when $z = 0.99$) (Figure 5.14a and 5.14b). Higher opportunities entail also higher numbers of active firms, explored TCs and innovative and imitative products; larger firm size (for both innovators and imitators) and lower prices (not shown here).

The mechanisms behind these results seem to be as follows: richer opportunities for innovation lead to more new drugs. More firms survive and some of them grow larger, through success-breeds success processes. Hence, within any TC concentration tends to increase. However, easier innovation implies also easier imitation and stronger competition from other innovative drugs, partially off-setting the rise of concentration and reducing prices. In the aggregate, given that more TCs are discovered, firms distribute their innovative and imitative activities over a wider spectrum of submarkets: aggregate concentration declines.

Cumulativeness

Next, we introduce in the model a higher degree of cumulativeness: technological advances of any one firm depend on accumulated technological capabilities and on previous technological efforts and successes. There are many possible alternative ways to model higher cumulativeness in this model. Here, we focus on search efforts: in this formulation the probability of finding new promising molecules is now positively affected by previous (successful) research efforts.[22] To do so, the search function is modified so that in each period the number of draws in the search space is an increasing function of the number of drugs owned by a firm $(J_{f,t})$. Thus, in equation (2), the number of draws a firm can make in each period is now defined as a function of the budget available for search activity $(B_{f,t}^{SR})$, cost of search (C^{SR}), plus an increasing function in the number of products owned by the firm:

---

[22]   Another straightforward and appealing formulation would focus on cumulativeness in development capabilities rather than search efforts: for example, development costs could be modeled as declining with each successive drug developed in a given TC. We did not pursue this line of exploration in this book and it remains an interesting subject for future work.

$$N_{f,t}^X = \frac{B_{f,t}^{SR}}{C^{SR}} + (\zeta^0 \cdot J_{f,t})^{\zeta^1} \tag{13}$$

where ζ^0 and ζ^1 are parameters.

Results (not reported here) show that in general more cumulative search processes – in the particular definition of Equation 13 – have little effects on concentration. When the exponent ζ^1 in Equation 13 is set equal to 1, higher cumulativeness (higher values of the parameter ζ^0) tends to lower the Herfindahl index. An "equalizing effect" prevails: all firms benefit from the cumulative effect in the process of search so that they increase their probability to develop more innovative products. This effect implies that also imitative firms have higher chances of surviving and prospering. Conversely, large firms with rich budgets benefit relatively less than small firms from cumulativeness, since they have already access to a large number of draws. On similar grounds, as long as development costs are fixed, the marginal payoff to additional draws is reduced. As a consequence, average concentration in each TC increases only slightly. But, as drug discoveries extend the market to new TCs, aggregate concentration declines.[23]

5.6.3 Market fragmentation

Results of our counterfactual simulations show consistently that the availability of imitation targets and the properties of the innovation process do indeed have the expected impact on innovation and market structure. In particular, stronger patent protection, higher opportunities to discover new drugs and higher degrees of cumulativeness (i.e. the variables that define a technological regime), positively influence the rate of innovation. In turn, more innovation entails moderately higher degrees of concentration within TCs but not in the aggregate. These results suggest that other factors are

---

[23] With higher values of the parameter ζ^1 (a quadratic and a cubic relationship between "extra draws" and "number of products") concentration does indeed increase, but the effect is still very small.

primarily responsible for the low levels of aggregate concentration. Indeed, one of the most important channels through which the variables that identify the technological regime exert their impact on market structure is through the discovery of new TCs. The crucial question, then, becomes: how and why do different degrees of market fragmentation affect concentration?

Recent contributions, mainly Sutton (1998) and Klepper (1997) and Klepper and Thompson (2006) explicitly identify in market fragmentation a main limit to concentration. Sutton (1998) provides a simple and compact framework in a game theoretic setting for analyzing this question. In his approach, the key determinant is an "escalation parameter": how large is the profit that a firm outspending its competitors may gain? If such profit is large, then an escalation mechanism is set in motion and this leads to high concentration. But, if the aggregate market is composed by many independent submarkets, then the value of the escalation parameter is lower. Klepper (1997) suggests that product differentiation and demand fragmentation into many niches may prevent shakeouts and the emergence of concentration in the standard model of the industry life cycle (as mentioned in the discussion in Chapter 1). Along these lines Klepper and Thompson (2006) develop a model in which the process of (exogenous) creation and destruction of submarkets drives industry evolution. Firms expand by exploiting new opportunities that arrive in the form of new submarkets, while they shrink when the submarkets in which they operate are destroyed. The model predicts that a shakeout occurs and concentration increases if the rate of creation of new submarkets slows down and/or a new very large submarket appears.

Our analysis fully recognizes the crucial role played by market fragmentation in limiting concentration. Here, however, we do not assume that the number of submarkets is fixed or exogenously generated, nor that any potentially profitable submarket is actually occupied (the "arbitrage principle," see Sutton, 1998). Although there is a fixed number of "potential" submarkets, the actual submarkets discovered are the result of firms R&D efforts. Thus, the degree of market fragmentation is partially endogenous and our analysis is cast in an explicit dynamic setting.

Thus, we explore the fragmentation issue by examining simulations with different numbers of TCs (keeping the value of the aggregate market unchanged[24]): from 200 TC in the Standard Set to 20 and (as an extreme case) to only 1. With twenty submarkets, the Herfindahl index is actually lower than in the Standard Set in the first part of the simulation and only slightly higher later on.[25] But with a homogenous market (only one submarket), concentration rises substantially and in most runs monopoly is approached. The Herfindahl index raises from 0.23 to 0.94 (Figures 5.15a and 5.15b).

This result further confirms the idea that market fragmentation is a powerful countervailing force to concentration. It suggests however that the existence of only few submarkets is sufficient to create this effect: in the runs with twenty submarkets aggregate concentration is not substantially higher as compared to the Standard Set. At the same time, though, within any one submarket powerful forces toward concentration are visible.

To probe this result, we reduce gradually the number of TCs from 200 to 1 and compute the corresponding aggregate Herfindahl index at the end of the simulation (Figure 5.16). Results are straightforward: concentration increases rapidly and substantially as market fragmentation falls below fifty submarkets.

---

24   The procedure is the following. Recall that the potential value of a TC is given by the number of patients q_h that is drawn from a normal distribution with mean μ^q and standard deviation σ^q. The total number of TCs is equal to H. Then, the potential number of patients of the aggregate market is: $q^H = H \cdot \mu^q$. When the simulation sets different values for H, then μ^q varies accordingly so that q^H is unchanged.

25   A plausible explanation runs as follows: In the case of twenty submarkets, after few periods, most of the few submarkets are already populated by innovators and imitators, and therefore are characterized by intense competition. Prices decline quickly (results for prices are not reported here) and many firms (mainly imitators) exit the market (only ten firms are in the market at the end of simulation). The opportunity to gain temporary monopoly power in new TCs is constrained because of the smaller number of TCs. Yet, over time the positive feedback from success-breeds-success processes allows a few firms to discover, develop and launch new products repeatedly, gaining significant market shares in most submarkets. Given the higher exit rates just mentioned, the aggregate outcome is higher aggregate concentration at the end of the simulation.

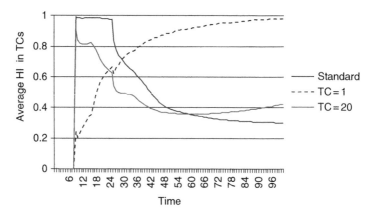

FIGURE 5.15A   Market fragmentation and average Herfindahl index in TCs.

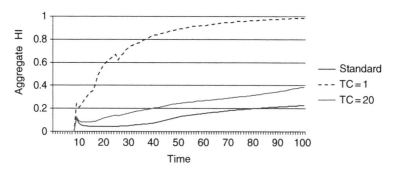

FIGURE 5.15B   Market fragmentation and aggregate Herfindahl index.

This observation raises the question of identifying even more precisely the forces generating and limiting concentration in this model of the pharmaceutical industry (Nelson and Winter, 1982a, 1982b). The obvious concentration-generating mechanism is the success-breeds-success process, that is, the positive feedback loop running from innovative success to profits to research budgets to search draws to

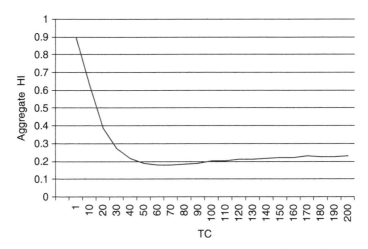

FIGURE 5.16 Aggregate Herfindahl index at the end of the simulation in different fragmentation settings.

further innovative success. This process is highly effective when some successful draws confer a disproportionate advantage on the lucky firm: In the model, hitting the jackpot – introducing a blockbuster – is the origin of the biggest competitive advantages.

The consideration of success-breeds-success processes suggest that it is not market fragmentation as such that matters, but the fragmentation of the value of the market. To check this interpretation, we ran the following exercise. We kept the number of submarkets unchanged as in the Standard Set ($H = 200$) but varied the distribution of the values of the submarkets: some TCs were randomly identified submarkets as "richer" in comparison with the others, according to the following specification. We selected 2 percent of the TCs (4 TCs out of the 200) and endowed them in alternative treatments with 15, 30, 45, 60 or 75 percent of the total patients in the aggregate market (the remaining patients assigned to other TCs). The results (Figures 5.17a and 5.17b) clearly show that as the share of patients of the 4 richer TCs increases, aggregate market concentration significantly increases (Figures 5.17a and 5.17b).

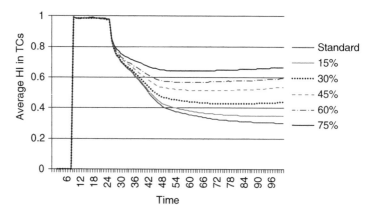

FIGURE 5.17A Average Herfindahl index in TCs under alternative distributions of the value of submarkets.

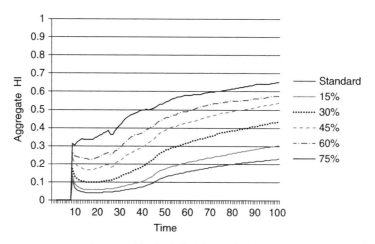

FIGURE 5.17B Aggregate Herfindahl index under alternative distributions of the value of submarkets.

We interpret these results as evidence that if the distribution of the market value is skewed, those few firms that conquer a very rich market are able to gain a significant advantage over competitors and therefore also a higher probability of finding new molecules. Success-breeds-success effects multiply these advantages, leading to market concentration. Conversely, when the distribution of the value of submarkets is sufficiently homogeneous, no firm can earn a disproportionate advantage by being leader in one submarket.

Our conclusions about the structural consequences of market fragmentation are quite similar to the findings obtained in Sutton (1998) and Klepper and Thompson (2006). However, our model suggests a further hypothesis: to the extent that early successful draws allow for the discovery of new very rich submarkets and provide a substantial differential in profits *vis-à-vis* competitors, first-mover advantages are likely to characterize industry dynamics. This appears to be indeed a distinctive feature of pharmaceuticals, where current industry leaders are almost all very early innovative entrants. We turn now to exploring this issue.

5.6.4 First-mover advantages

The empirical evidence suggests the relevance of innovative strategies and first-mover advantages in the evolution of the pharmaceutical industry. In the previous section, we noted also that the size of the submarkets entered early by firms should provide a strong advantage to innovators.

To explore these issues, we implement a simple econometric analysis with simulated data.[26] We define two different specifications of the model in order to test whether firms that dominate the market at the end of simulation are innovators and early entrants in large markets. We run 100 simulations and register values at the end of the simulation for about 50 firms per simulation, for the following variables[27]: *share* (firms' market share), and *survival* (status of

---

[26]   For a broader econometric analysis of the results of the model and a discussion of the methodology see Garavaglia *et al.* (2014).

[27]   The number of firms included in the regression should be 5,000 (50 firms for 100 simulations). However, among the 5,000 firms, 20 do not enter the market (i.e. they do not discover and sell any drug). These firms are not included in the regression sample.

firms). We also construct three dummies relating to the period of entry of firms: *cohort1* if the firm enters in periods [1–3]; *cohort2* if the firm enters in periods [4–8]; *cohort3* if the firm enters after period eight. We then introduce the variable *market size*, defined as the size of the TC (measured in terms of patients) in which firms enter first. Finally we define four dummies for the propensity of firms to invest in search φ^{SR} (as defined in Section 5.4.2): high propensity with φ^{SR} > 0.75; medium propensity with 0.75 < φ^{S} < 0.5; weak propensity with 0.5 < φ^{S} < 0.25 and low propensity (the excluded case in the regression) with φ^{SR} < 0.25.

We then estimate a Probit model (column 1 of Table 5.1) with firm survival as the dependent variable. The results show that the earlier the entry period and the larger the first market entered, the

Table 5.1 *First mover advantages*

Variables	(1) Probit survival	(2) OLS log(share)
Cohort1	0.87***	0.18**
	(0.064)	(0.085)
Cohort2	0.63***	0.057
	(0.073)	(0.093)
High propensity	0.062	1.47***
	(0.059)	(0.058)
Medium propensity	−0.015	0.37***
	(0.059)	(0.059)
Weak propensity	−0.031	0.12**
	(0.059)	(0.060)
log(Market size)	1.06***	0.35***
	(0.037)	(0.035)
Constant	−6.42***	−6.35***
	(0.20)	(0.22)
Observations	4980	1991
	(pseudo)	
R-squared	0.29	0.307

higher the probability of survival at the end of the simulation period. The dummy variables for research investment propensity are not significant. In another specification (column 2 of Table 5.1), we estimate an OLS regression on the subsample of firms conditional on survival at the end of the simulation. The dependent variable is the logarithm of share. Results are reported in column 2 of Table 5.1.

First, first mover advantages are substantial and they are stronger at the very beginning of the simulation, disappearing quickly later on. Firms entering during the first cohort have a significantly larger share at the end of the simulation as compared to later entrants. However, firms entering in the second cohort do not gain a similar advantage: The difference with later entrants is not statistically significant.

Second, results confirm that the size of the first TC explored by the firm affects positively the market share at the end of the simulation. Third, firms characterized by a high propensity to innovate reach on average a much larger market share than firms with a lower propensity.

In sum, the model reproduces the stylized fact that industry leaders are the early innovative entrants in large submarkets.

5.7   CONCLUSIONS

The model presented in this Chapter does a good job in reproducing the main stylized facts of the pharmaceutical industry. In the model, firms compete through innovation, imitation and diversification into new submarkets. Innovation constitutes a fundamental factor affecting firms' competitiveness. Over time, the stock of off-patent innovative products grows, presenting targets for imitation, and the share of imitative products in the total number increases continuously. As a consequence of these processes, firms grow and enjoy high levels of profitability. A skewed distribution of firms' size emerges with some larger firms (mainly innovators that are present in a large number of therapeutic classes) coexisting with many smaller companies (mainly imitators). Industry leadership is gained by innovative early entrants,

who are able to seize rich therapeutic classes (TCs) and to grow thereafter through success-breeds success processes. However, the industry
remains characterized by a high level of dynamic competition in the
form of R&D rivalry. In individual TCs, however, concentration is
higher but still moderate. Particularly at early stages of industry
history, it is high enough to dampen price competition, and thereby
affords protection to the "Schumpeterian rents" of innovators.

The counterfactual exercises we have run allowed us to explore
the relative importance of alternative possible explanations of the
peculiar market structure characterizing pharmaceuticals. More generally, the model highlights how the combination of different factors
prevents the onset of concentration in a highly R&D and marketing
intensive industry.

The first main point that emerges from the analysis of this chapter regards the crucial role of market fragmentation in limiting the
degree of aggregate concentration. Even in the presence of powerful
forces leading to market power in individual market segments, the
existence of multiple independent submarkets prevents the emergence
of a strong leader in the aggregate market. As mentioned previously, our
findings link closely with those recent contributions that assign a
crucial role to market fragmentation as a main factor preventing concentration in innovative industries (Klepper, 1996, 1997; Sutton, 1998;
Klepper and Thompson, 2006). The analysis in this chapter, however, is
cast in a dynamic evolutionary framework and new submarkets are
gradually activated endogenously over time as the outcome of processes
of search of new molecules and new submarkets.

A second related point resulting from this chapter is that concentration is not simply influenced by the degree of demand fragmentation as such, but by the distribution of the values of the various
submarkets. The emergence of market leadership depends on the
discovery of the first drugs in a very rich market segment – drugs
that become known as "blockbusters" – which confer a disproportio-
nately large advantage to the innovator and are subsequently reinforced by success-breeds-success processes. As a consequence, and

appropriately in a dynamic evolutionary analysis, time matters. Indeed, a third result achieved in this chapter concerns the relevance of the timing of entry and the existence of first mover advantages, even in a context where the ability to leverage past technological achievements for future innovation is limited.

More generally, the results of the model highlight the role of demand conditions in affecting the dynamics of market structure. As we shall elaborate in more depth in Chapter 6, the characteristics of the "demand regime" have to be considered as a fundamental factor in the explanation of the patterns of innovation and of the dynamics of concentration in an industry.

Still, a fourth broad conclusion from this chapter is that, jointly with demand conditions, the technological context in which firms operate remains a fundamental determinant of innovation and industry evolution. In this chapter, this context is defined in terms of technological opportunities, (lack of) cumulativeness of technological advances and appropriability conditions (specifically, length of patent duration in this model), i.e. attributes of the "technological regime" (Nelson and Winter, 1982a; Malerba and Orsenigo,1997; Winter, 1984). (We shall dwell on this point at greater length in Chapter 6.) Further, technological competition in our history-friendly model is set in a stylized historical context corresponding to the "golden age" of the pharmaceutical industry. At the start of this "age," there are new discovery methods on the scene and an untapped field of opportunity awaiting their application. By the end of the story, the actual or potential exhaustion of the opportunities puts a question mark over the future. In the intervening interval, the historical dynamics produce trends or broken trends in one descriptive variable after another. If the point of our efforts were to show how our model trajectories close on some long-run equilibrium that theory proposes as "the real answer," it would be a miserable failure – but that was not the point. These "historical" patterns in our simulation outputs have counterparts, and sometimes close counterparts, in the real-world history. That was the point. Our message to our colleagues, particularly to the ones who engage policy questions affecting dynamic industries, is this: Beware the timeless verities of the textbook! History is real, and it matters!

A fifth lesson emerging from this chapter concerns the complex dynamics that is created by the interactions between innovators and imitators. Innovation confers profits and competitive advantages to firms but at the same time opens up opportunities for imitators. Imitation, after a patent has expired, erodes the advantages of innovators, curbs monopolistic prices and allows for the survival of a large number of firms. In this respect, the model presented in this chapter replicates the classical Schumpeterian trade-off between static and dynamic efficiency and the policy dilemmas regarding the costs and benefits of a strong appropriability regime: stronger protection induces innovation, but it leads also to higher prices. However, the model highlights further complex dynamic mechanisms affecting this trade-off.

In the model stronger protection does indeed spur innovation and concentration within individual TCs. But more innovation implies also more imitation, the faster discovery of a larger number of new TCs and hence lower aggregate concentration. Moreover, to the extent that more innovative products within TCs compete with each other and with imitative drugs, monopolistic pricing is partially offset. Yet, the effects of stronger patent protection are crucially moderated by the values of other relevant variables, primarily those identifying the technological and demand regimes, the toughness of price competition and the other forces favoring or limiting imitation. These effects change also over the timing of the simulations.

More generally, the model suggests that arguments in favor or against a stronger patent regime should consider carefully that consequences depend on a large set of (sometimes non-linearly) interacting variables and on time. In this respect, we believe that our modeling style might be useful also for analyzing policy issues in complex dynamic environments.

APPENDIX 5.1   LIST OF VARIABLES AND PARAMETERS

Parameter	Symbol	Value / range
General indices		
Index for time periods	t	$\{1, \ldots, T\}$
Index for firms	f	$\{1, \ldots, F\}$
Index for markets (therapeutic classes – TCs)	h	$\{1, \ldots, H\}$
Index for molecules	x	$\{1, \ldots, X_h\}$
Index for products (drugs)	j	$\mathbb{N}$
Index for innovation / imitation	ι	$\{in, im\}$
Index for groups of patients within a TC (ordered by minimum quality requirements)	g	$\{1, 2, 3, 4\}$
Industry characteristics		
Periods of simulation	T	100
Number of potential firms	F	50
Probability of drawing a zero-quality molecule	z	0.97
Unit cost of search	C^{SR}	20
Unit cost of production	C^{PD}	1
Unit cost of development of innovative drugs	C_{in}^D	60
Unit cost of development of imitative drugs	C_{im}^D	20
Periods to develop an innovative drug	T_{in}^D	8
Periods to develop an imitative drug	T_{im}^D	4
Patent duration	T^{PT}	20
Patent width	W^{PT}	5
Minimum quality threshold of the drugs to be sold on the market	λ^Q	μ_Q
Interest rate	r	0.08
Indicator of market leaders power in Equation 6	ω	0.5
Perceived price elasticity of demand in Equation 6	ε	1.5
Scale parameter in Equation 7	a^0	1
Exponent in Equation 7	a^1	1

Parameter	Symbol	Value / range
Erosion rate of product image	η	0.01
Minimum market share threshold for survival of a firm in the market	λ^E	0.004
Minimum market share threshold for survival of a product in the market	λ^J	0.05
Periods without drawing a promising molecule after which an innovative firm exits	T^E	7
Scale parameter in Equation 13	ζ^0	0
Exponent in Equation 13	ζ^1	0
Scale parameter in Equation 9	v	1
Number of potential patients in the industry	q^H	$\mathbb{R}_+$
Therapeutic Classes, molecules and drugs characteristics		
Number of TCs	H	200
Number of molecules in TC h	X_h	200
Number of potential patients in TC h	q_h	$\mathbb{R}_+$
Mean of normal distribution of the number of patients per TC	μ^q	600
Standard deviation of normal distribution of the number of patients per TC	σ^q	200
Number of patients in group g of TC h	$q_{g,h}$	$\mathbb{R}_+$
Minimum quality threshold of group g	λ_g^Q	{30, 45, 60, 75}
Number of groups of patients buying a drug in TC h at time t	$G_{h,t}$	{1, 2, 3, 4}
Number of groups of patients in TC h that could buy drug j	$G_{h,j}$	{1, 2, 3, 4}
Set of all drugs in TC h with a quality higher than λ_g^Q	$\Im_{g,h}$	-
Economic value of a TC h	$V_{h,t}$	$\mathbb{R}_+$
Weight of product quality for TC h in Equation 9	δ_h^Q	[0.5, 0.6]
Weight of inverse of price for TC h in Equation 9	δ_h^P	[0.15, 0.2]

Parameter	Symbol	Value / range
Weight of product image for TC h in Equation 9	δ_h^A	$[0.35, 0.4]$
Quality of molecule x	Q_x	$\mathbb{R}_+$
Quality of drug j	Q_j	$\mathbb{R}_+$
Mean of normal distribution of positive quality molecules	μ^Q	30
Standard deviation of normal distribution of positive quality molecules	σ^Q	20
Residual length of patent protection for molecule x at time t	$T_{x,t}^{PT}$	$\{1, \ldots, T^{PT}\}$
Attractiveness of molecule x to be developed at time t	$v_{x,t}$	$\mathbb{R}_+$
Price of drug j at time t	$P_{j,t}$	$\mathbb{R}_+$
Markup of drug j at time t	$m_{j,t}$	$\mathbb{R}_+$
Launch period of drug j	T_j	$\{1, \ldots, T\}$
Advertising expenditures for drug j at launch period	B_j^A	$\mathbb{R}_+$
Product image of drug j at time t	$A_{j,t}$	$\mathbb{R}_+$
Propensity of patients in TC h to buy drug j at time t	$u_{h,j,t,}$	$\mathbb{R}_+$
Number of actual patients of drug j at time t	$q_{j,t}$	$\mathbb{R}_+$
Firm characteristics		
Fraction of budget invested in R&D activities by firm f	φ_f^{RD}	$[0.25, 0.75]$
Fraction of budget invested in search activities by firm f	φ_f^{SR}	$[0.05, 0.15]$
Initial budget of a potential firm	B^0	4000
Budget invested in search activities by firm f at time t	$B_{f,t}^{SR}$	$\mathbb{R}_+$
Budget invested in development activities by firm f at time t	$B_{f,t}^D$	$\mathbb{R}_+$
Budget invested in marketing activities by firm f at time t	$B_{f,t}^A$	$\mathbb{R}_+$
Number of new molecules drawn by firm f at time t	$N_{f,t}^X$	$\mathbb{N}$

Parameter	Symbol	Value / range
Number of drugs produced by firm f at time t	$J_{f,t}$	$\mathbb{N}$
Number of new projects started by firm f at time t	$N_{f,t}^{D}$	$\mathbb{N}$
Market share of firm f in TC h at time t	$s_{f,h,t}$	$[0,1]$
Number of patients of TC h buying from firm f at time t	$q_{f,h,t}$	$\mathbb{R}_{+}$
Profits from product j at time t	$\Pi_{j,t}$	$\mathbb{R}_{+}$
Profits of firm f in period t	$\Pi_{f,t}$	$\mathbb{R}_{+}$

APPENDIX 5.2   SENSITIVITY AND ROBUSTNESS ANALYSIS
In this section we adopt an ANOVA approach to test whether the results of the model are robust to small variations in the parameter settings (*robustness check*) and whether the main results described in the figures presented in Chapter 5 are statistically significant (*confirmation-test*).

Robustness check

With the robustness-check approach we aim at testing if a small variation in the input parameters of the model corresponds to a small variation in the output variables. We run the robustness check in three steps.

First, we identify a set of input parameters, which we consider crucial for the behavior of the model: patent duration, opportunities, market fragmentation, size of the aggregate market, quality requirements and number of firms. Then, we identify the output variables of main interest: the aggregate concentration index (aggregate H), the average concentration index in TCs (Avg. H in TC), and the number of innovative products.

Second, we consider three simulations of 1,000 runs for each pair parameter-output variable. The three simulations correspond to three different values of a given parameter: the value of the parameter as it is set in the standard simulation, the standard value increased by 2 percent and the standard value decreased by 2 percent.

Finally we test, for each pair parameter-output variable, the difference of the output means calculated in each of the three simulations. In order to test for mean differences we apply the one-way analysis of variance (ANOVA). We consider the output value measured in the last period of each run ($t=100$). Table A.5.1 shows the results.

We end our robustness check by increasing/decreasing at the same time all the parameters by 2 percent (upper/lower bound in Table A.5.1).

Some of the means in the three simulations (standard, +2 percent and –2 percent) are not significantly different despite the large number of observations in the three samples (1,000 observations each). In particular a variation of 2 percent of fragmentation, size of the market and number of firms does not affect much the three outputs considered (see ANOVA P-value column, Table A.5.1). Different values of the parameter give significantly different means in case of patent duration and quality requirements, although the output means do not actually vary much, as shown by the values reported in the three columns labeled avg. outputs. Their significance is mainly due to the large size of the samples.

These results suggest that the outputs of the model are robust to small variations (+2 percent/–2 percent) of the parameters. This is not the case for opportunities, where results are particularly sensitive to small input variations. This result reflects mainly our choice to set the parameter defining the probability of discovering new molecules at a low level, consistently with the history of the industry. At this low level, even a small change in the share of zero quality molecules produce a significant variation in concentration and in the number of innovative products.

We replicate the robustness check for larger variations of the parameter values, that is +/–5 percent and +/–10 percent. We expect that an increase in the variation of the parameters will result in larger difference among the output means: the larger the variation of

Table A.5.1 *Robustness check*

					Avg. outputs					
Input ->	Standard	+2%	-2%	Output (time 100)->	Standard	+2%	-2%	ANOVA P-value	ANOVA P-value +/- 5%	ANOVA P-value +/-10%
Patent duration	20	(21)20.4	(19)19.6	Aggregate H	0.23	0.22	0.23	0.027	0.027	0.000
				Avg. H in TC	0.30	0.30	0.29	0.000	0.000	0.000
				Inno. Prod.	165.51	173.87	156.56	0.000	0.000	0.000
Opportunities (% of zeros)	0.97	0.9894	0.9506	Aggregate H	0.23	0.31	0.19	0.000	0.000	0.000
				Avg. H in TC	0.30	0.28	0.32	0.000	0.000	0.000
				Inno. Prod.	165.51	74.49	218.75	0.000	0.000	0.000
Fragmentation	200	204	196	Aggregate H	0.23	0.23	0.23	0.915	0.026	0.000
				Avg. H in TC	0.30	0.30	0.30	0.705	0.213	0.000
				Inno. Prod.	165.51	164.56	167.95	0.095	0.001	0.000
Size of the whole market	120000	122400	117600	Aggregate H	0.23	0.23	0.23	0.771	0.958	0.586
				Avg. H in TC	0.30	0.30	0.30	0.915	0.019	0.000
				Inno. Prod.	165.51	168.57	163.39	0.007	0.000	0.000
Quality check	30	(31)30.6	(29)29.4	Aggregate H	0.23	0.24	0.22	0.002	0.000	0.000
				Avg. H in TC	0.30	0.30	0.30	0.989	0.228	0.001
				Inno. Prod.	165.51	159.39	175.12	0.000	0.000	0.000

	50	51	49			
Number of firms						
	Aggregate H	0.23	0.22	0.23	0.014	0.001	0.000
	Avg. H in TC	0.30	0.30	0.30	0.083	0.000	0.000
	Inno. Prod.	165.51	166.30	165.58	0.870	0.789	0.006
Upper/lower bound (all the variables de/increases by 2% except opportunities)	Aggregate H	0.23	0.23	0.23	0.532	0.607	0.086
	Avg. H in TC	0.30	0.30	0.31	0.075	0.588	0.177
	Inno. Prod.	165.51	166.27	169.92	0.016	0.000	0.013

Table A.5.2 *Confirmation of the results (over time)*

Output (time)->	20	50	100	ANOVA P-value
Aggregate H	0.04	0.13	0.23	0
Avg. H in TC	0.98	0.39	0.30	0
Inno. Prod.	62.68	111.78	165.51	0

Table A.5.3 *Confirmation of the results (prices)*

Output (time 100)->	In. Avg. price	Im. Avg. price	ANOVA P-value
Prices	1.31	1.1	0

parameters the smaller the P-value of the ANOVA test (see Table A.5.1, columns ANOVA P-value +/–5 percent and +/–10 percent). When we consider deviations from the standard value of a parameter to such an extent, we believe that they should be considered counterfactual exercises more than robustness checks and for this reason we expect (and desire) significantly different model outputs.

Confirmation of the results
The confirmation test consists again in an ANOVA. We aim to show that the main output variables change their values significantly over time for a given parametrization of the model. Table A.5.2 shows that average values of aggregate H, Avg. H in TC and Inno. Prod. are significantly different in three time periods: $t=20$, $t=50$, $t=100$. The simulation includes 1,000 runs and the input parameters are set according to the standard parametrization. The last column of the table (ANOVA P-value) shows that the averages in the three periods considered are significantly different.

We end our confirmation test by showing in Table A.5.3 that the average prices of innovative and imitative products are significantly different at the end of the simulation ($t=100$).

6 Reprise and conclusions

As we reach the end of our explorations, it is instructive to look back at the assessment of formal modeling that Alfred Marshall offered many years ago:

> It would be possible to extend the scope of such systems of equations as we have been considering... But while a mathematical illustration of the mode of action of a definite set of causes may be complete in itself, and strictly accurate within its clearly defined limits, it is otherwise with any attempt to grasp the whole of a complex problem of real life, or even any considerable part of it, in a series of equations. For many important considerations, especially those connected with the manifold influences of the element of time, do not lend themselves to mathematical expression; they must either be omitted altogether, or clipped and pruned till they resemble the conventional birds and animals of decorative art. And hence arises a tendency to assigning wrong portions to economic forces; those elements being most emphasized which lend themselves most easily to analytical methods.
>
> *(Marshall, 1890[1920], p. 850)*

We have been concerned in this book with grasping the decidedly complex real-life problems of innovation and industrial evolution. We have sought to capture in our dynamic models at least some of those "manifold influences of the element of time" of which Marshall spoke – though, of course, we do not make much progress on the full list. In choosing the "influences" to emphasize, we have tried in particular to bring to the fore the mechanisms that shape outcomes in ways that, while highlighted in many appreciative accounts of

217

technological and industrial dynamics, are quite often ignored in highly stylized, static models. These are mechanisms that, first of all, take some time to operate. They also tend to involve substantial momentum effects, and path dependence. That our models reflect those mechanisms and aspects forms the foundation of their claim to being called "history-friendly models." They portray the dynamic features of real economic causation, as described in empirical studies.

The constraints on mathematical analysis have obviously been relaxed a good deal since Marshall was turning out the successive editions of his *Principles*, roughly a century ago. From the many relatively recent advances in applied mathematics to the ever-expanding tool kits of economics graduate students, there is a lot more mathematical technique available for dealing with problems of dynamics. Much of this apparatus, especially the dynamic programming part, has found extensive application in mainstream economics. However, it still remains very difficult to reconcile even a moderate recognition of the complexity inherent in real economic problems with the tractability constraints of closed-form analytical models, whether static or dynamic. The sorts of considerations that are often pruned from mainstream models of industrial dynamics include such basic points as that firms generally lack insight into the structure of their competitive environments, that they have multidimensional policies that respond to different subsets of the system variables, and even that they are not infinitesimal relative to their markets. Further, mainstream models typically hew to a strictly economic logic, and thus do not make room for the extra-economic considerations that are prominent in some historical episodes – as illustrated by the discontinuities in semiconductor technology. When the modeling aesthetic also demands "optimal" solutions to firm problems – as is true in mainstream modeling by definition of "mainstream" – it is a foregone conclusion that the problem optimally solved will be drastically different from a real one. As Marshall emphasized, this is not to say that there is nothing to be gained by rigorous pursuit of such problems – but his warning about "assigning wrong proportions" clearly remains apropos, as does his comment about the "clipping and pruning" requirement.

In this book, we have taken advantage of the quite different relaxation of constraints provided by the enormous advances in information technology. Like many other scholars across virtually the entire post–World War II era, we have turned to computer simulation in a quest for greater modeling freedom. As the decades have passed, the technology has expanded the opportunity set for simulation methods more and more dramatically.[1] Several different constraints have been relaxed concurrently, but the difference that is most critical to the methods in this book is the opportunity to capture the insights of appreciative theorizing in a formal structure and then obtain, via computation, some conclusions about the implications of that structure. While the same set of dynamic equations could be viewed as an object for analytical study, there are well-known and formidable obstacles to deducing general qualitative conclusions from a complex model that is characterized only in qualitative terms. Simulation offers a way to circumvent those obstacles, partly because it draws on the strength of representations that have a rough quantitative plausibility.

Yet the necessity of clipping and pruning remains. While computer technology has greatly reduced the challenge presented by the sheer mass of computation in a simulation experiment, the tractability constraints reappear in the domain of interpretation of results. As has been well remarked, a model of baffling complexity can hardly be useful in probing the baffling complexity of the real world. When considering which mechanisms to represent in the model and how to represent them, it is necessary to balance the need to reflect those that seem to be key against the risk of overwhelming the interpretive powers of the investigators.

---

[1]   About three decades of technical progress are reflected in the many differences between the uses of simulation in this book and those in Nelson and Winter (1982a). Among the many important features of that, there is the great facilitation of the input-output functions and the programmable links to subsequent analysis. Output used to appear in thick sheaves of computer paper, and that was the starting point for interpretive analysis.

In constructing the models in this book, we have pursued the needed balance by, first, drawing on appreciative theory for guidance as to which mechanisms are key and therefore deserving of more careful representation. Beyond that, we have followed the general strategy of representing individual parts of the total decision problem faced by the firm by relatively simple descriptive rules – such as the simple cash-allocation rules for R&D, advertising and investment. Thus, we model firms that are plausibly responsive to the available information that is specific to particular domains, but do not have grand strategies that display the behavioral coherence expected of a "unitary rational actor." The extent to which real firm behavior has that sort of coherence is a complicated, matter-of-degree sort of question – and whether a real firm would actually be advantaged by the active pursuit of such coherence is another question of that sort. These are, in our view, questions that can be (and to some extent have been) explored by empirical inquiry.[2] They are not, in our view, questions that should be foreclosed for theoretical purposes by considerations of modeling aesthetics.

What deserves emphasis here is the fact that our choices of simple behavioral rules do not reflect an inability to think of anything subtler, more information-intensive, or more rationalistic. One decision domain at a time, we could certainly do that. The simplicity reflects the need to be wary of increasing the complexity and attendant interpretive challenges in the model as a whole. Restraint in the complexity introduced at the level of an individual firm decision smooths the way for subsequent efforts to interpret model output convincingly, for which we have employed a variety of specific devices. In general, we explore the model's functioning under a variety of parameter settings. We seek to understand apparently anomalous results when they appear, exploiting our designer understanding of

---

[2] See, for example, the careful study of pricing behavior in a large corporation recently reported by Zbaracki and Bergen (2010). The incoherence of the firm's pricing policy is quite apparent, both in the period before the crisis studied and after its resolution; the resolution displays a bureaucratic logic in operation rather than a comprehensive optimizing logic.

particular rules, and comparing results with expectations derived from appreciative theory. This tuning process permitted us to arrive at the history-friendly base cases that we used in particular studies. Contrary to some simplistic critiques of simulation methods, it is far from the case that such success is a foregone conclusion, or that the tuning process is uninformative. Quite the opposite is the case (see Chapter 2).

In this concluding chapter, we first highlight the causal mechanisms that were found to play an important role in many, if not all, of our individual studies. We then describe some of the more specific mechanisms and results, seeking to illustrate the historical content and to highlight some of the relatively unexpected conclusions. There are, of course, too many candidates for such a discussion to be accommodated in a short reprise, so we can present only a "sampler." In the final section, we look forward to consider how history-friendly modeling might evolve in the future, and how this current of evolutionary modeling might join with others that have appeared in recent years.

6.2 GENERIC MECHANISMS

6.2.1 *Firm growth and industry structure*

Firms in our models have lifetimes, during which they typically change considerably in scale. In any attempt to capture industrial dynamics in a realistic fashion, it is fundamental to recognize that large firms become so by growing over extended periods, in changing market conditions, and not by being born large. The giants grew by winning, for one reason or another, in the evolutionary struggle with other firms that prospered less. This rather obvious fact has implications for industrial concentration; it says that structure is endogenous in a dynamic, historical sense. This means that when industries differ substantially in structure, we are either looking at a historical life-stage phenomenon, or we are looking at the shaping influence of differing contexts – for example, differing technological or demand regimes. And, of course, we are also looking at the outcomes of processes involving the accumulation of chance events over time – processes that are well known to produce concentration by themselves, quite apart from any systematic relationships between the policies of firms and the requirements of the environments they face (Sutton, 1997; Geroski, 2000).

That the dynamics of firm growth are central to the appearance of concentration is an empirical reality that can be confirmed simply by viewing a "movie" of firm market shares in almost any industry, rather than a single snapshot. There are many things that might, as a matter of pure logic, be seen in such a movie: sudden appearances of new and very large firms, changes in firm size by multiple orders of magnitude in a month or two, or simply a quasi-random reshuffling of industry leadership from year to year. In fact, none of these things are seen. Rather, the real-world dynamics of firm growth involves substantial elements of inertia and continuity, with consequent slow evolution of concentration that is typically toward higher levels when the industry is young. These realistic patterns are seen consistently in our simulations. That this is the case is not surprising, given the power of the mechanisms adduced in the previous paragraph, which are common to the reality and the models.[3] It is a point worth emphasizing nevertheless, since the tradition of industrial economics was so long focused on static scale economies as a key determinant of concentration – with minimal attention both to the normal dynamics and to the role of exogenous shocks. The dynamic perspective makes a difference also to policy analysis, as we will discuss more in detail in section 6.3.

6.2.2   Innovation and increasing returns

Although details differ across models, the model environments in which our firms operate are ones in which innovation opportunities

---

[3]   There are some industries in which concentration had been significantly accelerated by merger and acquisition activity. However, merger and acquisition activity were of secondary importance in the focal industries of our study, and we have not attempted to capture its role in our models.

exist. Seizing these opportunities is typically a matter of costly expenditure on R&D. A key question is the scope of application of any innovations achieved. If benefits take the form of a reduction in production costs that applies to all the units of a given product that the firm produces, then benefits are closely related to firm scale, whereas innovation costs are not. Hence there is an informational economy of scale relating to R&D and innovation.[4] Such a scale economy gives larger innovative firms a doubled advantage over smaller ones: not only can they finance more R&D and achieve more frequent advances but they get a proportionally larger benefit from a given advance (much the same logic applies to advertising expenditure).

Over time, the scale-related advantages of innovation contribute to a competitive process that can have only a few winners, and perhaps only one. Thus, in the history-friendly base case of our computer industry model, we find the consistent emergence of a dominant firm – an "IBM" – in the early stages of the mainframe market. For something different to happen, there must be significant forces that undercut the ability of large firms to leverage achieved scale and other continuing advantages derived from past success. Such forces typically take the form of discontinuities of some sort – new opportunities in technologies and market that newer and smaller firms may be better equipped to perceive and address – as in the case of firms exploiting microprocessors and the PC market in our computer study.

When the market for final output is fragmented, the informational scale economy associated with R&D is attenuated. This is one key element of the contrast that our studies reveal between the pharmaceutical industry and the computer industry. The final market for pharmaceutical firms is fragmented into multiple therapeutic categories, and there is further fragmentation within categories, because of differences in product quality. For a firm active in multiple

---

[4] We assume that there are constant returns to scale in production, i.e., there are no technical scale economies in production. While such economies are doubtless present in reality, we believe that appreciative theory supports the view that the informational scale economies are much more important, and our modeling choices reflect this appraisal.

categories, there is an important causal linkage across categories by way of the feedback from product profitability to the financing of total R&D. That the fragmentation of the market has a powerful impact on the level and evolution of concentration is illustrated in Chapter 5 under a variety of conditions. See, for example, Figure 5.3, showing that different levels of fragmentation (number of therapeutic categories) has a much stronger effect on concentration in the aggregate market than does the strength (duration) of patent protection.

6.2.3   Technological regimes: opportunity

Over the years, a diverse range of studies have argued and documented the point that innovative opportunity comes to the individual firm from a variety of sources; it also displays a variety of different dynamic patterns at the firm, industry and economy-wide level. To understand the role of innovation in industry evolution, and the variation in innovative performance, it is crucially important to give heed to the nature of the variation in opportunity.

Broadly speaking, the challenge faced by an aspiring modeler of innovation presents the following face. We first recognize that innovation is costly, and this observation can be acknowledged by introducing "R&D expenditure" as a variable in the model. At the other end, successful innovation confers some sort of advantage in the marketplace. Such success can be represented in different ways, but in the literature and in our models, a common way is as a reduction in unit cost of production, possibly supplemented or qualified by quality considerations. In our model of the pharmaceutical industry, the R&D investments of firms enabled them to introduce new products. Similarly, in our model of the computer industry, the introduction of new types of computers was the fruit of firm R&D. With the end points of the exercise settled (partly by adhering to conventions in the literature), we confront the crucial question of what happens in between, and how to render that in a model. What process translates expenditure into competitive advantage, and how much detail about that should be visible in the model? It is not likely to be helpful to insert an elaborate submodel of a single R&D project into an industry model aimed at much larger questions. But the real complexity of innovative opportunity is very great, as appreciative studies have made clear, and this complexity demands judicious recognition in the formal modeling. In fact, our models of R&D activity introduce a considerable amount of significant structure into the linkage that runs from R&D expenditure to innovation. This structure underpins our simulation analysis of scale economies, cumulativeness and other issues highlighted in appreciative theory.

Our models share a common basic framework for the discussion of innovative opportunity. First, at any given time, a particular firm has a status quo technological position, an existing level of technological accomplishment, and it incurs R&D costs for the sake of improving that position. Second, while the firm can produce proportionally more "effort" by greater expenditure, the returns to effort depend on the status quo. Because opportunity at a point of time has limits that are defined in part by exogenous considerations that do not change quickly, a leader's effort to widen the lead is particularly subject to diminishing returns. Third, there is a chance element in the returns to effort, so initially identical firms will have derived different levels of success from the same effort. Fourth, in some cases, R&D effort can be economized by imitating the successes of other firms, or drawing on a pool of accomplishment to which all firms contribute. All of our models have some, if not all, of these general features.

6.2.4 Technological regimes: cumulativeness

A central element in our further characterization of the dynamics of opportunity is the concept of a *cumulative* technological regime. In a more cumulative regime, a firm can build on its previous innovative successes, without being much impeded by its proximity to the frontier (whether stationary or moving), or by the fact that it has advanced relative to the crowd of its rivals. While diminishing returns to effort still apply at each point of time, a step forward does not directly and immediately restrict the opportunity for further moves.

This formulation is in sharp contrast to one that has received great attention in the mainstream literature going back to Arrow (1962). That is the case of a single, discrete inventive opportunity, where the question of "further moves" cannot arise.

Considerations of cumulativeness enter in different ways into our various models. In general, it is clear enough that high cumulativeness enhances the ability of leaders to expand and retain their leads, and correspondingly presents late entrants with a major challenge of catching up – unless of course something fundamental has changed. Thus cumulativeness interacts with the considerations mentioned earlier as elements of the dynamic determination of structure.

6.2.5   Technological regimes: appropriability

It is widely agreed that innovation tends to prosper when innovators prosper, and innovators prosper only when they can appropriate some adequate share of the returns that their innovations produce.

But when is that? Much discussion seems to presuppose that *only* a strong regime of intellectual property rights can assure those returns for the innovator. That position has long been challenged in the literature of evolutionary economics, going back to Schumpeter (1950) and beyond. In that literature, there is in particular a strong emphasis on the scale of application for a particular advance that an individual firm can provide, a consideration that links appropriability to firm scale in the manner described earlier. See, for example, in this regard, Nelson and Winter (1982a, p. 279). Further, empirical studies of the patent system have raised doubts as to whether patents actually play the role typically envisaged for them in economic theory or some quite different but still important strategic role or perhaps little role at all. The answers clearly differ across sectors and situations (Levin *et al.*, 1987; Cohen *et al.*, 1999).

Thus, the overall picture is complex. While intellectual property rights certainly have something important to do with appropriability, their role is intermixed with other considerations of an institutional, industry-specific, firm-specific and even transaction-specific character. In our modeling, we have attempted to give due weight to intellectual property rights where they clearly matter a great deal (i.e., in pharmaceuticals), but in general our approach underscores the durable advantages of appropriation based on scale and reputation.

6.2.6 *Demand regimes*

While the research reported in this book was progressing, a rather broad consensus developed that the "demand side" had been neglected in much theorizing about competition, particularly the sort of inter-firm competition known as "rivalry" in strategic management or "Schumpeterian competition" in technology studies. As many scholars seemed to discover more or less in a parallel, standard images of competition grounded in markets for homogeneous products miss a lot of the interesting action. Imperfectly substitutable products, confronting differentiated demand, are pervasive and are important features of business strategies and of industry evolution. Our own investigations participated in the general "awakening" to the "demand side." We would now put "demand regimes" on a rough par with "technological regimes" in the context of understanding industry evolution – though in the still longer run, technology still has primacy as the key source of economic dynamism.

6.3 CONTEXTUAL SPECIFICITIES: A SAMPLER

It is the virtually universal practice of economic modelers to focus on causal mechanisms of an economic nature: What else would *economic* models be about? There is, however, no reason to imagine that observed economic outcomes, at whatever level, emerge from a strictly economic logic. Nature's grand domain is not so neatly partitioned into territories governed by particular logics, and certainly not according to the logics favored in particular academic disciplines. The observed phenomena of industry evolution, for example, are obviously shaped by a variety of causal cross-currents from politics and policy, scientific progress and demographic trends, to name just a few. Nevertheless, when economists seek to explain what happened in a particular industry, they naturally tend to underplay the causes arising from outside that industry and outside the domain of economics, while giving special attention to the ones inside those domains.

It is part of the intellectual program of the history-friendly approach to offer resistance to this general tendency to give too much emphasis to local economic causes. While our models doubtless participate in that general tendency to some extent, we at least illustrate the promise of trying to shift the allocation of emphasis. In this section, we highlight some of the cases where we have explored either the impact of (relatively) exogenous historical developments or the impact of specific contextual factors on the evolution of particular industries.

6.3.1   Computers and semiconductors: the role of exogenous change

As we explained in Chapters 3 and 4, the histories of the US computer and semiconductor industries were marked by a series of technical discontinuities that interrupted regimes of more incremental and cumulative change. If we look for the sources of the discontinuities – including the beginning of the electronic computer industry – we do not find examples of private, far-sighted, profit-motivated investment in R&D. Instead, we find structures of finance, goal-setting and coordination of R&D that derived from an array of government policies. Seeking the rationales for those policies in the United States, we find, primarily though not exclusively, national security concerns. In this sense, key events in the industry histories did not reflect the play of ordinary economic motivation. Attractive opportunities were created and profit-seeking firms responded to them, but the opportunities were created for other reasons and the funding of those opportunities did not derive from success in the marketplace.

In our modeling, we seek to capture the consequences rather than the causes of the discontinuities, placing the disruptive events in the simulated historical sequence at points corresponding to their places in the actual historical sequence. The analysis of Chapter 3 portrays first the capability growth of the transistor-based mainframe firms and the rapid growth of concentration in the industry once a few firms have met the threshold criteria of business customers in the dimensions of performance and cheapness. Then the story changes with the advent of the microprocessor. Some entry occurs in the established market, and the old firms either had to switch technologies or die. At the same time, the microprocessor opens up the new market of personal computers, by virtue of the new cheapness-performance combination it offers – which is more favorable in both dimensions, but particularly in cheapness. A flood of new companies enters that new market. In the period of the transition, the financial dimension of path-dependence is manifested. The previously dominant firm typically manages to weather the change in both technologies and markets, on the basis of the financial strength derived from past performance. Concentration in the mainframe market dips temporarily, while the PC market remains substantially less concentrated than the mainframe market throughout.

6.3.2 *Pharmaceuticals: market fragmentation and patent protection*

Our model of the pharmaceutical industry in Chapter 5 depicts the evolution of the research-based industry that emerged at the beginning of the last century and bloomed after World War II. Two features of that industry largely account for its quite distinctive character. First there is the structure of demand; the product market is divided into submarkets according to disease conditions or "therapeutic categories," and there is very little substitution across markets. Thus, even overwhelming dominance in a particular submarket does not translate into dominance of the market as a whole, though it facilitates it somewhat by way of the financing of R&D spending that can be re-deployed among categories. Complementing the role of market fragmentation are regulation and public policy that profoundly shape this industry. In particular, the patent system provided strong support for the monopoly pricing of drugs that, for the duration of the patent protection, were the best response to the needs of patients in a particular therapeutic category. Studies of the patent system are essentially unanimous and unequivocal in the conclusion that, whatever might be the case elsewhere, patents really matter in the pharmaceutical industry.

These contextual considerations presented distinctive problems for our modeling approach. The observable fragmentation of the market raises the question of whether the fragmentation is an exogenously given fact or is itself a feature of the evolution of the market. In our model, a therapeutic category is posited as a latent demand structure, which then becomes active when the first drug in the category is discovered by some firm. Thus, the list of active TCs evolves endogenously. Another modeling challenge specific to pharmaceuticals is the problem of patent scope. Precisely how far does the patent protection of a given drug extend? Our model accepts that distance metaphor and represents patent scope by a parameter that can be manipulated in the simulations. Aside from these aspects that are specific to pharmaceuticals, the model does incorporate the generic mechanisms described earlier.

Our simulations capture a much-remarked feature of the contemporary pharmaceutical industry, the tendency of follow-on or "me too" drugs to crowd the market space corresponding to a therapeutic category. Combined with the competition from generics that arises when a drug goes off patent, the result is declining prices and profitability at the level of a therapeutic category. While these are considered among the usual benefits of competition, less favorable implications arise by way of the feedback to R&D spending. There are complex countervailing forces at work, including effects on the rate at which new therapeutic categories become active.

6.4 EXPLORING MORE GENERAL QUESTIONS

The history-friendly models presented in Chapters 3, 4 and 5 were purposefully developed with the aim to investigate the factors and the causal mechanisms, that determined the observed patterns of evolution of individual industries. Attention to the industry-specific features, details and contexts is in fact a distinctive characteristic of this modeling approach that we certainly want to emphasize.

But, as discussed in Chapters 1 and 2, once the results of the specific modeling efforts are considered satisfactory, the analysis can proceed further. New models can be developed for different industries' histories. Comparisons between these models can be used to generate new and hopefully more general hypotheses about the factors shaping the interactions between technological change and industrial evolution. Indeed, as just mentioned, the models presented in this book share some generic mechanisms that appear to drive evolution in all the three industries that were the object of our analysis: to repeat, primarily the relationship between a firm's growth and industry structure, the link between innovation and increasing returns and the role of technological and demand regimes. At this stage, we believe, the models can then be used also to address new conceptual and more general questions.

Thus, modified versions of industry-specific history-friendly models can be built and used to investigate conceptual issues, which can be relevant for broader contexts and for different industries. These efforts might provide new insights on key questions in a variety of subfields like industrial economics, economics of innovation, strategy and technology management. Over the past years the models developed in the previous chapters have lent themselves to these purposes in various ways. We provide three examples and briefly discuss some of these efforts in what follows.

6.4.1 Demand regimes, technological regimes and industrial dynamics

A first question that we start to address concerns the role of demand and its interaction with technology – what we called demand and technological regimes – in affecting the dynamics of market structure and the evolution of industries. Using a modified version of the model of the pharmaceutical industry, in Garavaglia *et al.* (2012) we explore more systematically the relationships between technological and demand regimes and generalize the results obtained in Chapter 5. Fragmented markets are always associated with a lower degree of concentration as compared to homogeneous markets, irrespective of the characteristics of the technological regime: Concentration turns out to be low even when the degree of appropriability (e.g. patent duration) is very high and technological progress is strongly cumulative. These conditions generally lead to high concentration. And indeed they do so in pharmaceuticals, but only within submarkets (TCs). High quasi-monopolistic profits in a TC promote the discovery of new submarkets, and over time this leads to lower concentration – as was shown in Chapter 5. Of course, customers who need to purchase drugs in a particular submarket may find little comfort in the fact that the aggregate pharmaceutical market is not concentrated, if the specific drugs they need are offered by only one or two firms. A degree of comfort might perhaps be found in the recognition that their focal submarket might not exist were it not for the fact that firms do compete to open new submarkets, with funding provided from profits earned in previous submarkets.

A further important aspect of the demand regime and of market fragmentation in particular refers to the existence of niches of experimental users, or diverse preferences and needs among potential users, or both. These niches can play a crucial role in favoring the rise and diffusion of radical new technologies that are initially inferior to the dominant ones supported by incumbent firms. This hypothesis was virtually forced on us by our analysis of the evolution of computer technology and industrial structure in Chapter 3. Using a modified version of that model, Malerba *et al.* (2007) examine the case where new firms try to develop a new technology (e.g. microprocessors) and new products (e.g. personal computers) in a market dominated by a small collection of large firms using the older technology. Their analysis of the model indicates that the survival and success of these new firms depends crucially on the existence of fringe markets that the old technology does not serve well, or of experimental users that simply like to experiment with totally new technologies, or both. While established firms initially have little incentive to adopt the new technology, which is initially inferior to the technology they have mastered, new firms generally cannot survive in head-to-head conflict with established firms on the market well served by the latter. The new firms need to find some type of customers or a market that keeps them alive long enough to develop the new technology to a point where it is competitive on the main market. Niche markets, or experimental users, can provide that space. Without these niches, not only may the new firms fail to survive but also the new technology may fail to take off altogether, because incumbents face neither a positive incentive nor a competitive threat promoting adoption. Despite the opportunities afforded by a potentially powerful new technology, the industry will stay stuck with the old.

6.4.2   Entry and the evolution of industries

In a similar vein, a second broad theme that has been explored using modified versions of the models developed in this book concerns the role of entry and first mover advantages. In the models in this book (and as in most evolutionary models) entry has been considered as partly exogenous, meaning that the number of potential entrants is fixed at the outset of the simulations. The number and the fate of actual entrants – those who succeed in entering the market – are then determined by the specific dynamics of the model under consideration.

An immediate question that arises then is: How relevant is the size of the pool of potential entrants for the subsequent evolution of the industry? Most evolutionary models assume exogenous stochastic entry. Standard theories instead typically posit the existence of a pool or queue of potential entrants, the origin of which is unspecified and the size of which is assumed to be infinite or, again, is unspecified (see however Klepper and Sleeper (2005) for a significant improvement in this analysis. See also section 6.5.4 for some further comments on this point). However, in both cases, the size of the queue of the potential entrants might be crucial for determining the actual amount of entry. If the queue is small, entry will be limited irrespective of any other condition. When the pool is very large, "excessive entry" might take place. Thus, an effort toward beginning to disentangle the role played by the size of the queue and "real" entry might be a worthwhile undertaking.

A second set of issues relates to the post-entry performance of entrants. Under what conditions do they survive, grow and perhaps even displace incumbents? The models in this book and the extensions mentioned in the previous section provide answers that are specific to the model and the parameter values that were used. The contributions of Garavaglia *et al.* (2006) and Capone *et al.* (2013a) begin a more systematic analysis, by varying the number of potential entrants, the timing of entry and other conditions relating to the technological and demand regimes.

The simulations produce results that are broadly consistent with many of the stylized facts about entry and survival discussed in Chapter 1. Our results suggest also that the impact of the initial conditions defining the population of potential entrants and the performance of actual entrants are very sensitive to specific sectoral contexts, as summarized by the properties of the technological and demand regimes. For example, in the computer industry models, the initial number of entrants has little effect on subsequent evolution, while in the pharmaceuticals, a larger initial population of firms has long-lasting impacts on market structure and innovation.

In both cases, early movers enjoy an advantage over later entrants (Lieberman and Montgomery, 1988; Suarez and Lanzolla, 2007). The mechanisms behind these outcomes are, however, quite different. In the computer industry, first mover advantages arise from the cumulativeness of knowledge and bandwagon effects. Later entrants have an opportunity to challenge the incumbent monopolist by exploiting a technological discontinuity – a result that is not far from what is typically labeled as competence-destroying innovation (Tushman and Anderson, 1986; Christensen, 1997). In the pharmaceutical industry, the early mover advantage is based on a different mechanism, as we discussed in Chapter 5: the preemption of the technology and demand space by early innovators. More generally, the fate of new entrants is strongly dependent on the degree of market fragmentation: the chances of new firms are severely reduced in homogeneous markets.

One final point concerns the strength of selection and the exit rule. Entry may matter very little if the selection environment is tight and entrants struggle just to survive. New entrants may then lack the resources and time required to do what it takes to mount a real challenge – building a customer base, accumulating knowledge and searching the technology space.

These results, in our view, suggest the promise of further work aimed at building a longer and more solid bridge between fragmented empirical evidence and a dynamic theory of entry that is relevant to multiple industries.

6.4.3   Public policy in dynamic interdependent markets

A third broad topic that has been explored on the basis of history-friendly models is the role and scope of public policy in shaping the dynamics of market structure and industry evolution. A first question addressed was: Under what conditions might antitrust policy curb monopoly power over the evolution of industries characterized by increasing returns (e.g. in R&D, marketing, bandwagon effects, etc.)? In the computer model of Chapter 3 the outcome of these dynamic forces was the rise of "IBM" as a near monopolist in mainframes. Our simulations suggested that, given the assumed structure of dynamic increasing returns, this pattern was nearly inevitable. Using a modified version of that model, Malerba et al. (2001) explored whether antitrust policy can be successful in contrasting the emergence and persistence of monopoly power in such an industrial context. A first result was that if strong, dynamic, increasing returns are present, both through the accumulation of technological capabilities and through customer tendency to stick with a brand, the model suggests that there was little that antitrust intervention could have done to avert the rise of a dominant firm. On the other hand, if customer lock-in effects had been weaker (either by chance or through policies that discouraged efforts of firms to lock in their customers), the simulations say that the situation might have been somewhat different.

A second result from the simulations was an indication that the timing of intervention might be crucial in determining the efficacy of the policy. In general, anti-monopolistic action had only small and transitory effects on the simulated history. The source of this "policy ineffectiveness" result is to be found in the assumption that the evolution of technological capabilities is strongly cumulative. Small initial advantages tend to grow bigger over time and leaders run faster than laggards. Thus, simulations showed that an immediate intervention (breaking the monopolist into two smaller companies as soon as a threshold market share has been reached) succeeds only temporarily: Very quickly, dynamic increasing returns push another firm to dominance. Similarly, a later intervention is unable to curb the forces leading to monopoly. The two new firms resulting from the antitrust intervention are already very large with respect to competitors: as a consequence, one of them will quickly gain the leadership again.

The efficacy of antitrust action is, however, higher in two other cases. First, this policy is more successful in the intermediate stages of the industry life cycle, that is, when many firms have already entered the industry but are still small. The breakup of the largest firm then has the effect of making firms more similar in terms of size and resources, so that the emergence of a monopolist takes more time and concentration remains lower throughout the simulation. Second, in the very latest stages of the life cycle, antitrust action produces a duopoly. Yet, since technological opportunities are almost depleted and diminishing returns to R&D begin to bite, it is much more difficult for one of these new firms to gain a significant advantage vis-à-vis the competitor, and the duopoly remains relatively stable.

These results have been generalized looking also at different types of policy intervention. Using a modified version of the computer and semiconductor industry model of Chapter 4, Malerba *et al.* (2008b) show that alternative forms of intervention (not only antitrust but also support to new entrants, or to the diffusion of knowledge and to open standards) have quite different effects – or no effect at all – on some key policy targets such as market power or rate of technical progress. The results vary as a function of the strength of the forces that create increasing returns and of the magnitude and timing of the arrival of major technological discontinuities.

Lastly, Malerba *et al.* (2008b) examined the effects of various forms of public policy on the supply and on the demand side in vertically and horizontally related industries. The efficacy of the interventions depends on both the existence and strength of increasing returns on the supply and demand side but also – and crucially – on the nature of the feedback reactions governing the coupled dynamics of vertically and horizontally related industries. This analysis shows the possibility of important unintended consequences through the product markets, technological interdependencies and the changing boundaries of firms.

6.5   LOOKING FORWARD

What is the future of history-friendly modeling? We are confident that the approach lives in its own cumulative technological regime, for we have ourselves experienced the benefits of accumulating experience over the several years of this research effort. It is also clear that the opportunity is being renewed from exogenous sources. For example, the computers continue to get faster and the software more user-friendly. More important, the world continues to present interesting new phenomena, and our colleagues in diverse academic disciplines keep coming up with new ideas about how to understand those phenomena. Thus, from where we stand, we can see many attractive, and likely feasible, steps forward. We bring our book to a close by offering our thoughts on these possibilities.

6.5.1   Broadening horizontal scope

Our explorations have touched only a few industries; they are technologically progressive manufacturing industries in which formal R&D plays an important role. There are obviously other industries of that same general description that might be studied with the techniques of history-friendly simulation modeling. The aircraft industry appeals as one particularly intriguing example; medical devices might be another. Or the focus could be on so-called traditional sectors such as textiles or steel, which during their evolution have undergone major changes in the technologies used and the type of competition, and which illustrate the role of somewhat different factors than those examined in this book. Yet it could be argued that it would be a good idea for scholars of industry evolution to lean against the long-standing and widespread overemphasis on manufacturing industry – an overemphasis that, in the advanced countries at least, is further highlighted by the "National income originating" statistics of every passing year. The extension of our methods to examine the evolution of a major service industry would demand considerable effort and creativity. Doubtless it would be a good idea to keep the magnitude of the challenges under control, at least initially: How about hotels? For a mega-challenge, try health care!

6.5.2   Extending the analysis to comparisons across countries

Since the work by Mowery and Nelson (1999), a burgeoning empirical literature has emerged that investigates cross-country differences in innovation, patterns of evolution and industrial leadership in specific industries. For example, since the 1950s the semiconductor and computer industries in Europe and in Japan have followed a quite distinct path of evolution as compared to the United States (which is the focus of our analysis in this book). In Europe, the growth of these industries has been much slower and their international performance has not been so successful. The empirical literature suggests a variety of possible explanations, ranging from (in Europe) low rates of entry of new firms, the weakness of the venture capital sector or the lack of a supportive public policy (i.e. the R&D support by the American military) sustaining the growth of these industries in the early stages. Conversely, it has been suggested that the rapid growth of the semiconductor industry in Japan during the 1970s was related to the vertical integration of the large Japanese companies and to public policies fostering cooperation among existing incumbents (see Okimoto *et al.*, 1984, Malerba, 1985, Langlois and Steinmueller, 1999, Langlois and Steinmueller, 2000). History-friendly models look like good candidates for providing insights into such complex questions, assessing the relative strength of the factors deemed potentially responsible for the diverse evolutionary paths of the same industry in different countries and identifying possible interactions among them.

6.5.3   Explaining the dynamics of catching up and industrial development

In recent years a number of industry case studies have examined the processes of catching up in emerging countries, such as Korea, China, India and Brazil. One general result that emerges from these studies is that catching up is usually sector-specific, that is, for a particular country, it takes place in some industries and not in others (see, e.g., Malerba and Nelson, 2011 and Lee, 2013). These empirical studies provide rich material and a challenging starting point for the creation of history-friendly models aiming at replicating the catching-up process on the basis of alternative assumptions about the factors that affected the rise to sectoral leadership of these countries. For example, how important was the accumulation of technological and marketing capabilities by domestic firms for the catching-up process of Korea in electronics? What is the role played by public support of joint ventures in catching up in China in several manufacturing industries? How should we assess the role of different intellectual property rights policies in fostering or hampering innovation in a developing country, as, for example, in the case of the Indian pharmaceutical industry? How do capabilities, public policies and local demand conditions complement each other in the catching-up process of a country in a specific industry? Landini *et al.* (2016) provide a first step in the direction of these questions.

6.5.4   *Enriching the view of industry evolution*

In the years since we began the research reported in this book, a substantial revolution has occurred in the view of the early life stages of a new industry. In our models, potential entrants appear as a stock, and are differentiated by random effects. By contrast, the burgeoning literature on "spinoffs" now tells us very emphatically that "genealogy matters."[5] The proposition that "genealogy matters" is not the sort of proposition that an *evolutionary* theory should fail to take into account. Here, the "genealogy" in question is not, of course, the biological kind (though there may well be some correlations). It is the genealogy of descent by employment relationship, for which the iconic example is the "semiconductor family tree." Evidently, some important advantages accrue to employees of a strong founder firm in a new industry, when they take on an entrepreneurial role and found new firms in the same industry. Just what those important advantages are remains a subject of dispute, and an object of investigation. The question is obviously a key one in an evolutionary interpretation of the events. A history-friendly investigation of the phenomenon need not await the verdict of empirical research; on the contrary, it could assist the quest for such a verdict. While it may be too early to identify a history-friendly "base case," simulation affords the opportunity to discover the implications of alternative assumptions for a (possibly) counterfactual history – thus assisting in the discovery of the causal relations behind the facts.

---

[5]   Among the young classics of that literature, see Klepper (2002b). See also Agarwal *et al.* (2004), Capone *et al.* (2013b).

A different aspect of depth in the account of industry evolution relates to the question of industry origins. Our models share to a large extent in the prevalent *ex post* approach: A new industry appeared, and then what happened? Regarding what happened afterward, our history-friendly approach is vastly more aligned with the historical and behavioral realities than any alternative that makes any pretense to exploring a formal logic of the problem. Regarding the very complex question of origins, we have not been so "friendly."

Industries, like species, have their pre-emergent evolutionary origins in situations in which they played no role. So, what happened? It should be possible to explore this question in a history-friendly model, focusing in particular on the immediate prehistory of industry birth, and establishing links to the subsequent patterns of industry entry. It appears, from some accounts, that quite a number of stillbirths prefigure the appearance of a viable new industry. These issues are fundamental to the interpretation of the historical record. What, for example, accounts for the often-explosive increase in firm count that attended the birth of what we now see as major new industries? Possible answer: "It's all about selection in the market and selection in the data: You don't see the records of the new industries that died in their infancy. What's left is the record of success, or near-success." Because simulation models can afford a view of the selection mechanisms that edit both the reality and the data, they can play a role in correcting the strong perceptual bias involved in *ex post* assessments.

Finally, it is now widely acknowledged that institutions (broadly defined to include, e.g., standards and regulation, and non-firm organizations such as universities) play a fundamental role in innovation and the evolution of industries. Think of the role of standardization in software or of universities in biotechnology (Nelson, 2007). At the empirical level, the role of institutions and non-firm organizations in innovation and the organization and evolution of industries has been examined in detail for several industries by the literature on sectoral systems (see, e.g., the cases in Malerba,

2004 and Malerba and Adams, 2014). Here again history-friendly models can provide an appropriate methodology for illustrating and explaining the role of these institutions and organizations in industry evolution, and for checking the robustness of the hypotheses suggested by the empirical literature. Murmann (2003) and Murmann and Brenner (2003) are examples of this line of research, exploring the role of universities in the early development of the chemical industry in the United Kingdom and Germany.

6.5.5   Examining firms' strategies in dynamic environments

Last but certainly not least, history-friendly models can assist the analysis of strategic behavior in different industrial contexts. The models discussed in the previous chapters assumed relatively simple and inertial strategic orientations by firms, ranging from the decisions regarding the expenditures and the directions of R&D, the investments in marketing, the pursuit of innovative and imitative strategies, the timing of entry, diversification, vertical integration, etc. As we just mentioned in the first section of this chapter, this conscious choice was determined by a need to preserve transparency in the interpretation of the results of the simulations, but it does not preclude, in principle, further steps toward a more detailed and subtler analysis of the firms' strategic behavior, after the fundamental causal mechanisms driving the model have been identified and probed.

In this respect, a first move forward in this direction is to examine the implications and consequences, for individual firms and for the evolution of the industry as a whole, of alternative strategic rules – in a spirit closely akin to the counterfactual analysis performed in our models. For example, our basic treatment of the diversification of "IBM" followed the historical example; we assumed that the dominant mainframe firm created an independent PC division. The model, however, could certainly be used to explore historically counterfactual situations in which dominant mainframe firms in the computer industry followed a different diversification strategy into the new emerging PC market. What would have happened if entry had instead taken place through the application of existing competencies that proved quite successful in the established market? (We performed this exercise in Malerba *et al.*, 2001). Or, under what alternative structural conditions (regarding, e.g., the properties of the new technology, the behavior of new firms, etc.) could this strategy have been (more) effective? This kind of analysis might be useful at least in providing an understanding of the possible virtues and limits of those strategies in specific contexts, and perhaps in allowing some generalizations, after the key conditions have been identified.

A more ambitious research program would attempt at going deeper inside the firms, making the strategic choices more sophisticated (if needed) and partly endogenous. For example, it would certainly be consistent with the evolutionary view to represent firms as differing in their R&D spending policies, and allowing those policies to adapt slowly to the profitability feedback that the firms receive.

6.5.6   *Going inside the firm: contrasting opportunities*

As we have explained, the behavioral rules that we impute to firms are justified by (1) their responsiveness to real-time information that is both available (in the real-world counterpart) and relevant to the specific question, and (2) the cognitive tractability advantages of adopting rather simple formulations at the micro level, when the real quarry is an understanding of dynamics at the system level. Two quite different lines of intellectual development in recent years suggest correspondingly different approaches to improving the representation of firm behavior in the models.

Over a time span roughly coincident with the research program reported in our book, the "NK modeling approach" has exploded in the literature, particularly in the management literature.[6] To describe

---

[6]   The application of NK methods to management questions was inaugurated by Levinthal (1997). A recent example of the genre is Knudsen *et al.* (2014).

"NK" in its technical details is a task well beyond the scope of the present chapter. Suffice it to say, first, that NK models implement a particular metaphor for boundedly rational decision making, the idea of searching for the highest point on a landscape. When firms fail to locate that optimum, they fail because they face difficulties heuristically related to the "complexity" of the problem they face. In the NK scheme, the vague idea of "complexity" is transformed into a specific idea represented by a parameter that can be manipulated. Thus, simulation experiments can be used to explore such questions as "What happens if the problem faced by firms is more or less complex than our base case assumes?" – as in Rivkin (2001).

In the context of history-friendly modeling, such a question might be posed in relation to the complexity of the technologies employed by the firms.[7] It seems plausible that "complexity" in a technology might well relate directly to its "cumulativeness": Experience with a large number of interrelated component technologies provides a firm with a platform for success in the future. In real-world technological contexts, it is observed that major "system integrators" in complex system industries seem to display both a command of high complexity and the ability to sustain industry dominance over long periods (see Hobday *et al.*, 2000; Orsenigo *et al.*, 2001; Brusoni *et al.*, 2001). The relationship between the complexity and the dominance seems like a tempting subject for a history-friendly analysis.

A contrasting approach to strengthening the representation of firm behavior would be to turn clearly in the "behavioral" direction. Instead of taking guidance from some notional "black box" treatment of the inner workings of firms, we could imagine trying to capture, in quantitative terms, the main thrust of the behavioral rules that firms actually follow. Such an approach would represent a belated attempt to follow the lead of Cyert and March (1992 [1963]). Their studies – in

---

[7]   Note that NK would then be the basis of only a segment of the full model of the firm, replacing our distributions and draw schemes. This would be consistent with an apparent existing trend toward more flexible use of NK as a building block.

particular, the account of department store pricing in Chapter 7 (with C.G. Moore) – still represent something of a high-water mark for this craft (Winter, 1986). More recently, the cause of "behavioral economics" has prospered, and today it is widely seen as the leading alternative to the rational choice theorizing that defines the mainstream. This contemporary behavioralism, however, is strongly focused at the individual level – or even at the neurophysiological level. For qualitative insight into the organizational level, there is much to draw upon in the literatures of organizational behavior, strategic management, business history and the daily press, among other sources. But the true inheritors of the Cyert and March empirical paradigm – inside the firm, empirical, routines-oriented and quantitative – have yet to appear. For a potential practitioner of history-friendly modeling, the challenging message is this: First, someone has to do a good deal more of that kind of empirical research. And then, we can figure out how to reflect it in the model.

6.6   SOME CONCLUDING REFLECTIONS

With these observations on how the research program associated with history-friendly modeling might go forward, we bring this report on the current state of the art to a close. Our purpose in writing this book has been not only to generally inform our colleagues and to enlist some but also to reach out to the broad community of scholars interested in economic dynamics and help to structure what we think may be a common cause.

We believe that there is a broadly shared view in this community that much of the modeling that has been done by economists over the past half century has not provided much insight into how the economy really works. Modeling efforts often aim at elucidating causal mechanisms, and may succeed at least in sharpening intuitions about particular mechanisms. Most of the models, however, have been too stylized to give us an understanding that is relevant to the complicated economic reality we need to know about, where multiple mechanisms are typically in play. To acquire such an understanding, it is necessary to face up to the intrinsic difficulty of the task, rather than assuming it away. We argue that in the future the models we build should be oriented more closely by what we know about particular segments of that complex reality, so as to provide more believable insight into those aspects that we are struggling to understand. This, of course, is the basic commitment of history-friendly modeling. But there is wider recognition today of the need to engage with the complexity of economic reality, even at the price of seeing it in "a much messier, less pretty view" (Krugman, 2009).

We certainly have many companions among economists who, like us, believe that the behavioral theory built into the core of neoclassical economics gets in the way of understanding much of economic behavior, and that a more explicitly behavioral approach, based on observation of how economic actors actually arrive at the actions they make, is needed. The modern behavioral economists obviously are committed to just this point of view. In the social sciences outside of economics, a substantial range of empirically grounded, more "behavioral" approaches are employed, with guidance from diverse disciplinary perspectives. There is, of course, little support there for the specific formulations of neoclassical economics. The portion of this work that deals with behavior in large organizations is particularly relevant to projects like our own, and, in our view at least, to economics generally. We believe, also, that many economists today are in accord with our argument that to understand how an economy works, it often is important to consider influences that fall outside of the generally accepted domain of economics as an independent science. An important class of these involves the impetus to technological advance that comes from fundamental science, or from developments outside the for-profit sector. They also prominently include the factors that influence how markets are structured and how they work. There is a considerable overlap of interest here between evolutionary economists and economists who study economic institutions as "the rules of the game" of economic activity, and how those rules are formed and changed.[8]

In short, we see our development of history-friendly modeling as part of a broader scholarly movement that is moving research on how our economy actually works in the right direction. We are optimistic about the future.

[8]   Among others, see the special issue of the *Journal of Institutional Economics* (December 2014) and in particular the Introduction (Hodgson and Stoelhorst, 2014).

References

Abernathy, W.J., 1978. *The Productivity Dilemma: Roadblock to Innovation in the Automobile Industry.* Baltimore, MD: Johns Hopkins Press.

Abernathy, W.J., and Clark, K.B., 1985. Innovation: Mapping the Winds of Creative Destruction, *Research Policy* **14**: 3–22.

Abernathy, W.J., and Utterback, J., 1978. Patterns of Innovation in Industry, *Technological Review* **80**: 41–47.

Acs, Z.J., and Audretsch, D.B., 1989. Small-Firm in U.S. Manufacturing, *Economica* **56**: 255–265.

Acs, Z.J., and Audretsch, D.B., 1990. *Innovation and Small Firms.* Cambridge, MA: MIT Press.

Agarwal, R., Echambadi, R., Franco, A.M., and Sarkar, M.B., 2004. Knowledge Transfer Through Inheritance: Spin-Out Generation, Development and Survival, *Academy of Management Journal* **47**(4): 501–522.

Agarwal, R., and Gort, M., 1996. The Evolution of Markets and Entry, Exit and Survival of Firms, *Review of Economics and Statistics* **78**(3): 489–498.

Aghion, P., and Howitt, P., 1992. A Model of Growth through Creative Destruction, *Econometrica* **60**(2): 323–351.

Andersen, E.S., 1994. *Evolutionary Economics: Post-Schumpeterian Contributions.* London: Pinter Publisher.

Arora, A., Fosfuri, A., and Gambardella, A., 2001. *Markets for Technology.* Cambridge, MA: MIT Press.

Arora, A., Landau, R., and Rosenberg, N. (eds.), 1998. *Dynamics of Long-Run Growth in the Chemical Industry.* New York, NY: John Wiley & Sons.

Arrow, K.J., 1962. Economic Welfare and the Allocation of Resources for Invention, in Nelson, R. (ed.) *The Rate and Direction of Inventive Activity: Economic and Social Factors.* Princeton, NJ: Princeton University Press, pp. 609–625.

Arthur, W.B., 1989. Competing Technologies, Increasing Returns and Lock-In by Historical Events, *The Economic Journal* **99**(394): 116–131.

Baldwin, J., and Gorecki, P., 1998. *The Dynamics of Industrial Competition.* Cambridge: Cambridge University Press.

Barnett, W.P., and Glenn, C.R., 1995. Modeling Internal Organizational Change, in Hagan, J. (ed.) *Annual Review of Sociology*. Vol. **21**. Palo Alto, CA: Annual Reviews, pp. 217–236.

Bartelsman, E., and Doms, M., 2000. Understanding Productivity: Lessons from Longitudinal Microdata, *Journal of Economic Literature* **38**(3): 569–594.

Bartelsman, E., Scarpetta, S., and Schivardi, F., 2005. Comparative Analysis of Firm Demographics and Survival: Evidence from Micro-Level Sources in OECD Countries, *Industrial and Corporate Change* **14**: 365–391.

Becker, M.C., 2008. *Handbook of Organizational Routines*. Cheltenham: Edward Elgar.

Becker, M., Knudsen, T., and Swedberg, R. 2011. *The Entrepreneur: Classic Texts by Joseph A. Schumpeter*. Stanford, CA: Stanford University Press.

Beesley, M.E., and Hamilton, R.T., 1984. Small Firms, Seedbed Role and the Concept of Turbulence, *Journal of Industrial Economics* **33**: 217–232.

Bloom, N., and Van Reenen, J., 2010. Human Resource Management and Productivity, NBER Working Papers 16019, National Bureau of Economic Research, Cambridge, MA.

Boero, R., and Squazzoni, F., 2005. Does Empirical Embeddedness Matter? Methodological Issues of Agent-Based Models for Analytical Social Science, *Journal of Artificial Societies and Simulation* **8**(4): 6.

Boslaugh, S., 2008. *Encyclopedia of Epidemiology*. Thousand Oaks, CA: Sage.

Bottazzi, G., Dosi, G., Jacoby, N., Secchi, A., and Tamagni, F., 2010. Corporate Performances and Market Selection: Some Comparative Evidence, *Industrial and Corporate Change* **19**(6): 1953–1996.

Bottazzi, G., Dosi, G., Lippi, M., Pammolli, F., and Riccaboni, M., 2001. Innovation and Corporate Growth in the Evolution of the Drug Industry, *International Journal of Industrial Organization* **19**(7): 1161–1187.

Bottazzi, G., and Secchi, A., 2006. Explaining the Distribution of Firms Growth Rates, *RAND Journal of Economics* **37**: 234–263.

Breschi, S., Malerba, F., and Orsenigo, L., 2000. Technological Regimes and Schumpeterian Patterns of Innovation, *Economic Journal* **110**: 388–410.

Bresnahan, T.F., and Greenstein, S., 1999. Technological Competition and the Structure of the Computer Industry, *Journal of Industrial Economics* **47**: 1–40.

Bresnahan, T.F., Greenstein, S., and Henderson, R., 2012. Schumpeterian Competition and Diseconomies of Scope: Illustrations from the History of Microsoft and IBM, in Lerner, J., and Stern, S. (eds.) *The Rate and Direction of Inventive Activity Revisited*. NBER University of Chicago Press, pp. 203–271.

Bresnahan, T.F., and Malerba, F., 1999. Industrial Dynamics and the Evolution of Firms' and Nations' Competitive Capabilities in the World Computer Industry, in Mowery, D., and Nelson, R. (eds.) *The Sources of Industrial Leadership: Studies of Seven Industries*. New York: Cambridge University Press, pp. 79–132.

Brusoni, S., Cefis, E., and Orsenigo, L., 2006. Innovate or Die? A Critical Review of the Literature on Innovation and Performance, KITeS Working Papers 179, KITeS, Centre for Knowledge, Internationalization and Technology Studies, Universita' Bocconi, Milano, Italy, revised September 2006.

Brusoni, S., Prencipe, A., and Pavitt, K., 2001. Knowledge Specialization, Organizational Coupling, and the Boundaries of the Firm: Why Do Firms Know More Than They Make? *Administrative Science Quarterly* **46**(4): 597–621.

Cabral, L.M.B., and Mata, J., 2003. On the Evolution of the Firm Size Distribution: Facts and Theory, *American Economic Review* **93**(4): 1075–1090.

Capone, G., Malerba, F., and Orsenigo, L., 2013a. Are Switching Costs Advantages Effective in Creating First-Mover Advantages? The Moderating Role of Demand and Technological Regimes, *Long Range Planning* **46**(S 4–5): 348–368.

Capone, G., Malerba, F., and Orsenigo, L., 2013b. Spinoffs in Different Contexts: Theory and Empirical Evidence, *Academy of Management Proceedings* **2013**(1): 16387.

Chandler, A.D., 1990. *Scale and Scope: The Dynamics of Modern Capitalism*. Cambridge, MA: The Belknap Press of Harvard University Press.

Chandler, A.D., 2005a. *Shaping the Industrial Century: The Remarkable Story of the Modern Chemical and Pharmaceutical Industries*. Cambridge, MA: Harvard University Press.

Chandler, A.D., 2005b. *Inventing the Electronic Century: The Epic Story of the Consumer Electronics and Computer Industries*. Cambridge, MA: Harvard University Press.

Chetley, A., 1990. *A Healthy Business? World Health and the Pharmaceutical Industry*. London: Zed Books.

Chien, R.I., 1979. *Issues in Pharmaceutical Economics*. Lexington, MA: Lexington Books.

Chong, J., Crowell, H., and Kend, S., 2003. *Merck: Refocusing Research and Development*. Claremont, CA: Blaisdell Consulting, Pomona College.

Christensen, C.M., 1997. *The Innovators Dilemma: When New Technologies Cause Great Firms to Fail*. Boston, MA: Harvard Business School Press.

Christensen, C.M., and Rosenbloom, R., 1994a. Explaining the Attacker's Advantage: Technological Paradigms, Organizational Dynamics, and the Value of Network, *Research Policy* **24**: 233–257.

Christensen, C.M., and Rosenbloom, R., 1994b. Technological Discontinuities, Organizational Capabilities and Strategic Commitments, *Industrial and Corporate Change* **3**: 655–686.

Clark, K.B., 1985. The Interaction of Design Hierarchies and Market Concepts in Technological Evolution, *Research Policy* 14: 235–251.

Cohen, W.M., 2011. Fifty Years of Empirical Studies of Innovative Activity and Performance, in Hall, B., and Rosenberg, N. (eds.) *Handbook of Economics of Innovation*. Amsterdam: Elsevier, pp.129–213.

Cohen, W.M., and Levin, R.C., 1989. Empirical Studies of Innovation and Market Structure, in Schmalensee, R., and Willig, R. (eds.) *Handbook of Industrial Organisation*. Amsterdam: North Holland, pp. 1059–1108.

Cohen, W.M., Nelson, R., and Walsh, J., 1999. *Protecting Their Intellectual Assets: Appropriability Conditions and Why U.S. Manufacturing Firms Patent (or Not)*. Pittsburgh: Carnegie Mellon University.

Comanor, W.S., 1986. The Political Economy of the Pharmaceutical Industry, *Journal of Economic Literature* 24: 1178–1217.

Cyert, R.M., and March, J.G., 1963. *A Behavioral Theory of the Firm (1992 Edition)*. Malden, MA: Blackwell.

Darwin, C., 1859. *On the Origins of Species by Means of Natural Selection (1872 Edition)*. London: John Murray.

David, P.A., 1985. Clio and the Economics of QWERTY, *American Economic Review* 75(2): 332–337.

DiMasi, J.A., Hansen, R.W., and Grabowski, H.G., 2003. The Price of Innovation: New Estimates of Drug Development Costs, *Journal of Health Economics* 22: 151–185.

Dorfman, N., 1987. *Innovation and Market Structure: Lessons from the Computer and Semiconductor Industries*. Cambridge, MA: Ballinger.

Dosi, G., 1982. Technological Paradigms and Technological Trajectories, *Research Policy* 11: 147–162.

Dosi, G., 1984. *Technical Change and Industrial Transformation*. London: Macmillan.

Dosi, G., 2007. Statistical Regularities in the Evolution of Industries: A Guide through Some Evidence and Challenges for the Theory, in Brusoni, S., and Malerba, F. (eds.) *Perspectives on Innovation*. Cambridge: Cambridge University Press, pp. 155–186.

Dosi, G., Fagiolo, G., and Roventini, A., 2010. Schumpeter Meeting Keynes: A Policy-Friendly Model of Endogenous Growth and Business Cycles, *Journal of Economic Dynamics and Control* 34(9): 1748–1767.

Dosi, G., and Marengo, L., 1993. Some Elements of an Evolutionary Theory of Organizational Competence, in England, R.W. (ed.) *Evolutionary Concepts on Contemporary Economics*. Ann Arbor, MI: University of Michigan Press, pp. 157–178.

Dosi, G., Marsili, O., Orsenigo, L., and Salvatore, R., 1995. Learning, Market Selection and the Evolution of Industrial Structures, *Small Business Economics* 7(6): 411–436.

Dosi, G., and Nelson, R., 1995. An Introduction to Evolutionary Theories in Economics, *Journal of Evolutionary Economics* 4: 153–172.

Dosi, G., Nelson, R., and Winter, S. (eds.), 2000. *The Nature and Dynamics of Organizational Capabilities*. Oxford: Oxford University Press.

Dunne, T., Roberts, M. J., and Samuelson, L., 1988. Patterns of Firm Entry and Exit in US Manufacturing Industry, *Rand Journal of Economics* 19(4): 495–515.

Ericson, R., and Pakes, A., 1995. Markov-Perfect Industry Dynamics: A Framework for Empirical Work, *Review of Economic Studies* 62: 53–82.

Fisher, R.A., 1958. *The Genetical Theory of Natural Selection*. Mineola, NY: Dover.

Flamm, K., 1988. *Creating the Computer*. Washington DC: The Brookings Institution.

Fontana, R., Guerzoni, M., and Nuvolari, A., 2008. Habakkuk Revisited: A History Friendly Model of American and British Technology in the Nineteenth Century, Jena Economic Research Papers 64, Friedrich Schiller University and Max Plank Institute of Economics, Jena.

Foster, J., 1987. *Evolutionary Macroeconomics*. London: Allen and Unwin.

Fransman, M., 1994. Different Folks, Different Strokes – How IBM, AT&T and NEC Segment to Compete, *Business Strategy Review* 5(3): 1–20.

Freeman, C., Clark, J., and Soete, L., 1982. *Unemployment and Technical Innovation: A Study of Long Waves in Economic Development*. London: Frances Pinter.

Friedman, M., 1953. *The Methodology of Positive Economics*. Chicago: University of Chicago Press.

Galambos, L., and Sewell, J.E., 1996. *Network of Innovators. Vaccine Development at Merck, Sharp & Dohme and Mulfor, 1895–1995*. Cambridge: Cambridge University Press.

Galambos, L., and Sturchio, J., 1996. The Pharmaceutical Industry in the Twentieth Century: A Reappraisal of the Sources of Innovation, *History and Technology* 13(2): 83–100.

Gambardella, A., 1995. *Science and Innovation in the US Pharmaceutical Industry*. Cambridge: Cambridge University Press.

Garavaglia, C., Malerba, F., and Orsenigo, L., 2006. Entry, Market Structure and Innovation in a History-Friendly Model of the Evolution of the Pharmaceutical Industry, in Dosi, G., and Mazzucato, M. (eds.) *Knowledge Accumulation and*

Industry Evolution: The Case of Pharma-Biotech. Cambridge: Cambridge University Press, pp. 234–266.

Garavaglia, C., Malerba, F., Orsenigo, L., and Pezzoni, M., 2012. Technological Regimes and Demand Structure in the Evolution of the Pharmaceutical Industry, *Journal of Evolutionary Economics* **22**(4): 677–709.

Garavaglia, C., Malerba, F., Orsenigo, L., and Pezzoni, M., 2013. A Simulation Model of the Evolution of the Pharmaceutical Industry: A History Friendly Model, *Journal of Artificial Societies and Social Simulation* **16**(4): 5.

Garavaglia, C., Malerba, F., Orsenigo, F., and Pezzoni, M., 2014. Innovation and Market Structure in Pharmaceuticals: An Econometric Analysis on Simulated Data, *Journal of Economics and Statistics* **234**(2–3): 274–298, April.

Geroski, P.A., 1995. What do We Know About Entry?, *International Journal of Industrial Organization* **13**(4): 421–440.

Geroski, P.A., 2000. The Growth of Firms in Theory and Practice: Competence, Governance and Entrepreneurship, in Foss, N., and Mahnke, V. (eds.) *Competence, Governance and Entrepreneurship.* Oxford: Oxford University Press, pp. 168–186.

Gort, M., and Klepper S., 1982. Time Paths in the Diffusion of Product Innovations, *The Economic Journal* **9**: 630–653.

Grabowski, H., and Vernon, J., 1977. Consumer Protection Regulation in Ethical Drugs, *American Economic Review* **67**(1): 359–364.

Grabowski, H., and Vernon, J., 1994a. Innovation and Structural Change in Pharmaceuticals and Biotechnology, *Industrial and Corporate Change* **3**(2): 435–449.

Grazzini, J., Richiardi, M.G., and Sella, L., 2013. Analysis of Agent-Based Models, Working Paper no. 135, Labor – Laboratorio R. Revelli, Turin.

Greenstein, S., 2010. The Emergence of the Internet: Collective Invention and Wild Ducks, *Industrial and Corporate Change* **19**(5): 1521–1562.

Griliches, Z., and Mairesse, J., 1997. Production Function: The Search for Identification, in Strom, S. (ed.) *Econometrics and Economic Theory in the Twentieth Century: The Ragnar Frisch Centennial Symposium*, Econometric Society Monograph Series. Cambridge: Cambridge University Press, pp. 169–204.

Heaton, C.A., 1994. *The Chemical Industry.* New York, NY: Springer.

Helfat, C.E., 2003. The Dynamic Resource-Based View: Capability Life Cycles, *Strategic Management Journal* **24**(10): 997–1010.

Helfat, C.E., and Lieberman, M.B., 2002. The Birth of Capabilities: Market Entry and the Importance of Pre-history, *Industrial and Corporate Change* **11**(4): 725–760.

Henderson, R., and Clark K.B., 1990. Architectural Innovation: The Reconfiguration of Existing Product, Technologies and the Failure of Established Firms, *Administrative Sciences Quarterly* **35**: 9–30.

Henderson, R., Orsenigo, L., and Pisano, G.P., 1999. The Pharmaceutical Industry and the Revolution in Molecular Biology: Exploring the Interactions between Scientific, Institutional and Organizational Change, in Mowery, D.C., and Nelson, R. (eds.) *The Sources of Industrial Leadership: Studies of Seven Industries*, Cambridge: Cambridge University Press, pp. 267–311.

Hobday, M., Howard, R., and Tidd, J., 2000. Innovation in Complex Products and Systems, *Research Policy* **29**(7–8): 793–804.

Hodgson, J., and Stoelhorst, J.W., 2014. Introduction to the Special Issue on the Future of Institutional and Evolutionary Economics, *Journal of Institutional Economics* **10**(4): 513–540.

Holland, J.H., 1998. *Emergence: From Chaos to Order*. Boston, MA: Addison-Wesley.

Jacobides, M., and Winter, S., 2005. The Co-Evolution of Capabilities and Transaction Costs: Explaining the Institutional Structure of Production, *Strategic Management Journal* **26**: 395–413.

Jacobides M., and Winter, S., 2012. Capabilities: Structure, Agency and Evolution, *Organization Science* **23**(5): 1365–1381.

Jacobides, M., Winter, S., and Kassberger, S., 2012. The Dynamics of Profit, Wealth and Competitive Advantage, *Strategic Management Journal* **22**(12): 1384–1410.

Jovanovic, B., 1982. Selection and the Evolution of Industry, *Econometrica* **50**(2): 649–670.

Kim, C.W., and Lee, K., 2003. Innovation, Technological Regimes and Organizational Selection in Industry Evolution: A "History Friendly Model" of the DRAM Industry, *Industrial and Corporate Change* **12**(6): 1195–1221.

Kitcher, P., 2003. Darwin's Achievement, in Kitcher, P. (ed.) *In Mendel's Mirror*. Oxford University Press, pp. 45–93.

Klein, B., 1977. *Dynamic Economics*. Cambridge, MA: Harvard University Press.

Klepper, S., 1996. Entry, Exit, Growth, and Innovation over the Product Life Cycle, *American Economic Review* **86**: 562–583.

Klepper, S., 1997. Industry Life Cycles, *Industrial and Corporate Change* **6**(8): 145–181.

Klepper, S., 2002a. Firm Survival and the Evolution of Oligopoly, *Rand Journal of Economics* **33**(1): 37–61.

Klepper, S., 2002b. The Capabilities of New Firms and the Evolution of the US Automobile Industry, *Industrial and Corporate Change* **11**: 645–666.

Klepper, S., and Graddy, E., 1990. The Evolution of New Industries and the Determinants of Market Structure, *The RAND Journal of Economics* **21**(1): 27–44.

Klepper, S., and Simons, K., 2000a. Dominance by Birthright: Entry of Prior Radio Producers and Competitive Ramifications in the US Television Receiver Industry, *Strategic Management Journal* **21**: 997–1016.

Klepper, S., and Simons, K., 2000b. The Making of an Oligopoly: Firm Survival and Technological Change in the Evolution of US Tire Industry, *Journal of Political Economy* **108**: 728–760.

Klepper, S., and Sleeper, S., 2005. Entry by Spinoffs, *Management Science* **51**(8): 1291–1306.

Klepper, S., and Thompson, P., 2006. Submarket and the Evolution of Market Structure, *RAND Journal of Economics* **37**: 861–886.

Klette, T.J., and Kortum S., 2004. Innovating Firms and Aggregate Innovation, *Journal of Political Economy* **112**(5): 986–1018.

Klevorick, A., Levin, R., Nelson, R., and Winter, S., 1995. On the Sources and Significance of Interindustry Differences in Technological Opportunities, *Research Policy* **24**(2): 185–205.

Knudsen, T., Levinthal, D.A., and Winter, S.G., 2014. Hidden but in Plain Sight: The Role of Scale Adjustment in Industry Dynamics, *Strategic Management Journal* **35**(11): 1569–1584.

Kricks, G.A., 1995. Vertical Integration in the Mainframe Computer Industry: A Transaction Cost Interpretation, *Journal of Economic Behavior and Organization* **26**(1): 75–91.

Krugman, P., 2009. *A Few Notes on My Magazine Article. The Conscience of a Liberal.* New York: New York Times.

Lancaster, K.J., 1966. A New Approach to Consumer Theory, *Journal of Political Economy* **74**(2): 132–157.

Landini, F., Lee, K., and Malerba, F., 2016. A History-Friendly Model of the Successive Changes in Industrial Leadership and the Catch-up by Latecomers, *Research Policy*, Forthcoming.

Langlois, R.N., 1990. Creating External Capabilities: Innovation and Vertical Disintegration in the Microcomputer Industry, *Business and Economic History* **19**: 93–102.

Langlois, R.N., and Robertson, P.L., 1995. *Firms, Markets and Economic Change: A Dynamic Theory of Business Institutions.* London, Routledge.

Langlois, R.N., and Steinmueller, E., 1999. The Evolution of Competitive Advantages in the Worldwide Semiconductor Industry 1947–1996, in Mowery, D., and Nelson,

R., (eds.) *Sources of Industrial Leadership*. Cambridge: Cambridge University Press.

Langlois, R.N., and Steinmueller, W.E., 2000. Strategy and Circumstance: The Response of American Firms to Japanese Competition in Semiconductors, 1980–1995, *Strategic Management Journal* 21(10–11): 1163–1173.

Lee, K., 2013. *Schumpeterian Analyses of Economic Catch Up*. Cambridge: Cambridge University Press.

Levin, R.C., Cohen, W.M., and Mowery, D.C., 1985. R&D Appropriability, Opportunity and Market Structure: New Evidence on Some Schumpeterian Hypotheses, *American Economic Review* 75(2): 20–24.

Levin, R.C., Klevorick, A., Nelson, R., and Winter, S.G., 1987. Appropriating the Returns from Industrial Research and Development, *Brookings Papers on Economic Activity* No. 3: 783–820.

Levinthal, D., 1997. Adaptation on Rugged Landscapes, *Management Science* 43: 934–950.

Lichtenberg, F.R., 2006. The Impact of New Laboratory Procedures and Other Medical Innovations on the Health of Americans, 1990–2003: Evidence from Longitudinal, Disease-Level Data, NBER Working Papers 12120, National Bureau of Economic Research, Cambridge, MA.

Lieberman, M.B., and Montgomery, D.B., 1988. First-Mover Advantages, *Strategic Management Journal* 9: 41–58.

Lomi, A., and Larsen, E.R., 2001. *Dynamics of Organizations: Computational Modelling and Organization Theories*. Cambridge, MA: MIT Press.

Luttmer, E.F.P., 2007. Does the Minimum Wage Cause Inefficient Rationing?, *The B.E. Journal of Economic Analysis & Policy* 7(1): 1–42.

Malerba, F., 1985. *The Semiconductor Business*. Madison, WI and London: The University of Wisconsin Press and Frances Pinter.

Malerba, F., 2004. *Sectoral Systems of Innovation*. Cambridge: Cambridge University Press.

Malerba, F., and Adams P., 2014. Sectoral Systems of Innovation, in Dodgson, M., Gann, D., and Phillips, N. (eds.) *The Oxford Handbook of Innovation Management*. Oxford: Oxford University Press, pp.183–203.

Malerba, F., and Brusoni, S. (eds.), 2008. *Perspectives on Innovation*. Cambridge: Cambridge University Press.

Malerba, F., and Nelson, R., 2011. Learning and Catching Up in Different Sectoral Systems. Evidence from Six Industries, *Industrial and Corporate Change* 20(6): 1645–1675.

Malerba, F., Nelson, R., Orsenigo, L., and Winter S., 1999. History Friendly Models of Industry Evolution: The Computer Industry, *Industrial and Corporate Change* **1**: 3–41.

Malerba, F., Nelson, R., Orsenigo, L., and Winter, S., 2001b. Product Diversification in a History-Friendly Model of the Evolution of the Computer Industry, in Lomi, A., and Larsen, E.R. (eds.) *Dynamics of Organizations: Computational Modelling and Organization Theories*. Cambridge, MA: MIT Press.

Malerba, F., Nelson, R., Orsenigo, L., and Winter, S., 2007. Demand, Innovation, and the Dynamics of Market Structure: The Role of Experimental Users and Diverse Preferences, *Journal of Evolutionary Economics* **17**: 371–399.

Malerba, F., Nelson, R., Orsenigo, L., and Winter, S., 2008a. Vertical Integration and Disintegration of Computer Firms: A History-Friendly Model of the Co-Evolution of the Computer and Semiconductor Industries, *Industrial and Corporate Change* **17**: 197–231.

Malerba, F., Nelson, R., Orsenigo, L., and Winter, S., 2008b. Public Policies and Changing Boundaries of Firms in a "History Friendly" Model of the Co-Evolution of the Computer and Semiconductor Industries, *Journal of Economic Behaviour and Organization* **67**: 355–380.

Malerba, F., and Orsenigo, L., 1995. Schumpeterian Patterns of Innovation, *Cambridge Journal of Economics* **19**(1): 47–65.

Malerba, F., and Orsenigo, L., 1997. Technological Regimes and Sectoral Patterns of Innovative Activities, *Industrial and Corporate Change* **6**(1): 83–118.

Malerba, F., and Orsenigo, L., 2002. Innovation and Market Structure in the Dynamics of the Pharmaceutical Industry and Biotechnology: Towards a History Friendly Model, *Industrial and Corporate Change* **11**(4): 667–703.

Malerba, F., and Orsenigo, L., 2010. User-Producer Relations, Innovation and the Evolution of Market Structures under Alternative Contractual Regimes, *Structural Change and Economic Dynamics* **21**(1): 26–40.

Malerba, F., Nelson, R., Orsenigo L., and Winter, S., 2001a. Competition and Industrial Policy in a History Friendly Model of the Evolution of the Computer Industry, *International Journal of Industrial Organization* **19**: 635–664.

Malerba, F., and Yoon, M., 2011. Modelling the Evolution of Firm Boundaries: A History Friendly Model of the Emergence of the Fabless Ecosystem, Working Paper, Milan and Seoul.

Marshall, A., 1890. *Principles of Economics (1920 Edition)*. New York, NY: Macmillan.

Marsili, O., 2001. *The Anatomy and Evolution of Industries*. Cheltenham: Edward Elgar.

Matraves, C., 1999. Market Structure, R&D and Advertising in the Pharmaceutical Industry, *Journal of Industrial Economics* **47**(2): 169–194.

Metcalfe, S., 1998. *Evolutionary Economics and Creative Destruction*. London: Routledge.

Miller, R., Hobday, M., Leroux Demers, T., and Olleros, X., 1995. Innovation in Complex Systems: The Case of Flight Simulation, *Industrial and Corporate Change* **4**(2): 363–400.

Mirowski, P., 1989. *More Heat than Light: Economics as Social Physics, Physics as Nature's Economics*. Cambridge: Cambridge University Press.

Moore, G.E., 1995. Lithography and the Future of Moore's Law, *Proceedings SPIE*, Volume **2440**, pp. 2–17.

Mowery, D., and Nelson, R. (eds.), 1999. *Sources of Industrial Leadership*. Cambridge: Cambridge University Press.

Mowery, D.C., and Rosenberg, N., 1982a. The Influence of Market Demand upon Innovation: A Critical Review of Some Recent Empirical Studies, in Rosenberg, N. (ed.), *Inside the Black Box: Technology and Economics*. Cambridge: Cambridge University Press, pp. 193–242.

Mowery, D.C., and Rosenberg, N., 1982b. Technical change in the commercial aircraft industry 1925–1975, in Rosenberg, N. (ed.), *Inside the Black Box: Technology and Economics*. Cambridge: Cambridge University Press, pp. 163–178.

Mowery, D.C., and Rosenberg, N. (1998). *Paths of Innovation: Technological Change in 20th Century America*. Cambridge, UK: Cambridge University Press.

Murmann, P., 2003. *Knowledge and competitive advantages: the coevolution of firms, technology and national institutions*. Cambridge: Cambridge University Press.

Murmann, J.P., and Brenner, T., 2003. The Use of Simulations in Developing Robust Knowledge about Causal Processes: Methodological Considerations and an Application to Industrial Evolution, Papers on Economics and Evolution #0303, Max-Planck-Institute of Economics, Jena.

Nelson, R., 1961. Uncertainty, Learning, and the Economics of Parallel Research and Development, *Review of Economics and Statistics* **43**: 351–368.

Nelson, R., 1968. A Diffusion Model of International Productivity Differences in Manufacturing Industry, *American Economic Review* **58**(5): 1219–1248.

Nelson, R., 1991b. Why Do Firms Differ and How Does it Matter?, *Strategic Management Journal* **12**: 61–64.

Nelson, R., 2007. What Enables Rapid Economic Progress: What Are the Needed Institutions?, *Research Policy* **37**: 1–11.

Nelson, R., 2008. Economic Development from the Perspective of Evolutionary Economic Theory, *Oxford Development Studies* **36**(1): 9–21.

Nelson, R., and Winter, S., 1977. Simulation of Schumpeterian Competition, *American Economic Review* **67**(1): 271–276.

Nelson, R., and Winter, S., 1982a. *An Evolutionary Theory of Economic Change*. Cambridge, MA: The Belknap Press of Harvard University Press.

Nelson, R., and Winter, S., 1982b. The Schumpeterian Trade-Off Revisited, *American Economic Review* **72**: 114–132.

Nelson, R., and Winter, S., 2002. Evolutionary Theorizing in Economics, *Journal of Economic Perspectives* **16**(2): 23–46.

Nelson, R., Winter, S., and Schuette, H.L., 1976. Technical Change in an Evolutionary Model, *Quarterly Journal of Economics* **90**(1): 90–118.

Nightingale, P., and Mahdi, S., 2006. The Evolution of the Pharmaceutical Innovation, in Mazzucato, M., and Dosi, G. (eds.) *Knowledge Accumulation and Industry Evolution: The Case of Pharma-Biotech*. Cambridge University Press, pp. 73–111.

Nightingale, P., and Martin, P., 2004. The Myth of Biotech Revolution, *Trends in Biotechnology* **22**(11): 564–569.

Okimoto, D.I., Sugano, T., and Weinstein, F. B. (eds.), 1984. *Competitive Edge: The Semiconductor Industry in the U.S. and Japan*. Stanford: Stanford University Press.

Oltra, V., and Saint Jean, M., 2005. The Dynamics of Environmental Innovations: Three Stylized Trajectories of Clean Technology, *Economics of Innovation and New Technology* **14**(3): 189–212.

Orsenigo, L., 1989. *The Emergence of Biotechnology*. London: Frances Pinter.

Orsenigo, L., Pammolli F., and Riccaboni M., 2001. Technological Change and Network Dynamics, *Research Policy* **30**(3): 485–508.

Pammolli, F., 1996. *Innovazione, Concorrenza a Strategie di Sviluppo nell'Industria Farmaceutica*. Milan: Guerini Scientifica.

Pammolli, F., Riccaboni, M., and Magazzini, L., 2011. The Productivity Crisis in the Pharmaceutical R&D, *Nature Reviews Drug Discovery* **10**(6): 428–438.

Pavitt, K., 1984. Sectoral Patterns of Technical Change: Towards a Taxonomy and a Theory, *Research Policy* **13**(6): 343–373.

Pavitt, K., Robson, M., and Townsend, J., 1987. Technological Accumulation, Diversification and Organization in UK Companies, 1945–1983, *Management Science* **35**(1): 81–99.

Peltzman, S., 1973. *Regulation of the Pharmaceutical Innovation: The 1962 Amendments*. Washington, DC: American Enterprise Institute for Public Policy.

Phillips, A., 1971. *Technology and Market Structure: A Study of the Aircraft Industry*. Lexington, MA: DC Heath.

Pisano, G., 1996. *The Development Factory: Unlocking the Potential of Process Innovation*. Boston, MA: Harvard Business School Press.

Richiardi, M., Leombruni, R., Saam, N., and Sonnessa, M., 2006. A Common Protocol for Agent-Based Social Simulation, *Journal of Artificial Societies and Social Simulation* **9**(1): 15.

Rivkin, J., 2001. Reproducing Knowledge: Replication without Imitation at Moderate Complexity, *Organization Science* **12**: 274–293.

Rosenberg, N., 1976. *Perspectives on Technology*. Cambridge: Cambridge University Press.

Rosenberg, N., 1982. *Inside the Black Box: Technology and Economics*. Cambridge: Cambridge University Press.

Schumpeter, J.A., 1934. *The Theory of Economic Development: An Inquiry into Profits, Capital, Credit Interest and the Business Cycle* (English edition, German original 1911). Oxford University Press.

Schumpeter, J.A., 1950[1942]. *Capitalism, Socialism and Democracy*. New York, NY: Harper and Row.

Silverberg, G., Dosi G., and Orsenigo, L., 1988. Innovation, Diversity and Diffusion: A Self-Organization Model, *The Economic Journal* **98**(393): 1032–1054.

Simon, H.A., 1955. A Behavioral Model of Rational Choice, *The Quarterly Journal of Economics* **69**(1): 99–118.

Simon, H.A., 1976. *The Sciences of the Artificial*. Cambridge, MA: MIT Press.

Simon, H.A., 1991. Organizations and Markets, *Journal of Economic Perspectives* **5**(2): 25–44.

Solow, R.M., 1957. Technical Change and the Aggregate Production Function, *Review of Economics and Statistics* **39**(3): 312–320.

Stigler, G.J., 1951. The Division of Labor is Limited by the Extent of the Market, *Journal of Political Economy* **59**: 185–193.

Suarez, F., and Lanzolla, G., 2007. The Role of Environmental Dynamics in Building a First Mover Advantage Theory, *Academy of Management Review* **32**: 377–392.

Sutton, J., 1997. Gibrat's Legacy, *Journal of Economic Literature* **35**: 40–59.

Sutton, J., 1998. *Technology and Market Structure: Theory and History*. Cambridge, MA: MIT Press.

Sutton, J., 2001. The Variance of Firm Growth Rates: The "Scaling" Puzzle, Economics of Industry EI/27, Suntory and Toyota International Centres for

Economics and Related Disciplines, London School of Economics and Political Science, London.

Syverson, C., 2011. What Determines Productivity?, *Journal of Economic Literature* **49**(2): 326–365.

Teece, D.J., 1986. Profiting from Technological Innovation: Implications for Integration, Collaboration, Licensing and Public Policy, *Research Policy* **15**: 286–305.

Teece, D.J., 2009. *Dynamic Capabilities and Strategic Management*. Oxford: Oxford University Press.

Teece, D.J., and Pisano, G., 1994. The Dynamic Capabilities of Firms: An Introduction, *Industrial and Corporate Change* **3**(3): 537–556.

Teece, D.J., Pisano, G. and Shuen A., 1992. Dynamic Capabilities and Strategic Management, Working Paper, Center for Research in Management, University of California, Berkeley, CA.

Teece, D., Pisano, G.P., and Shuen, A., 1997. Dynamic Capabilities and Strategic Management, *Strategic Management Journal* **18**: 509–533.

Tripsas, M., 1997. Surviving Radical Technological Change through Dynamic Capability: Evidence from the Typesetter Industry, *Industrial and Corporate Change* **6**(2): 341–377.

Tripsas, M., and Gavetti, G., 2000. Capabilities, Cognition, and Inertia: Evidence from Digital Imaging, *Strategic Management Journal* **21**(10–11): 1147–1161.

Tushman, M.L., and Anderson, P., 1986. Technological Discontinuities and Organizational Environments, *Administrative Science Quarterly* **31**: 439–456.

Usselman, S.W., 1993. IBM and its Imitators: Organizational Capabilities and the Emergence of the Computer Industry, *Business and Economics History* **22**(2).

Utterback, J.M., and Suarez, F., 1993. Innovation, Competition, and Industry Structure, *Research Policy* **22**(1): 1–21.

Verspagen, B., 2002. Evolutionary Macroeconomics: A Synthesis between Neo-Schumpeterian and Post-Keynesian Lines of Thought, *The Electronic Journal of Evolutionary Modeling and Economic Dynamics* **1007**: 1–21.

Werker, C., and Brenner, T., 2004. Empirical Calibration of Simulation Models, ECIS Working Paper 04.13, Eindhoven Centre for Innovation Studies, Eindhoven.

Williamson, O., 1975. *Markets and Hierarchies: Analysis and Antitrust Implications*. New York: Macmillan.

Williamson, O., 1979. Transaction Cost Economics: The Governance of Contractual Relations, *Journal of Law and Economics* **22**: 3–61.

Williamson, O., 1985. *The Economic Institutions of Capitalism*. New York: Free Press.

Williamson, O., 1999. Strategy research: Governance and competence perspectives, *Strategic Management Journal* **20**: 1087–1108

Windrum, P., Fagiolo, G., and Moneta, A., 2007. Empirical Validation of Agent-Based Models: Alternatives and Prospects, *Journal of Artificial Societies and Simulation* **10**(2): 8.

Winter, S., 1964. Economic "Natural Selection" and the Theory of the Firm, *Yale Economic Essays* **4**: 225–272.

Winter, S., 1971. Satisficing, Selection, and the Innovating Remnant, *Quarterly Journal of Economics* **85**(2): 237–261.

Winter, S., 1984. Schumpeterian Competition in Alternative Technological Regimes, *Journal of Economic Behavior and Organization* **5**: 287–320.

Winter, S., 1986. The Research Program of the Behavioral Theory of the Firm: Orthodox Critique and Evolutionary Perspective, in Gilad, B., and Kaish, S. (eds.) *Handbook of Behavioral Economics, Vol. A: Behavioral Microeconomics.* Greenwich, CT: JAI Press, pp. 151–188.

Winter, S., 1987. Knowledge and Competence as Strategic Assets, in Teece, D.J. (ed.) *The Competitive Challenge.* Cambridge, MA: Ballinger, pp. 159–184.

Winter, S., 2006. The Logic of Appropriability: From Schumpeter to Arrow to Teece, *Research Policy* **35**(8): 1100–1106.

Yoon, M., 2011. A History-friendly Model on the Relationship between NISs and Performances in Frontier Industries of Korea and Taiwan, Working Paper, Kyungpook National University, Korea.

Zbaracki, M.J., and Bergen, M., 2010. When Truces Collapse: A Longitudinal Study of Price-Adjustment Routines, *Organization Science* **21**(5): 955–972.

Author index

Subject index